SOROROPHOBIA

SOROROPHOBIA

Differences Among Women in Literature and Culture

HELENA MICHIE

New York   Oxford
OXFORD UNIVERSITY PRESS
1992

Oxford University Press

Oxford   New York   Toronto
Delhi   Bombay   Calcuta   Madras   Karachi
Petaling Jaya   Singapore   Hong Kong   Tokyo
Nairobi   Dar es Salaam   Cape Town
Melbourne   Auckland

and associated companies in
Berlin   Ibadan

Copyright © 1992 by Oxford University Press, Inc.

Published by Oxford University Press, Inc.
200 Madison Avenue, New York, New York 10016

Oxford is a registered trademark of Oxford University Press

Portions of this book have previously appeared in other publications. Parts of Chapter 1
were published in *ELH* Vol. 56, No. 2 (Summer 1989). Material from Chapter 5 was
published in *Literature and Psychology* Vol. 32, No. 2, and in *Discontented Discourses: Psychoanalysis, Textual Interventions, Feminism,* Marleen Barr and Richard
Feldstein, eds. (Chicago: University of Illinois Press, 1989). I am grateful to everyone
for the permission to reprint my work.

Library of Congress Cataloging-in-Publication Data
Michie, Helena.
Sororophobia : differences among women / Helena Michie.
p. cm.   Includes index.
ISBN 0-19-507387-8
1. American literature—Women authors—History and criticism.
2. English literature—Women authors—History and criticism.
3. Difference (Psychology) in literature.   4. Feminism and
literature.   5. Women and literature.   6. Women—Psychology.
I. Title.
PS152.M5   1992   810.9'32042—dc20   91-30648

135798642

Printed in the United States of America
on acid-free paper

*To Colleen Lamos
and Gladys Michie*

CONTENTS

SOROROPHOBIA

INTRODUCTION

The terms "other" and "woman" form a familiar pairing. In popular culture the anxiety generated by both words is contained within a single figure: "other woman" points to and indicts the mistress. For feminists since Simone de Beauvoir, the two words are virtually synonymous, the pairing redundant: all women are in some sense other. The trajectory of the phrase as it moves through those two frequently opposed discourses—popular culture and feminism—is illustrative. Popular culture uses the transfiguration of female otherness into the mistress to locate it outside the family; the mistress, as the not-wife, becomes the locus of all that is troubling, problematic, unfamiliar about female sexuality and sexual difference. The discourse of contemporary feminism within the United States works in a different register toward a disturbingly similar end: the equation of "other" and "woman" that makes *all* women other threatens to make all women the same. Once again we might have recourse to the family idiom that is one of the central concerns of this book: if the mistress presupposes a family based on a husband, wife, and children, feminism proposes a new family of sisters based on their presumed psychological, biological, and cultural identity to and with each other. If the figure mistress protects the family through her exile from it, the figure of the sister protects a new, feminist family by suggesting that the family of women is capacious enough to contain all women no matter how different from each other they may appear to be.

The choice between exile and absorption of the other or, more properly, of otherness—for the embodiment of otherness in the figure of the other is already a domestication—is articulated by Roland Barthes in *Mythologies* in his entwined images of the mirror and the spectacle. In the mirror, "any otherness is reduced to sameness. . . . The spectacle or the tribunal, which are both places where the Other threatens to appear in full view, become mirrors."[1] Sometimes, however, the otherness of the other cannot be reproduced as a mirror image of the gazer: "Sometimes—rarely—the Other is revealed as irreducible: not because of a sudden scruple, but because *common sense* rebels: a man does not have white skin, but a black one, another drinks pear juice, not *Pernod*. How can one assimilate the Negro, the Russian? There is a figure for

3

emergencies: exoticism. The Other becomes pure object, a spectacle, a clown.'' (Barthes, p. 151)

Barthes' specular strategies for the deployment of otherness, for all of their masculine markings, can be read for their resonances with the two words ''other'' and ''woman'' with which we began. The mistress, in this gendered translation from the world of what Barthes calls the ''petit bourgeois man,'' becomes the irreducible other, the clown, the exotic, the scandal. The feminist sister, on the other hand, becomes the cultural marker of ''otherness reduced to sameness,'' the mirror in which we,[2] as feminists, look anxiously for ourselves. This process of translating the other into the self, becomes, in Gayatri Spivak's resistant discourse, a common matter of mainstream feminist ''selfing''; the self we see in the mirror is, herself, a sign of process, construction, erasure.[3]

This book situates itself in and reacts to a culture whose two options for the understanding of otherness are the mirror and the spectacle, to look specifically at otherness between and among women, at women's differences from each other. De Beauvoir's notion of the ''other'' based on a heterosexual difference, and a heterosexual economy in which women take their place from and in relation to, men, places difference at a relatively comfortable distance across the barrier of gender. The story of second-wave feminism in the United States is, by and large, the story of the translation of difference from the space on the other side of the gender marker to places between and among women, as sexual, racial, and other minorities have challenged feminism from within by insisting upon their difference from the hegemonic ''woman'' safely ensconced at the political and rhetorical center of feminist discourse. As I will be discussing later, conflicts within feminist subcultures have repeatedly proven that no community, be it lesbian-feminist, black or hispanic feminist, is immune to the movement of difference within it: lesbian communities have had to face the challenge of racism, internalized homophobia, and conflicts over sexual lifestyles, while black communities have had to deal with conflicts within their ranks over homophobia, male-identification, classism, and competition.

This place of difference is a troubling one; it is more comforting to imagine that difference can be contained and kept at bay by the construction of a single, powerful identity, whether that identity be ''woman,'' ''lesbian,'' ''woman of color,'' ''Third-World woman'' ''matriarchal feminist,'' ''hag,'' or even, I would argue, ''self.'' It is tempting to treat these words as talismans against difference, these identities as sanctuaries of sameness. This political project out of which this book is written insists that differences between women cannot be contained, no matter how refined, how small, or how specific the operative category. No political or physic marker from ''human'' to ''self'' can exclude division, conflict, duplicity, or multiplicity. It is toward this end that I want to recall a litany of words from the shadows within feminism: competition, racism, betrayal, argument, homophobia, classism, jealousy, envy, hostility.

If the list I have provided above seems to contain what in feminist discourse are not culturally or perhaps even syntactically parallel terms, it is because in pairing, say, racism and jealousy, I am trying to juxtapose two kinds of differences: one, the discourse of "isms" which seems to suggest structural or institutional divisions, and the other, which we might call the discourse of the individual, which suggests more "personal" divisions. I want to argue first that in creating a dichotomy between individual and personal discourse, feminism has been untrue to the simplest and the most profound of its foundational insights: that the personal is political and vice versa, and that making these distinctions allows feminists to trivialize and to despair over differences among women.

Race, class, and sexual preference are clearly fundamental categories for the deployment of differences among women. Bonnie Thornton Dill's germinal essay, "Race, Class, and Gender: Prospects for an All-Inclusive Sisterhood," brought to the attention of mainstream feminists the tensions at work within so many of their assumptions.[4] As the word "prospects" in the title suggests, however, Dull's essay keeps in place the possibility of the sisterhood whose conflicts she explores; the article is indexical in two senses, as it simultaneously calibrates and categorizes differences and points to a future in which such differences would in some sense be resolved. Elizabeth V. Spelman's *The Inessential Woman* speaks to how mainstream feminists have too often ignored these categories of race and class, positing a "generic 'woman'" who operates, according to her, "much the way the notion of generic 'man' has functioned in Western Philosophy: it obscures the heterogeneity of women and cuts off examination of the significance of such heterogeneity for feminist theory and political activity."[5] The generic "woman" posits a connection between women that transcends race, class, and other differences, translating them all too easily into a master-category of gender. Spelman also points out feminist strategies for relatively easy gestures toward the potentially divisive problems of race and class; she names and locates "the ampersand problem," or the too-easy addition of race and class to categories already worked out in terms of gender. Phrases like "women and blacks" add to the problem precisely by that she calls their "additive analysis"; it is as if race and class can merely be used as another in a long series of nouns that do not change the truth value or even the syntax of a particular declarative sentence.

While race, class, sexual preference, age, and disability, to risk a canonically feminist additive structure, are obviously crucial categories, I feel strongly that difference cannot be frozen into these relatively safe and abstract forms. I say "relatively" safe, to paraphrase Mary Daly, by way of an overstatement and a pun.[6] While racism and homophobia are profoundly troubling concerns, the categories of race and sexual preference allow us to talk as if all women of color, all lesbians, all white middle-class feminists are alike. Difference can and has been managed by racism, but it cannot be contained by it; difference spills over into, for example, lesbian communities and lesbian couples: one cannot rid oneself of difference by staying within the confines of a particular race, class, or sexual preference. This has been made abundantly clear by two essays in the recent anthology, *Competition: A Feminist Taboo?*, in which psychotherapist Joyce P. Lindenbaum reports on her work with competition between members of lesbian couples and Daphne Muse interviews a series of young black women about their competitive feelings for each other to see how these feelings are negotiated by teenage pregnancy, rivalry for men, or desire for financial or academic success.[7] It is no more true, satisfying, or useful, no less racist, to talk, for instance, of "black women," than to talk, as Spelman suggests white middle-class feminists too often do, about "woman."

It is perhaps for the negotiation of difference within what is too often and too easily assumed to be a community of sameness that the anthology form, recently so popular with feminists, is especially useful. Anthologies allow for a sense of connection and divergence within particular communities as *Home Girls,* an anthology of black women's writings, *With Wings,* a collection of pieces by disabled women, or *Companeras,* a collection of Latina writings, so aptly demonstrate. While the anthology form is of course bound up in problems of exclusion and canonization, it is, I think, one of the most fertile places for the relatively safe and relatively public expression of difference; this difference has, I think, been interestingly thematized in the recent wonderfully combative anthology, *Conflicts in Feminism.*

If an institutional lexicon of "isms" has allowed for abstraction within feminism, the discourse of personal difference has trivialized and localized it. This discourse tends to be absorbed in the idiom of the therapeutic, as if all female difference is something that needs to be gotten over, grown out of, or projected onto patriarchal power structures. Over the past few years a number of books about women's relations have taken on this idiom and this valence; Luise Eichenbaum and Susie Orbach's *Between Women* has been helpful in exploring how differences between women can accommodate and be controlled by patriarchal structures; in the process, however, it assumes all differences among women to be a by-product of internalized patriarchal norms.[8] Even Valerie Miner and Helen Longino's title essay in their collection seems sometimes to assume that female competition is simply a matter of patriarchal structures: "If we could stop feeling defensive and fearful long enough to consider how we compete not only for money but also for attention and affection and righteousness, we might be better able to eliminate the negative elements of competitiveness from our lives. If we could muster the courage to examine the functions that competitiveness serves under both capitalism and patriarchy, we might feel less guilty about being caught in its web.'' (Miner, pp. 1–2) While Miner and Longino carefully use the term ''negative elements of competitiveness'' presumably to distinguish these from potentially positive aspects, the movement of their argument is toward the center of a patriarchal and capitalist ''web'' that immediately appropriates all forms of healthy competition between women for its own purposes. What remains to be imagined is what women under patriarchy and capitalism should do with competition, and whether, in the process of trying to dismantle forms of hegemonic power, they should also be dismantling all forms of competition between women.

It seems important here, having invoked personal ''differences'' in the sense of arguments or debates, to set up the relation between these differences and the larger category of difference. It can be argued that one does not, for instance, compete with any one who, for whatever reason, seems entirely different from oneself; competition is in some sense a mark of sameness, if only of shared goals. In addition, it suggests at least a minimal degree of equality between competitors. While it is certainly true that competition arises as much from a perception of sameness as from difference, or, more properly, that it takes place on a complex grid of sameness and difference, competition involves a fundamental ''othering,'' a cognitive and psychological intuition that if an other person ''wins'' it is not the same as winning oneself.

Both institutional and personal forms of difference are forms of what I will be calling ''otherness,'' a term I use almost spatially as a place in which differences between women are played out. In using the abstract noun ''otherness'' and the verb ''othering'' I am consciously echoing the work of such diverse thinkers as Mary Louise Pratt, Luce Irigaray, Jacques Derrida, and Roland Barthes. The word ''other'' affects and infects all grammatical forms; the very clumsiness of its renominalization as ''otherness'' or its transformation into a verb as ''othering'' serves my purpose of defamiliarization, of, as it were, keeping otherness other.

Defamiliarization is, in fact, one of the strategies that underlies this book, I am interested in investigating feminist dependence on the concept and idiom of the family, in its entanglement with the figures of the sister and the mother. Often accused by critics of being anti-family, feminists have instead chosen to reproduce familial configuration both in their critiques of existing structures and in their visions of the future. The word ''patriarchy'' itself, so central to the feminist lexicon, locates power in the literal and metaphorical fatherhood, and defines the family as the scene, if not the source, of women's oppression.

There is within feminism, however, a mirror tendency to reclaim the family and reproduce it, albeit in significantly altered form. The figural response to patriarchy is the sisterhood invoked as its challenge. The attack, then, comes both from within the family and from within the familial idiom. Sisterhood disrupts the symmetry of familial relations, and even of Oedipality, by evoking the struggle of *many* sisters with a single father; more important, perhaps, sisters usurp the father's reproductive powers and privilege by reproducing themselves through political action. Still, politics remains a family affair.

If the clash between sister and father produces the rhetorical energy that fuels feminist *practice,* it is the relation between mother and daughter that has become the locus of the reproduction of much feminist psychoanalytic, and, I would argue, more generally, feminist literary and academic discourse. The canonical narrative of feminist canon revision tells the story of the search for lost foremothers. Object relations theorists posit the relation between mother and daughter as central to the construction and articulation of the female self, while other psychoanalytic feminists like Helene Cixous and Luce Irigaray turn the mother-daughter relation as the model for the production of women's language. Psychoanalytic feminism has, largely, turned its gaze from the Oedipal triangle to the pre-Oedipal period in which the girl struggles with her likeness and unlikeness to her mother before her entrance into and her inscription within the law of the father. It is in relation to the maternal body that the female "I" and the female speaking subject have been produced and reproduced.

Feminist discourses, "American" and "French," "activist" and "academic," to make some provisional distinctions, simultaneously depend on and problematize their own investment in the family. Certainly this is true of the figure of the mother around whom feminism has begun to construct a useful discourse of matrophobia that encompasses fascination and repulsion, identity and separation, competition and cooperation, on the part of both mother and daughter. Feminists as diverse as Susan Suleiman, Sue Miller, Luce Irigaray, Alice Walker, Adrienne Rich, and Audre Lorde have taught us to talk in complex and often contradictory ways about mothers and daughters; the maternal lexicon has been opened up to the specter of difference.

Sisterhood, however, remains a distressingly utopian term despite the acknowledgment from a number of feminists that, as Eichenbaum and Orbach put it in their discussion of female friendship, "the ideology of 'sisterhood is powerful' has, in some ways, served to obscure much . . . pain." (Eichenbaum, p. 21) Still, the icon of the sister, if not sisterhood itself, has an almost uncanny power; only a few pages later in *Between Women* Eichenbaum and Orbach describe conflict in a woman's legal practice in Boston by explaining "warmth was replaced with suspicion, sisterliness with competition and envy." (Eichenbaum, p. 23) Why should the concept of sisterliness not include, among other elements, competition and envy? Certainly the few sociologists and biographers who write about actual sisters, as we shall see in Chapter 1, suggest that envy and competition can be thought of as constitutive factors in sisterly dynamics. Even in the act of dismantling the ideology sisterhood, of pronouncing it coercive and obscurantist, Eichenbaum and Orbach cannot completely block its return as fantasy.

For many feminists sisterhood in turn depends on a trope of similarity that cannot entirely be denuded of its physical component. In her remarkable book *A Passion for Friends*, Janice G. Raymond posits a familiar specialness to feelings that women have for each other, feelings for which she coins the term "Gyn/affection." Raymond argues for the "liberating potential of Gyn/affection where women turn to their Selves and others like their Selves for empowerment," for the power of "the female Self in affinity with others like her Self—her sisters."[9] This likeness on which so much depends is both empowering and potentially sinister. Who is to decide who is enough "like" someone else to be part of the family? Is biological womanhood a guarantor, the only guarantor of likeness? Are black women "like" white women? Sisterhood, and indeed all familial discourse, is inevitably tangled up in the question of biologism, which is why Christine Downing's suggestion that the problem of the sororal idiom would be solved by a return to the realities of relations between biological sisters seems unsatisfactory to me. While she acknowledges that feminist sisterhood depends on an utopian notion of relations between women she advocates "real" sisterhood as a corrective. While this would certainly mean that feminist sisters would have a larger and more inclusive emotional lexicon available to them, it would not resolve the exclusionary tendency of any discourse about family.[10]

My own partial "solution" moves in two opposite directions. One is to acknowledge, as Downing does, the cracks in metaphorical and literal sisterhood, and the other is to try to move outside the family to look at figures excluded from the familial lexicon. The first move, the acknowledgment of differences within the family, is marked in my text by the regular appearance of the term "sororophobia," a term, which like "otherness," and like the clitoris in the work of Jane Gallop, "sticks out" of text and of its reproductive economy. Sororophobia also obviously has much in common with, owes its very existence to, is even we might say a daughter of "matrophobia." Like all daughters, however, "sororophobia" is always in negotiation with her mother about her separateness. Indeed, sororophobia is about negotiation; it attempts to describe the negotiation of sameness and difference, identity and separation, between women of the same generation, and is meant to encompass both the desire for and the recoil from identification with other women. Sororophobia is not so much a single entity as it is a matrix against and through which women work out—or fail to work out—their differences.

The second impulse of this book—the move outside the family—finds its textual location in the infinitely capacious figure of the "other woman." The other woman is culturally present in many guises: from the mistress, to the woman of color, to the foreigner, the lesbian, the anti-feminist, the dop-pelganger, and many other others. Each of the chapters in this book deals with a different impersonation or embodiment of the other woman and with the process by which that otherness is constructed, displayed, and negotiated. I try to look for otherness between women and for the provisional and always probematic embodiment of that otherness in unexpected places; it is partially for this reason that I do not talk explicitly in the body of this book about the most obvious impersonation of female otherness, the one with which I began this preface: the mistress. My decision to exclude the mistress does not, however, exclude the erotic from this text; I want explicitly to talk about the erotics of female difference in the absence of the mistress, in the absence of explicit rivalry for the sexual attentions of men. For this purpose I have tried to do with the familiar feminist term "sexual difference" what I did earlier to the term "other"; I have translated it from a heterosexual to a female economy. I speak then of "sexual difference" between women when I want to describe the different positions individual women take up with respect to the sexual.

Although there is no chapter or inter-chapter on the mistress, this text is of course haunted by her presence. It is she, after all, who most easily becomes a sign of familial anxiety. Missing too is a figure which, for all her differences, I find in many ways analogous to the mistress: the domestic worker, who, like the mistress, hovers on the border of the family to serve not only its household needs but also its need to name itself as a family apart from her. I mention the domestic worker and her role in the family because it is Alice Childress' novel about domestic labor *Like One of the Family* that first forced me to think about the connections between family, race, and exclusion in the ideology of the United States. I mention both the domestic worker and the mistress before I proceed with my account of what and who is in this book because it seems only fitting to begin with an acknowledgment of figures I have chosen to exclude.

This book consists of four chapters and five shorter pieces I call inter-chapters. Each chapter looks at how difference between women has been represented, managed, and deployed at a particular historical moment, al-though the book does not move in strict chronological order. Chapters 1 and 2 focus on the representation of otherness in Victorian literature and culture; the first posits literary and historical sisterhood as a relatively safe place where differences between women could be worked out, and where the problems of heterosexual difference, embodied in the novel in the marriage plot and in lived experience in the institution of marriage, can be anticipated, rehearsed, and deferred. I use Victorian melodramatic adaptations of *Jane Eyre* as my starting point in identifying a powerful sororophobic subplot at work in many literary texts of the period, including George Eliot's resolutely anti-melodramatic *Middlemarch* with which I end the chapter.

The second and later Victorian chapter moves within the individual female subject to find and project difference. Using Victorian sensation novels and their preoccupation with female self-replication across class lines, and mid-century cultural insistence on marriage as a form of self-replication and class transcendence, I open up and reread *Tess of the D'Urbervilles* in the context of Victorian anxiety about adultery and female duplicity, as a text about women's power to duplicate herself. In both chapters I use texts from outside the Victorian canon as more overt and more overtly troubling attempts to manage female difference as a way of rereading texts enshrined at the center of the canon.

The third and fourth chapters of this book deal with contemporary material; the third with difference within lesbian communities and the fourth with how differences between women are negotiated and eroticized in three novels by Afro-American women writers. The chapter on lesbian difference looks first at competing accounts of lesbianism that alternately locate lesbianism in the idiom of sameness and of difference. I then move to painful sites of difference within lesbian-feminist communities in the United States: sadomasochism, butch-femme role playing, and race. The chapter then moves to an exploration of sameness and difference as tropes in lesbian-feminist poetry. The chapter on Afro-American woman's literature begins with Nella Larsen's *Quicksand* and *Passing* and with her improvisations on the figure of the mulatto she has inherited from nineteenth-century literature written by both blacks and whites. It then takes up the question of differences among women in the absence of the mulatto figure in Toni Morrison's *Sula;* in all three novels difference is deeply rooted in the idioms of sexuality and community building.

I find myself, in the third and fourth chapters, writing, to a variable extent, from the position of outsider. I am aware, in a general way, of the irony of writing about differences within communities of which I am outside. By problematizing the notion of "inside," I hope I am not permitting myself to speak from positions not my own. I hope instead to speak as part of a dialogue, a debate, a quarrel, that recognizes both the authority of positionality and the necessity to investigate the sources of that authority. Toward that end, I want to invoke the notion of "correctability," a term I first heard in the sense I am using it here by Amy Curtis-Weber in a feminist theory class at Brandeis University. As I understood it then, and as I am using it now, correctability allows one to speak, to speculate, to try to formulate ideas about experiences and communities that are somehow "other" in the full knowledge that one can and will be corrected and challenged. This does not, of course, mean that we are not responsible for our words or that we should not be as accurate, as careful, and as scrupulous as possible; it merely suggests that words are there to be answered, and that revision is always both possible and necessary.

In both chapters I have chosen to let other voices, other critics, speak as much as possible. I am aware, as I hope I make clear in Chapter 5, of the politics of quotation; but, particularly in Chapter 4, I attempt to position myself in dialogue with another voice, in this case Deborah McDowell's. In foregrounding both the similarities and differences between our positions, I hope I am being true to my position on the fertility of sororophobic exchange, and, in some limited sense, to both McDowell's voice and my own.

My final chapter looks at how a variety of feminist theorists have gestured toward, cathected, and ultimately contained the specter of otherness between women by embodying it in the figure of the other woman who appears and disappears in various forms—as colleague, as maid, as Third-World woman, at crucial and crucially marked moments in the text. I identify the other woman in a series of textual and paratextual places—conclusions, footnotes, parentheses—that typically serve as containers for the other woman. This chapter posed, in the writing of it, an opposite challenge to the one offered by the two preceding it. If I had somehow to situate myself outside Chapters 4 and 5, I had somehow to place myself within the community of academic feminist theorists about whom I was writing. Rather than biographizing my position, as so many feminists, including those in this chapter, have chosen to do, I chose instead to construct and at times to undercut an implied "I" through the juxtaposition of other voices, other women.

The five chapters are inter(penetrated) with what I am calling inter-chapters: shorter, less academic pieces on how difference between women has been put on cultural display. Some of the inter-chapters—notably those on the Olympic ice-skaters Katarina Witt and Debi Thomas and on the country-Western mother-daughter singing duo, the Judds—are popular, topical, containing material that dates quickly. Two others—on the film *Fatal Attraction* and on the portrait of the Brontë sisters by their brother Branwell—make a bridge between what we usually think of as high and low culture. I do not want to make a distinction between chapter and inter-chapter based on content or on their relation to the canon, especially since many of the chapters contain uncanonical material. Rather, I see the inter-chapters as an alternative way of writing and thinking about the same phenomenon. If there is a difference in content, it is that the inter-chapters, by and large, focus on how patriarchal culture has managed and displayed difference, while the chapters offer a less unified picture of hegemonic culture, more of a place for resistance and undoing.

My final inter-chapter is a response, in part, to those who have asked, when reading the rest of it, where I am, where I stand in this dance of otherness. Entitled "Helena and Elizabeth," an account of one encounter between myself, as a rape-crisis counselor, and a rape survivor, it is intended both as compensation for and a corrective to any moments in the body of my work where I might seem to imply that I have transcended the problem of otherness between women, or that I am in any position to judge other women's struggles to negotiate that otherness. I prefer to tell the story of my fumblings with otherness than to announce my presence at the beginning of this text, or freeze myself into a series of epithets that might explain my interest, my qualifications, or my hesitations about this project. I have delayed as long as possible the obligatory feminist confessional moment by speaking in the sustained first-person only in this final inter-chapter. The delay may in fact be purely a sign of cowardice; "my" linked choices to wait and to narrativize did, however, provide me with an alternative to the list of positional adjectives with which I automatically began the first draft of my introduction: I owe their absence to Robyn Warhol who reminded me of my own argument that such adjectives— "white," "married," etc.—would be both obscurantist and boring. The final few pages also make room—between parentheses of course—for my mother, whose presence throughout is too powerful for articulation. For this reason her name also appears on the first, dedicatory page of this book.

I close this introduction with an attempt to relate my project to two key terms for feminism and for social change in general: history and community. As I hope I make clear, this book is not historical in a strict sense, or even in the expanded sense that has produced and continues to produce the "New History"; while I focus intimately on specific historical moments and concerns— Victorian attitudes toward sisters, the development of lesbian-feminist sado-masochism in northern California in the mid-eighties—I juxtapose them without supplying an intervening narrative, a reason or reasons for the change in emphasis from sister to lesbian. Juxtaposition, borrowing as it does from the spatial idiom that shapes so much of this book, is, I think, the key term of my enterprise; in inviting readers to make connections between, say, "Goblin Market" and *Sula* as I do in Chapter 4, or, more generally, between the Victorian discourse about marriage and recent discourse about sadomasochism, I hope I am not eliding the differences between them that the goal of this project is to protect. History, too, operates between sameness and difference; for this reason the chapters—separated as they are by inter-chapters—must in some sense be read as much for their differences as for their continuities.

This project's relation to community and to community making is simpler if no less vexed. As I suggest in Chapter 4, I see the lexicon of community, like the lexicon of family, as both empowering and coercive.[11] If I seem to stress difference at the expense of community it is because, politically, I prefer the concept of coalition. Coalition building is not easy—I speak now as an activist as well as a literary critic—and it provides few of the stable comforts of community. "Coalition" as itself an awkward and compound word—does one hyphenate or not?—does, however, suggest the possibility of dissolution, and, insofar as this is possible, voluntary affiliation. Perhaps most important, I do not see coalition as inevitably tied to identity or exclusion; if one is, as "one" might very well be, excluded from a coalition, there is always the possibility of re-formation, of a next time, of, once again, "correctability."

I am grateful to those many people who have already stepped in to correct me. Many have heard or read parts of this under many names, and for this reason I have many people to thank. First, I am deeply grateful to the National Endowment for the Humanities for their funding of this project, and to Brandeis University for their financial and logistical support. Most important to the shapes this book has taken are the members of my writing group—JoAnn Citron, Beth Kowaleski-Wallace, and Robyn Warhol. I would have written something without them, but it would not have been this book. They have argued with, praised, laughed at, understood, and misunderstood portions of my project. They have embodied the wonders and the frustrations of otherness between women, and they have done it with great wisdom and affection.

I thank also my colleagues at Brandeis, especially Paul Morrison, William Flesch, Michael T. Gilmore, Allen Grossman, and Susan Staves. I am also indebted to the members of the Feminist Literary Theory Seminar at Harvard for an evening of comments that changed the shape of the final chapter, and to Jonathan Loesberg who helped me transform Chapter 2. Many thanks also to Julie Burnham who came in contact with this project at this crucial moment as a researcher and proofreader.

Finally I turn to my family: to my mother who officially appears only parenthetically and on the last few pages of this text, but who is everywhere within it, and to Scott Derrick who was always with me as I wrote 400 miles away. Finally, I thank my friend, and now once again my colleague, Colleen Lamos, who taught me the pleasures and pains of negotiating difference between women.

Chapter 1

"There Is No Friend Like a Sister": Sisterhood as Sexual Difference

In 1879, some thirty years after the publication of Charlotte Brontë's *Jane Eyre*, James Willing and Leonard Rae adapted the novel for the melodramatic stage. While there had been previous adaptations of *Jane Eyre* both in England and on the continent, Willing and Rae's simultaneously represents the most dramatic departure from the original storyline and the most interesting interpretation of the novel.

In the Willing and Rae version, Blanche is seduced and ruined by an adult John Reed after Rochester has rejected her in favor of Jane. Abandoned and starving, Blanche searches the countryside for shelter, much as Jane does in the second half of the novel. Blanche stumbles upon Mr. Brocklehurst's house where Jane—through a series of bizarre plot twists—has been working as a teacher. Jane has just learned through Brocklehurst that she is the heiress to her uncle's fortune; John Reed, transformed into a melodramatic villain, has tried unsuccessfully to persuade Brocklehurst to sign a paper certifying that Jane died in infancy, so that he, John, could become heir to the money. When Jane opens the door, Blanche greets her with a flow of enraged language denied to her by Jane's first-person narrative in the novel:

> Whose fault was it that I fled with that villain—yours, Jane Eyre! The guilt, the sin of my elopement lies at your door—I loved Fairfax Rochester—You, with your smooth face and mock humility tore his love away and crushed my heart. John Reed poured into my ears the taunt—I was a jilted woman. Furious at Rochester's preference for you, I threw myself into the tempter's arms.[1]

Jane's response to this rhetoric of rivalry and opposition is to stress the similarities between her situation and Blanche's by invoking a third woman, Bertha Mason, who has come between herself and Rochester. Within the parallel that Jane offers as consolation lurks, however, the specter of the difference between herself and Blanche:

> BLANCHE: Then you too have been deceived?
> JANE: Cruelly—but—
> BLANCHE: Not fallen, you would say—Don't spare me—I deserve it all.
>   . . .   (Willing and Rae, p. 53)

The poignant play of sameness and difference between Jane and Blanche embodied in Jane's pregnant "but" is quickly transformed in Jane's next speech into an idiom that would seem to repress and rewrite the distinction between the fallen and the unfallen woman so crucial to Victorian culture and to the play's retelling of *Jane Eyre:*

> JANE: . . . I long for the ties of home and friends—Blanche, will you be my sister?
> BLANCHE: Your—sister—am I awake. . . . I came here to curse you—and I stay—to bless—to adore you.   (Willing and Rae, p. 54)

Jane and Blanche embrace in a tableau of sisterly love that works against the psychological and visual grain of the novel and is one of the play's climactic moments.

The play reiterates the promise of sisterhood even when Rochester is reintroduced onto the scene. Blanche, moved by Jane's generosity, reveals that she knows Rochester's whereabouts and that he has been asking for Jane. Together, the two women hurry to his sickbed, where John Reed, also mysteriously in attendance, misreads the relationship between Blanche and Jane as one of simple rivalry. "Well—Blanche," he says, "I suppose you'll come with me? You can't both marry Mr. Rochester." (Willing and Rae, p. 62) The power of this newly forged sisterhood lies, of course, in the interruption and subversion of the heterosexual binarism that structures the novel. While in Brontë's version Rochester must choose between Blanche and Jane, and Jane between St. John and Rochester, the play allows for an alternative that transforms the discourse of opposition into the idiom of family. Jane renews her promise, in Rochester's presence, that her home shall be Blanche's. In doing so, she reiterates the promise of sisterhood over the bed of her future husband.

> JANE: Call me sister?
> BLANCHE: Sister—dear Sister.   (Willing and Rae, p. 62)

The word "sister," repeated so often within this scene and the one that precedes it, is central both to an understanding of how the play reads and rewrites the novel and to how Victorian culture understood and represented relations between women.

While Brontë's novel has frequently been read as the story of a young woman's successful struggle to establish an identity and a family, it ends, as many critics have remarked, with a strangely monogamous and isolated vision. Although Jane has discovered the joys of family life with her cousins, the Rivers, they drop from the story when Jane leaves them to find Rochester. St. John is rejected by Jane and then killed off by the author; Diana and Mary, for all practical purposes identical to each other, remain in the home that Jane provides for them so she may set up her own with her husband.

It is, perhaps, predictable that the emotional energy of the novel should not center on Jane's relations with her female cousins. Throughout the novel, Jane has asserted her identity in opposition to a series of other women. Jane must learn that she is *not* Helen, Eliza, Georgiana, Blanche, or Bertha before she can emerge as an independent woman. She must learn, even—and perhaps especially—after Rochester falls in love with her, to resist the pressure to become a woman she is not, to deny the seductive power of his rhetoric that would turn her into a fairy, an elf, or an angel. The teleology of the novel propels Jane past other women; her journey is fueled by rejection of and hostility toward a veritable gallery of female figures whom she must learn to reject as models. Diana and Mary Rivers, appearing as they do at the end of the novel, cannot mitigate the flamboyant hostility of its first and most memorable five hundred pages, cannot erase Jane's uncomfortably articulate anger toward so many other women.

Willing and Rae's adaptation simultaneously dramatizes and domesticates the anger of the novel by containing it within a master trope of sisterhood. The play's reiterated tableaux of sisterly love by no means deny the differences between the two women; indeed, they depend for their emotional effect on moral contrast. This is why the play twists the plot of the novel to create Blanche's sexual fall and why Jane's invocation of Blanche's fall precedes her declaration of sisterhood; sisterhood, in Victorian culture, depends on differences between women, and provides a safe, familiar, and familial space for its articulation. Victorian melodrama abounds with pairs of sisters who work out issues of identity and difference with relation to each other. Difference between sisters is often visually and spectacularly rendered; dark and light, blind and seeing, healthy and sick sisters compose themselves for the audience in tableaux of physical contrast.

Difference between sisters, in this adaptation as well as in many other Victorian texts, is also reproduced explicitly as *sexual* difference, that is, the difference between the fallen and the unfallen, the sexual and the pure woman. The capacious trope of sisterhood allows for the possibility of sexual fall and for the reinstatement of the fallen woman within the family; fallen sisters, as we shall see in later discussions of works by Christina Rossetti and Wilkie Collins, are frequently recuperable through their sisters' efforts in a way forbidden to other Victorian fallen women. Sisterhood acts as a protecting framework within which women can fall and recover their way, a literary convention in which female sexuality can be explored and reabsorbed within the teleology of family.

While sisterhood may indeed be powerful, it is by no means simple or completely benign. Jane's offer to Blanche that she make a third in the Rochester household has, quite clearly, its sadistic side. Blanche, prevented forever by her ruin from marrying or from striking out on her own, must live daily with the evidence of her rival's sexual triumph. Permanence is both the promise and the nightmare of sisterhood; to be absorbed into the family is to know no escape from its idiom, its pleasures, and its punishments. While the convention of sisterhood can offer an emotional home for the fallen woman, it can also, by operating precisely on a system of sexual contrast, become a constant reminder of the evils of female sexuality. The pure sister loves and protects the fallen one precisely by participating in a system that allows for the opposition between pure and fallen.

By insisting on the translation of the sororophobic undercurrents of the novel into its most vivid tableaux, and by simultaneously displaying and containing sexual rivalry between women within the trope of sisterhood, Willing and Rae produce a version of *Jane Eyre* whose ambivalence about family takes center stage and locates itself in the play's subtitle, *Poor Relations*. The existence of the play frees us to see the novel as something other than a simple search for and journey toward family. Blanche's transformation into Jane's sister, along with the insistence of the subtitle that Jane must, throughout the play, be concerned with her status as "poor relation," attests to the uneasy power of the family as metaphor and institution. Other melodramatic adaptations of the play take the novel's uneasiness about family even further. In several versions of the play, including *Jane Eyre: A Drama in Four Acts* by Mme. von Heringen Hering, the role of rival for Rochester's love is taken on by Jane's cousin Georgiana (Georgina in Hering's play), who, in the company of her mother, visits Thornfield as Rochester's fiancée. While this doubling of characters clearly had practical advantages for small companies of players who would typically have only one actress suitable for the part of the wicked rival, the collapsing of cousin and sexual rival is loyal both to the novel's structure of character repetition, and to the claustrophobic sense of family which that repetition produces.[2] In the novel Jane finally works out her relation to the Reeds through transference: Diana, Mary, and St. John, as several critics have noted, are clearly benign repetitions of Georgiana, Eliza, and John Reed. Jane also, of course, returns to the Reed household and to Mrs. Reed's deathbed after she has been at Thornfield some time; in this sense, the characters reappear in the novel as more benign versions of themselves. Despite Jane's new control over her past and the family members who were once so cruel, however, the very fact of their reappearance, in so many forms at so many crucial moments, attests to the power of past and family to reassert itself. The appearance of Georgiana/ Blanche and her mother at Rochester's home, their penetration into the erotic and—for all Jane knows—safe space of Thornfield make vivid the matrophobic and sororophobic tensions of the novel and simultaneously underscore the erotic dimension of Jane's childhood rivalries and conflicts with the Reeds, exemplified by Mrs. Reed's explicit and formative comparisons between Georgiana's curly-headed beauty and Jane's plainness.

This chapter will explore both sisterhood as institution and narrative structure and sororophobia as a prevailing narrative tension as it explores the relation between light and dark, pure and fallen sisters. In readings of Wilkie Collins' *No Name,* Christina Rossetti's "Goblin Market," and Thomas Hardy's *Tess of the D'Urbervilles,* I will examine sisterhood as a structure for the containment and representation of sexual differences among women. Before discussing the Victorian texts that work with the convention of contrasting sisters, it will be useful to look briefly at the scant sociological material on relations between sisters available to us today.

Like Victorian novels, plays, and poems, contemporary sociological accounts of relations between sisters take their shape from tropes of opposition and difference. Like the melodramatic version of *Jane Eyre,* and like the sensational *No Name* discussed below, sociological constructions of sisterhood depend on the notion of role-play. Toni McNaron notes that sisters frequently take on opposing "roles" within the family: "Either one sister encourages the other to play out some complementary self that she does not or cannot become, or forces around them are such that complementarity becomes the pattern within which they both act out their adult lives."[3] Each sister, then, is assigned and/or assigns herself a role in relation to the other. As McNaron points out, this structuring trope of difference can have the sinister effect of producing "an unspoken, probably unconscious pact, that neither sister need develop all her potential." (McNaron, p. 8)

This configuration of complementarity works, to a certain extent, for all siblings, but especially, according to family psychologists Steven Bank and Michael Kahn in their central theoretical work on the subject, for sibling pairs who are similar in both age and gender.[4] It seems likely, given the tenuous sense of self and other that Chodorow and others attribute to girls and to women, that sister pairs would engage especially acutely in these specular and spectacular choreographies of self. Bank and Kahn cite the example of a pair of female twins whose "solution" to the issue of contrast and identification was to choreograph their respective weights so that one became anorexic while the other forced herself to eat and grow fat. The sisters were only "comfortable" when a certain number of pounds separated them, when, in effect they produced between them a sense of visual contrast. (Bank and Kahn, pp. 42–45) In stressing contrast as a structure for sisterly relations, I do not mean to imply simple difference. Contrast depends as much on likeness as unlikeness; sisters might be said to work out issues of difference within a framework of genetic and cultural similarity. Christine Downing, in her provocative Jungian study of sisterly relations, suggests that sisters do not have to choose to be "utterly dependent" or "utterly free" of each other as daughters might have to do with respect to mothers.[5] Sisterhood, according to Downing, is not as extreme a relation as that between mother and daughter; Greek myths about sisters tend also to be about mortals, while myths about mothers project those mothers as goddesses. Sisterhood, then, becomes a playground, or, more sinisterly, a battlefield, in which issues of the outside world can be rehearsed and worked out in the relative safety of a relation between female equals.

It should not be surprising that the enterprise of contrast should both depend on physical spectacle and be caught up in the theatrical idiom of role playing. Sisterhood, like the Oedipus complex, is fundamentally family drama. This is, of course, not to say that the drama of sisterhood is not "real," or that sisters do not feel real pain, real love, real ambivalence for each other. These feelings, however, like the identities that in turn shape and are shaped by them, are at least partially the products of roles frequently assigned to children before birth, worked out and staged by the children themselves over the period of their entire lives.

> Differences in temperament . . . among infants of the same biological family often result in an early identity imposition and role assignment for each child by older family members. They often do this by contrasting one child's reactions with those of another. A placid baby girl may become identified as "the calm one" or "the easy one," while a more active, stimulus-sensitive sister may become known as "the excitable one," "the lively one," or "the trouble-maker" . . . it appears that in most families there is only one person who can occupy a certain psychological space . . . at one time. One child's identity is cultivated as "gentle," "kind," "dependable," "the little one," and so on, and, as such, pre-empts the possibility that any of his or her siblings can take over that role. (Bank and Kahn, p. 23)

Role assignment, interwoven as it is with sibling temperament, family expectation, and the need for contrast, is not merely the artificial imposition of an identity on a formless human psyche; identity is itself inextricably linked with role playing.

Nowhere is the staging of female identity through sisterhood more dramatically rendered than in Victorian melodrama, sensation novels, and canonical literature. Captivated by contrasts between women, and uneasy about alliances among them, Victorians took advantage of the domestic, often sentimentalized, trope of sisterhood simultaneously to contain and project hostility, competition, and sexual rivalry among women. From the melodramatic sibling relations in Christina Rossetti's "sister" poems, a series of ballads about rivalrous and sometimes murderous sisters, to the more realistic but equally fertile contrast between Celia and Dorothea Brooke in George Eliot's *Middlemarch*, to Tess' abrupt and sentimental invocation of her sister Liza-Lu at the very end of *Tess of the D'Urbervilles*, relations among sisters in Victorian texts are competitive, problematic, and theatrical.

Since so many contemporary American feminists depend on the trope of a political sisterhood that emphasizes love between and unity among women, these Victorian depictions of sisters might seem reactionary, male-identified— in a word, "unsisterly." In positing a place for sisterhood in Victorian literary tropology that allows for the expression of hostility among women, I want to insist first that such a place was historically necessary, and, second, that contemporary feminists need themselves to provide rhetorical and political room for the expression of female difference, for anger and mistrust between and among women. Allowing women to express negative or ambivalent feelings toward one another should not, must not, undo the work of centuries of feminists who have struggled to maintain that relations between women are primary and vital connections. In making a place for difference we are adding a dimension of dignity and choice to friendships between and among women. The fact that sisters in Victorian texts frequently compete with and replace each other should not blind us to the fact that within the protective idiom of sisterhood, women could express anger and sexuality in a way unavailable to them in the context of other relations, certainly including those with men.

If Virginia Woolf needed in *A Room of One's Own* to plead for books about how women liked each other, she was ignoring a rich tradition of Victorian representations of sisters for whom "like" was too simple a term. Relations between sisters in Victorian texts can, of course, be flat and stereotyped, simply catty or simply benign. Structurally, however, fictional representations of sisterhood provide a place and a vocabulary for the representation of a range of stereotypically unfeminine feelings and behaviors. Victorian texts frequently enrich and complicate feminist notions of sisterhood, as they undermine our most dearly cherished tropes of female unity. While some Victorian depictions of sisterhood are troubling for feminists to read, I think they are useful and necessary in producing a richer and more complex feminism that recognizes and supports differences among women.

If Victorian fictions of sisterhood demarcate relatively free psychological and representational space, it might follow that historical sisterhood—the relations between "real-life" Victorian sisters—might also provide an escape from proscriptions against anger or sexuality; one might also expect, from the indications of literary sources, that a psychological space for this escape might be made available through psychological contrast. It is, for many reasons, very difficult to find historical traces of anger or competition between sisters. Historical reconstructions of Victorian sisterhood run into predictable problems of methodology: the sources that are available to contemporary scholars— letters, journals, biographies, and conduct books, for example—each follow conventions of their own and produce, in effect, their own fictions of sister- hood. Caroll Smith-Rosenberg's pioneering study of the correspondence and journals of nineteenth-century American women reveals some of the problems inherent in depending on personal sources to reconstruct family life. In recording the textured and elaborate expressions of affection between women that she finds in her sources, Smith-Rosenberg presents a glowing portrait of a loving female subculture, a "female world in which hostility and criticism of other women were discouraged."[6] At one point, searching in vain for signs of conflict between mothers and daughters, she concludes:

> One could speculate at length concerning the absence of that mother-daughter hostility today considered almost inevitable to an adolescent's struggle for autonomy and self-identity. It is possible that taboos against female aggression and hostility were sufficiently strong to repress even that between mothers and their adolescent daughters. Yet these letters seem so alive, and the interest of daughters in their mothers' affairs so vital and genuine, that is is difficult to interpret their closeness exclusively in terms of repression and denial. (Smith-Rosenberg, p. 65)

One need not have recourse to the vocabulary of the troublingly ahistorical discourse of psychoanalysis—"repression and denial"—to posit the possi- bility of unexpressed hostility between sisters as well as between mothers and daughters. The very reasons Smith-Rosenberg cites for female closeness— unmarried sisters sharing bedrooms or even beds for their entire lives, the fact that middle-class girls were usually educated at home until late in the century— are also powerful reasons not to express anger or difference. While prolonged physical proximity may have in many cases produced great affection, we can also surmise that it must sometimes have produced feelings of claustrophobia. In using the word "taboo," Smith-Rosenberg opens up the issue of generic convention as powerfully operative in documents of private life as in, for example, fictional forms. While on the one hand one cannot ignore the words of the women who wrote so movingly about female affection, one must also be aware of the historical constraints on self-expression.

One cannot look for the "truth" about sisters in a single place, a single series of sources. The task of reconstructing sisterhood is made more difficult by the poverty of historical material on relations between women; it is a commonplace that most women's letters available to contemporary scholars were preserved because of the woman's relation to a male public figure: of the Victorian women who were famous enough to have letters preserved, only the Brontës' and the Webbs' deal directly and in detail with relations between sisters. We must look for parenthetical comments about sisters in legal documents, family conduct books, biographies, and letters, alive to the formal requirements of each genre and to distinctions among them.

Legal documents pertaining to sisterly relations would seem to be a stable starting point from which to come to terms with at least the most canonized ideas about proper sisterly relations; to invoke Victorian law regulating these relations is, however, at once to invoke instability, conflict, and oddity in what came to be satirized as "the annual blister," the Deceased Wife's Sister's Act and the controversies surrounding it. These controversies, as Margaret Morganroth Gullette persuasively points out, themselves relied on the almost endless proliferation of competing fictions.[7]

The act, passed into law in 1835 and not repealed until 1907 despite considerable protest throughout the nineteenth century in many forms—from sermons to legal pamphlets, to novels, to flagrant and widespread violation of the law—is often considered an arcane footnote to the progress of English Law. Dismissed in most history books as controversy over little or nothing, the law, which prohibited a widower from marrying his late wife's sister, can nonetheless be seen as a symptom of a series of cultural anxieties about the family and sexuality. Gullette identifies in the act a need to construct and to regulate middle age and, in particular, the notion of middle-aged sexuality; in her argument the act serves as a legal parallel to the "second chance" of second marriage novels. In this way, it becomes one of a series of Victorian discourses struggling to name and contain emerging ideas about the sexual and familial self.

The act can also be seen as an attempt to construct a notion of sisterhood and to regulate the sexual relation of sisters. Gullette argues that although the act was supposedly based on the interpretation of biblical taboos, public discourse about it tended to focus on jealousy between sisters. (Gullette, p. 20) She sees the debate over the repeal of the act in terms of two competing fictions featuring the domestic relations of an imagined couple: the sister and widower of the deceased wife. According to Gullette, defenders of the act tended to portray the widower and the surviving sister as a "vicious, often un-English couple who seduced or teased each other during the lifetime of the wife and could hardly wait until she died to legalize their criminal union" (Gullette, p. 19), while advocates of repeal imagined and represented a sober, middle-aged couple whose main concern was often the care of the deceased wife's children and a mutual commitment to the memory of a beloved wife and sister. Both narratives focus on this limited cast of characters—the sister and widower who want to marry—although the act also affected, for example, men who wanted to marry their deceased brothers' wives and women who were deserted by their sisters' widowers under the protection of the law.

The two narratives—the two sets of fictions Gullette has identified in the context of the discovery of middle age—work together as dramatizations of the two sides of sororophobia, as investigations into contradictory relations between sisters, and separately as conflicting accounts of the nature of sisterhood. Both are essentially domestic fictions in which the dead and the surviving sister struggled with the question of their relationship. One can pose the question of the relation between sisters a number of different ways: are sisters reiterations of each other? Metaphoric replacements? Competitors? Is the deceased sister primarily replaced as wife or mother or as both? Is one sister the most natural or the most unnatural replacement for another? Is marrying your sister's widower the ultimate act of betrayal or the ultimate act of loyalty to her memory? Are sisters too much the same (incest), or comfortingly similar (familial bliss)?

While these questions are, within the context of the act, being worked out, as it were, over the body of the dead sister and through the body of the survivor, they obviously have repercussions for the relations between living sisters. If we look at the first few divorces granted to women by Parliament in the beginning of the nineteenth century, we will see the same issues of sisterly jealousy, reiteration, and substitution at work in the logic of the law. While men could sue for (and be granted) a divorce based solely on the "proven" adultery of the wife, women could not get a parliamentary divorce on the grounds of adultery alone. Two out of the first three divorces granted to women in England involved the "aggravating" grounds of "incest" added to adultery; in both cases the husband's adultery had been with the wife's sister.[8] These two cases not only pitted wife against husband but sister against sister.

While the law by definition treats aberrations from the norm at the same time that it constructs and produces normative relations, the domestic discourse of conduct books purports to treat the normative itself in some detail. Conduct books offer, then, a more benign version of sisterhood, although they too implicitly ask similar questions of relations between sisters. What I am calling family conduct books—those advice manuals that address themselves, for example, to the upbringing and education of children—have, by and large, much more to say about relations between brothers and sisters than relations between sister pairs. Perhaps the most complete and interesting account of sisterhood I have been able to find is in Sarah Ellis' unjustly infamous *Women of England*. Ellis provides us with two counter-narratives of sisterhood: the first a picture of the problems of sisterhood, the second a more predictable eulogy to its joys. The first, interestingly enough, is far more detailed and evocative:

I am . . . inclined to think that the strength of this (sisterly) bond arises chiefly out of their mutual knowledge of each other's capability of receiving pain; because, in families whose circumstances are uniformly easy . . . we often see the painful spectacle of sisters forming obstacles to each other in their progress both to temporal and eternal happiness. . . . I have heard of hackney-coachmen in a certain highly civilized metropolis, who adopt the cruel practice of lashing a galled or wounded part, if they can find one in the wretched animals they drive; but I hardly think the practice, abhorrent as it is, demands our condemnation more than that of the women who are thus false and cruel to each other—who, because they know exactly where to wound, apply the instrument of torture to the mind, unsparingly, and with the worst effect.[9]

In this more sinister narrative of sisterhood, Ellis depends for her effect on the language of "spectacle," and on the translation of intimacy into pain. She contains the nightmare of this sort of sisterhood within the framing contrast of good and bad sisterly relations. As if to assure the reader that the horrors of sisterly sadism are avoidable, she deliberately stops herself and presents a happier alternative:

But let us change this harsh picture, and turn to the sunnier hours of youthful love, when sisters who have shared one home in childhood, then separated by adverse circumstances, return, after the lapse of years, to enjoy a few brief days of heart-communings beneath the same roof again. How lovely then are the morning hours, when they rise with the sun to lengthen out the day! (Ellis, p. 70)

The sunnier second picture cannot entirely eclipse the memory of the first, especially when sisterly love in the second seems to depend on separation and more painful life circumstances. One discovers the joys of sisterhood, it seems, only through separation and privation: a happy life and continued physical intimacy between sisters makes for unhappiness, competition, and emotional violence.

Later in the century, in 1876, Charlotte Yonge crossed, as did so many female novelists of the period, the line between domestic fiction and family conduct books. Her *Womankind* specifically sets off the relations between sisters from other relations between women. Her argument against sending girls to large schools is based precisely on the fact that schoolgirls are *not* related:

Spite and jealousy are dangers among girls thrown together without relationship, and without the gradations of age necessarily modifying family rivalries. . . . And as all parties are too old to fight it out, the tongue is employed to taunt and teaze, and a lasting habit is formed. Such things do prevail among sisters, but less commonly.[10]

It is in this passage and elsewhere in Yonge that we might begin to hear echoes of structuring fictional tropes of contrast. If sisters are at least relatively safe from this kind of mutually destructive relationship, it is only, it seems, because of contrast in age. Yonge observes: "Many an elder sister is as kind as possible to the babies, while she is harsh and impatient to the middle-sized children." (Yonge, p. 31) Again, effective sisterhood depends on contrast, rendered in girlhood as contrast in age. As sisters grow older, according to Yonge, other contrasts seem to come into play. This is particularly true of unmarried sisters who become, in adulthood, everything to each other:

> Besides, owing to the much-talked-of redundancy of females, sisters often remain the first with each other through life, lean on one another, suffer and rejoice together, and preserve the same relative position with which they started as soon as their age brought them such an equality that force of character could assert itself. One remains leader and originator, housekeeper and manager; the other is her complement for life, and the tie is never loosened. (Yonge, p. 142)

The "relative position" of sisters is once again construed here as complementarity; contrast in age gives way, in Yonge's narrative of sisterhood, to contrast of "character."

Yonge, like Ellis, acknowledges the possibility of rivalry between sisters by consecrating it as a taboo. Her position on jealousy between sisters is unequivocal:

> Rivalry and jealousy are the most terrible of all foes to sisterly love. Let them never be spoken of lightly, or treated as a kind of evidence of fine feelings. They are hateful passions, destructive of all good, and should be prayed and struggled against as belonging to the spirit of Cain. (Yonge, p. 145)

The vehemence of Yonge's protest is revealing; like Ellis' sinister portrait of sisterly relations, this passage, with its sarcastic invocation of "fine feelings," also seems to have something to do with social class. We have no way of knowing the exact context for what seems to be an indictment of sisters with the leisure to think about their "fine feelings," but it does seem as though jealousy between sisters of a certain class was common enough for Yonge to bring the weight of biblical prohibition to bear on its display.

What emerges from both Yonge and Ellis is an ideal sisterhood that absorbs conflict into meticulously choreographed *contrast*. Like the more contemporary sisters discussed by McNaron, Victorian sisters, it seems, worked on resolving conflict through role playing. Biographies of Victorian sisters carry out the theme of role assignment, none more flamboyantly than Nina Auerbach's biography of Ellen Terry. In describing Terry's relation to her sister, Auerbach says: "Theatrical sisters are popularly supposed to hate each other offstage, but the tension between Kate and Ellen Terry was more complex: their early fusion was so intense that as adults, they could separate only by playing utterly distinct parts.''[11] Because the Terrys were such startlingly public figures, both as actresses and as models for G. F. Watts, metaphors of contrast and role playing develop a glowing literalness. Kate and Ellen actually posed for Watts' *The Sisters:* "Ellen Terry sprang to life on Canvas as the vivid, yet movingly crumpled and clinging girl who invited sympathetic tears. In *The Sisters,* Kate is a hazy characterless mass, present only to be leaned on by the compelling Ellen.'' (Auerbach, pp. 82–83)

Whether the aesthetics of physical contrast recorded in this passage are Auerbach's, Watts', the Terrys' or some combination of all of these, there can be no doubt that Ellen Terry saw herself throughout her life as the naughty sister and Kate as the demure one who caused ''no trouble'' to her parents or audiences. Kate and Ellen, as they posed with and against each other in countless on- and offstage tableaux, are only the most unabashedly theatrical embodiment of common Victorian assumptions about sisterhood. When these assumptions get translated into the fiction, poetry, and drama of the time, the space of opposition—the space between sisters—becomes an even more fertile, more capacious exploration of difference.

Sisters, Melodrama, Allegory, and Sensation

Wilkie Collins' *No Name* is a sophisticated and sensational exploration of the iconography of sisterhood, an almost parodically complex improvisation on the standard contrast between the good and the bad, the fair and the dark sister. With its heavy reliance on melodramatic conventions and scenes that take place in the theater, *No Name* acknowledges sisterhood as spectacle. Throughout the novel, characters and readers alike are invited to compare the two sister-heroines and to draw first the excitement and then the moral of the tale from the contrast between them.

Norah and Magdalen Vanstone, two pampered sisters, find themselves orphaned about one-third of the way through the novel. More important, they find out that they are illegitimate and that the considerable inheritance they had always been led to expect goes to an uncle. For various reasons, none of them to his credit, this uncle refuses to help the sisters financially. Against the background of this shock the differences in character between Norah and Magdalen, always present in descriptions of their looks and character, begin to make themselves felt as a structuring narrative principle. Magdalen vows revenge; Norah advises caution. The sisters take on opposite roles in the spectrum of possibilities open to them in the Victorian marketplace; Norah moves into a new domestic space to become a governess, while Magdalen runs away from the home her sister prepares for her to become an actress. Once she has made enough money to support herself in further adventures, Magdalen disguises herself in one of her theatrical costumes and begins to act out an elaborate plan in which she tries to entice her hated uncle into restoring her legacy. The plan backfires when the uncle dies. Magdalen finds out that he has left his money to his equally unattractive and stingy son, and, with the help of a self-proclaimed lovable rogue named Captain Wragge, she creates a new identity and family for herself as a Miss Byfield and begins the work of inveigling her cousin into marrying her. Although Magdalen does succeed in marrying her cousin, he discovers her treachery with the help of his house-keeper and disinherits her just before he dies. In the meantime, Norah, who has remained passively at home, has attracted the attention of a George Bartram, who is, coincidentally, the same person to whom Magdalen's husband has left the money. Magdalen's repeated disappointments as well as her attendant moral collapse lead to a brain fever from which she is rescued first by a naval captain who is a friend of her father's and then by Norah, who takes her home to heal. Magdalen, after an appropriate period of repentance and soul searching, marries her naval rescuer and refuses what becomes, through a legal quirk, her share of the fortune in favor of whatever money her husband and her sister choose to give her.

The moral of the story, depending as it does on the symmetry of the two sisters' relation to marriage, family, and inheritance, is that feminine passivity will reap the very rewards that female aggression seeks and fails to achieve. Norah not only ends up with the inheritance, she does so by an appropriately feminine replication and inversion of her sister's tactics; her happy marriage, which rewards her both emotionally and financially, is a gentle but effective parody of the marriage that Magdalen has risked her life to forge between herself and her hated cousin. The novel offers us opposition and inversion within a confining framework of symmetry; the sisters search for the same solution through opposite means and with opposite results.

The symmetry of the novel, with its careful opposition between the two sisters, is undercut by a close reading of the sisters' early relationship and by the character(s) of Magdalen herself. The contrasting ways in which the sisters react to their disinheritance has a psychological history of its own; until roughly a third of the way through the novel, it was Magdalen who was the fair sister and Norah who was repeatedly figured by images of darkness and gloom. The novel disrupts its own easy system of oppositions by reminding us that the dark and the fair sister are *positions,* not characters, and that dark and fair can change places with changing material conditions. Soon after the crisis of the sisters' disinheritance, Miss Garth, the family governess, is forced to invert the opposition between Norah and Magdalen that has structured her (and the reader's) relationship with the sisters: ''For the first time in the long companionship of her pupils and herself, a doubt whether she, and all those about her, had not been fatally mistaken in their relative estimate of the sisters, now forced itself on her mind."[12]

The phrase "relative estimate" speaks to the structure of sisterhood as I have outlined it; the two "relatives" come to textual and emotional life in relation to each other: to reevaluate the character of one is to do the same for the other. In this way the novel anticipates what have become familiar to us as poststructuralist notions of language and identity by making visible the interdependence of the dark and fair sisterly roles. "Dark" and "fair" are positions that must be occupied and inhabited; if one sister switches roles, the other must do the same. Female identity in *No Name* is always contingent, specular, always in flux within the structuring and enabling framework of sisterhood.

No Name also disrupts the tempting symmetry of the opposition between Magdalen and Norah by making Magdalen herself an embodiment of female difference. While difference *between* the sisters provides a formal and moral structure to the novel, differences *within* Magdalen's body and psyche give the novel its energy. Magdalen's acting, disguises, and indecision, her discomfort with the restricted roles assigned to her by Victorian society, make her into a seductively self-contradictory heroine. Not surprisingly, given Victorian conventions of physiognomy, we can read the contradictions of Magdalen's character in and on her body during her first entrance into the text:

> Her eyebrows and eyelashes were just a shade darker than her hair, and seemed made expressly for those violet-blue eyes, which assert their most irresistible charm when associated with a fair complexion. But it was here exactly that the promise of her face failed of performance in the most startling manner. The eyes, which should have been dark, were incomprehensibly and discordantly light. . . . Thus quaintly self-contradictory in the upper part of her face, she was hardly less at variance with established ideas of harmony in the lower. (Collins, p. 16)

Discordance and self-contradiction inhabit Magdalen's body; while her physical contrast to her sister will be emphasized later in the novel, we can read Magdalen's body during this carefully staged entrance for signs of the multiple women already at work within it.

Miss Garth and other characters in the novel locate the crucial moment when the sisters exchange roles in their divergent reactions to the discovery of their illegitimacy; it is also, for Miss Garth, a moment of family breakdown. The novel has, however, already begun the work of breaking down the Vanstone family and of choreographing the differences between sisters.

It is not illegitimacy but sexuality that has already marked the sisters off from one another. Before the tragedy that disinherits the sisters is exposed, Magdalen has met and fallen in love with a man patently unworthy of her: Frank Clare, a passive good-for-nothing neighbor of the family. Frank makes her feel for the first time "the master-passion of sex in possession of her heart" (Collins, p. 80), and her love for him that first divides her from her sister.

Norah is the first to be suspicious about Magdalen's feelings for Frank; she grows bitterly resentful of her sister and follows her to the shrubbery where Magdalen has gone to meet him. Norah discovers them and accuses her sister of impropriety and betrayal: "'You are treating me heartlessly,'" says Norah, "'For shame, Magdalen—for shame!'" (Collins, p. 63) For the first time in the novel the two sisters meet face to face in a tableau of difference: "For a moment, the two sisters—so strangely dissimilar in person and character— faced one another, without a word passing between them. For a moment, the deep brown eyes of the elder and the light gray eyes of the younger looked into each other with steady unyielding scrutiny on either side." (Collins, p. 63)

Until this point in the novel, the sisters, for all their dissimilarities, have not been directly compared; indeed, they make their entrances into various scenes in the novel as they do into the novel's opening chapter—completely sep- arately. The awakening of Magdalen's sexuality brings the differences between the two sisters into intimate focus. The scene in the shrubbery is intensely physical; Norah, for instance, grabs Magdalen's parasol from her and twists her arm. The specter of physical difference, which makes its way into the passage quoted above in the form of contrasting bodily description, is also, of course, the specter of Magdalen's sexuality, which will separate her from Norah in a variety of different ways. It is important to understand that this is no simple scene of sexual rivalry; there is no particular indication that Norah fancies Frank for herself. What is at stake is the betrayal of one sister by the other, Magdalen's separation and differentiation from her sister.

It is significant, especially in view of the theatrical dynamics of sisterly role playing, that Magdalen and Frank should have fallen in love during the process of putting on an amateur production of *The Rivals* at the house of another neighbor. Amateur theatricals are used, of course, in nineteenth-century literature from *Mansfield Park* onward, as vehicles for the expression of inappropriate erotic feelings: Magdalen and Frank predictably fall in love as they play lovers on stage. There is, however, another important element at work here; Magdalen discovers in the process of rehearsal that she is a "born actress," and indeed when another neighbor quits her part, she takes on two roles at once. Magdalen, then, embodies three major Victorian anxieties about acting and actresses: the blurring of distinctions between fiction and reality, the promiscuous multiplication of (especially female) identity, and the corporeal and erotic dimension of life on stage. All these anxieties get projected in

Victorian culture onto the mendacious and multiplicitous female body—in this case, of course, Magdalen's.

Perhaps the most frightening thing about Magdalen's performance—and what marks her as an actress—is her ability to be many women at once, or at least in quick succession. She is able, to the surprise of the audience, to keep her two roles distinct: "Failing in many minor requisites of the double task which she had undertaken, she succeeded in the one important necessity of keeping the main distinctions of the two characters thoroughly apart. Every body felt that the difficulty lay here—every body saw the difficulty conquered—every body echoed the manager's enthusiasm at rehearsal, which had hailed her as a born actress." (Collins, p. 59)

This drama of internalized difference is further complicated by the method that Magdalen uses to keep her two roles separate; for her role as lover she imitates the physical and verbal mannerisms of her sister. By playing her sister on stage she dramatizes the difference between them; by casting her sister as a lover she parodies Norah's prudishness and celebrates her own eroticism. Magdalen, as Norah appreciates, transforms her sister's body into public spectacle despite Norah's refusal to take any part in the theatrical proceedings.

Indeed, Magdalen's greatest crime throughout the novel is prcisely that she makes family differences—both in the sense of familial disputes and of difference in character between family members—public. When she becomes a professional actress she not only disgraces her sister by falling in caste, but by using both Norah and Miss Garth as models for characters in her famous one-woman show. The theater completes the punishment that the law has perpetrated on the Vanstones; family business moves beyond the Vanstone shrubbery into the sphere of public discourse as family differences become public property.

While Norah shuns the publicity of the theater, she cannot, especially after Magdalen has run away, retreat from the publicity of the law. In fact, with Norah's help, the law makes Magdalen's body public in a way even the Victorian theater would not allow. Two times in the novel Norah and Miss Garth between them provide full physical descriptions of Magdalen, down to a significantly double mole on the nape of her neck. In the first instance, the description is reproduced on a bill that is posted in public buildings all over the seaside town to which Magdalen is supposed to have escaped. The descriptions—particularly the mention of the mole—make Magdalen extremely angry. While in the theater she could control the scrutiny of the audience with lighting, costume, and makeup, when she becomes Miss Byfield she loses control over her body. Noël Vanstone, his suspicions aroused, actually looks for the mole on Magdalen's neck; ironically, it is in "private" life, after she has given up the theater, that Magdalen is most vulnerable to the gaze of other characters.

It is tempting to see Norah's embarrassingly explicit description of her sister and her "innocent" betrayal of information to Noël Vanstone's housekeeper as strategies of revenge. Despite Norah's dislike of publicity, she, like Magdalen, moves into the public arena to do battle with her sister in the name of bringing her home. Interestingly, it is when she is searching for Magdalen that she meets her cousin, George Bartram, the man whom she will eventually marry. The pathos of Norah's story moves Bartram to admiration; the story she tells is, of course, Magdalen's. Both sisters use the differences between them to advantage; each turns the other into spectacle and parades signs of identity and difference.

The ending of *No Name* works hard to repress the differences between the sisters and to forget or gloss over Magdalen's sexual history. It is quite surprising, in view of the exchange of her physical charms for money in her marriage to Noël, that Magdalen is allowed by Collins to marry again. This is, I think, possible only within the framing convention of sisterhood. Norah, like Lizzie in "Goblin Market," erases her sister's fall through her own purity. Sisterhood and a proper marriage come together to absorb Magdalen's wayward sexuality and to channel it into family. Norah joins Magdalen's naval suitor as a principle of narrative closure, comfort, and containment; her own romantic life well in place and suitably de-eroticized by her choice of her cousin as a husband, Norah, as married woman, can restore Magdalen's fortune, name, and innocence. Norah's own retention, or rather reappropriation, of the Vanstone name through her marriage can be read simultaneously as a sign of her individual power over the law and her own personal history, and as a retreat into a dream of undifferentiated familial bliss that is finally the source of both her power and her weakness. Like Jane Eyre in Willing and Rae's adaptation, Norah absorbs the woman who has so repeatedly hurt her into her family under the name of sister; like Jane, she uses marriage as a vehicle that makes sisterhood, with all its attendant pains and pleasures, possible. We do not know if Magdalen, unlike Blanche, resists her own domestication; we do know that she does marry and that her husband is a world traveler. The novel does not tell us whether Magdalen moves away from the family she has almost died to regain. If she does leave, the conventions of Victorian literature and culture prevent us from following her on her journey.

Christina Rossetti's "Goblin Market," like *No Name,* ends with two marriages that attempt to erase the difference between sisters. The poem closes with a tribute to the integrative powers of sisterhood in the voice of Laura, the once-fallen sister:

For there is no friend like a sister
In calm or stormy weather;
To cheer one on the tedious way,
To fetch one if one goes astray[13]

"Goblin Market" is precisely about the process that enables one sister to speak for the other and that transforms sexual difference between sisters into replication and reproduction. While the action of the poem depends on Lizzie's and Laura's contrasting reactions to the tempting cries of the goblin men, it ends with Lizzie's and Laura's twin wifehood and motherhood and with Laura's apparent affirmation of sisterly sameness to an audience of her children and her nephews and nieces. Lizzie has reproduced Laura in her own image, and together, it seems, they have reproduced an undifferentiated circle of children, "joining hands to little hands." Like Norah, who pulls Magdalen into her domestic orbit at the end of *No Name*, Lizzie seems to see a proper marriage as a joint sisterly venture, as an institution that de-emphasizes sexual difference in favor of reproduction.

Despite "Goblin Market"'s happy ending, despite the cheerful closure of the family circle under the benediction of sisterhood, the poem and the sisterhood that shapes its moral are always in danger of falling apart, of being dismantled from within. "Goblin Market," most frequently read as an allegory of sexual fall, is perhaps more accurately also a poem about sexual difference; its moral center is not so much virginity as the undifferentiation of which virginity is only a sign. Lizzie, the good sister, privileges innocence as a state of sororal fusion; the power of her rhetoric and of her moral life depends on sameness and repetition: the repetition of words and phrases like "no, no, no," of images like the lily to which both sisters are frequently compared, and of tasks like the routine household chores in which she takes so much pleasure. These structural and rhetorical repetitions are linked throughout to Lizzie's conservative counter-quest for sameness, and for the erotic stasis that characterizes her unfallen girlhood. Even the logic of Lizzie's position is the logic of sameness and of analogy; she repeatedly warns Laura to "remember Jeanie" who died taking the same action that Laura takes.

If Lizzie's is the discourse of sameness, Laura's, like the goblin men's and like Magdalen's, is the discourse of difference. Importantly, the temptations that interrupt the poem are structured as a series of lists. The seductiveness of the goblin cries lies in their power to specify, to list, one after the other, a series of fruits:

Apples and quinces,
Lemons and oranges,

> Plump unpecked cherries,
> Melons and rasberries,
> Bloom-down-cheeked peaches,
> Swart-headed mulberries   (Rossetti, lines 5–10)

The temptation of fruit, is, of course, the temptation of difference, of sexual knowledge and the knowledge of difference. The items that compose this litany of temptations, however, are not merely "fruit," although Lizzie resists their specificity in calling them "fruits" or "gifts"; each kind of fruit is articulated and made separately real; the generic association of fruit and temptation is particularized until particularization itself, the ability to generate lists of objects, becomes the temptation to which Laura, the poet, and the reader succumb.

The goblin men themselves take the form of difference. While Lizzie dismisses temptation with the generic and collective "we must not look at goblin men," Laura "lingers":

> Wondering at *each* merchant man.
> One had a cat's face,
> One whisked a tail,
> One tramped at a rat's pace,
> One crawled like a snail,
> One like a wombat prowled obtuse and furry . . .   (Rossetti,
>   lines 70–75, my italics)

The use of "each" and the repetition of the initial "one" sets each individual goblin man off from the others; Laura's sinful gaze particularizes, prefiguring a time when she too will be set apart, when she too will be "one" instead of two.

Individuation threatens familial discourse as it threatens this family of sisters; as the poem progresses, words from the safe familial lexicon become themselves violently separated from each other. The goblin men approach Laura:

> Leering at each other,
> Brother with queer brother;
> Signalling each other,
> Brother with sly brother.   (Rossetti, lines 93–96)

Sexual difference is doubled and redoubled here, as pairs of words ("brother": "brother," "each other": "each other") and pairs of phrases ("leering at each other": "signalling each other," "brother with queer brother": "brother with sly brother") tantalize with sameness and symmetry only to disrupt it. Brothers, separated from each other by "queerness" and "slyness," as the repetitions of "brother" are separated by disruptive and disorienting modifiers, are separated from the sisters they are tempting by sexual difference. Moreover, they enact the separation of gender difference by producing sexual difference between the sisters, by awakening the sexuality that makes Laura different from her sister.

Part of the poem's erotic power, however, lies in its ability to undercut the distinction between the sexual Laura and the innocent Lizzie. Erotic temptation is so powerful, so fertile in this poem that it invests all aspects of it, including, as a number of critics have pointed out, the relationship between Laura and Lizzie. Interestingly, most readings of the poem's homoeroticism focus on the lines that follow Laura's capitulation to the goblin men, where Lizzie and Laura are virtually indistinguishable:

> Golden head by golden head,
> Like two pigeons in one nest
> Folded in each other's wings,
> They lay down in their curtained bed:
> Like two blossoms on one stem,
> Like two flakes of new-fall'n snow,
> Like two wands of ivory
> Tipped with gold for awful kings.
>
> Cheek to cheek and breast to breast
> Locked together in one nest.   (Rossetti, lines 184–91, 197–98)

It is easy to see these lines as an erotic invocation of sameness, even as an alternative female erotics based on sisterhood, identity, and similarity. Such interpretations leave unanswered the important question: Why is this idyll of sameness not, then, presented at the beginning of the poem? Why does it only take textual place after Laura's fall into difference? The answer, I think, has implications beyond the poem in the place(s) of difference between women. Many homophobic and lesbian-feminist accounts of lesbianism, as I explain in more detail in Chapter 4, share a dependence on tropes of sameness; women's attractions to other women have until recently almost always been seen, for better or for worse, as attractions produced by or at least enabled by morphological and psychological similarity. The erotics of sisterhood in "Goblin Market" suggest something more complicated; even the rhetoric of sameness insisted on by almost incantatory repetition of the word "like" and seemingly identical body parts (head, cheek, breast) depend for their articulation on prior difference, on Laura's assertion of self that removes her from Lizzie. Lizzie's attempt to pull Laura back into domestic sameness succeeds as eroticism because it depends on difference; it fails, however, as an integrative gesture. The next morning the two sisters do their chores in separate worlds:

> Lizzie with an open heart,
> Laura in an absent dream,

> One content, one sick in part;
> One warbling for the mere bright day's delight,
> One longing for the night.   (Rossetti, lines 210–14)

The three "one"'s that begin the lines quoted above are, of course, marks of the
goblin men. It is as if their cry that haunts the sisters and the poem were not so
much "come buy" as the contagious and, in the world of the poem, sinister
"one" that signifies sexual experience.

Lizzie and the poem must at this point assert their teleology and save Laura
from sexual difference. Lizzie's heroism consists not so much in the potential
sacrifice of her life and world as she beckons to the goblin men, but in her
refusal to admit difference. This is why her rescue of Lizzie takes the familiar
form of sharing, of reiteration:

> Tender Lizzie could not bear
> To watch her sister's cankerous care
> Yet not to share.   (Rossetti, lines 299–301)

Lizzie's sacrifice allows her to reconstruct a shared sororal space that is once
again rhetorically defined by sameness, analogy, and iterability. She fuses with
Laura in the act of replacing her, and, in announcing her heroism, seduces
Laura into fusing with her:

> Come and kiss me
> Never mind my bruises,
> Hug me, kiss me, suck my juices
> Squeezed from goblin fruits for you,
> Goblin pulp and goblin dew.
> Eat me, drink me, love me;
> Laura, make much of me . . .   (Rossetti, lines 466–72)

Lizzie's desire is for the incorporation and introjection articulated for psychoanalysis in Melanie Klein's attempt to reproduce the fantasies of children. For
Klein, and for Lizzie, the fantasy of incorporating or being incorporated by the
other is simultaneously hostile and loving, destructive and recuperative. It is
even unclear who is incorporating whom in Lizzie's fantasy; while she begs
Laura to drink her, to eat her, and to take her in, Lizzie herself seems to swell
into a sort of pregnancy of heroic origin and dimension as she commands her
sister to "make much of" her. This double pregnancy foreshadows the linked
images of motherhood with which the poem comes to a close.

What Lizzie fails to realize in her fantasy, however, is the extent to which
even incorporation depends on difference. Lizzie's act, like all mirror images,
is as much an inversion of Laura's as it is a replication and reiteration of it. By
keeping her mouth shut to temptation, Lizzie marks herself off from Laura and

makes the oral fantasy of incorporation impossible. We can hear the echoes of resistance, the muted rhetoric of difference, in Laura's seemingly integrative last words:

> For there is no friend like a sister
> In calm or stormy weather;
> To fetch one if one goes astray,
> To lift one if one totters down,
> To strengthen whilst one stands.

Even in this apparent triumph of sameness, Laura's language reproduces the call of the goblin men; the last four lines of the poem are marked by a series of "one"'s that return as repressed memories to Laura in her compound role of wife, mother, and sister. The return of the repressed and the unfamiliar is established precisely through the return to the family; sisterhood is finally the place that allows for oneness within the rhetoric of sameness. Again, the power of sisterhood is by no means simple. Its energy lies not in the desperate prescription of sameness, but the highly sexual, deeply political power of difference, in the conversion of sororophobia into the comforting institutional framework of sisterhood.

Tess of the D'Urbervilles, unlike "Goblin Market," does not appear on the surface to be about sisterhood. It operates within the space of sexual difference as it is most commonly understood, structuring itself around Tess' twin relationships with Alec D'Urberville and Angel Clare. It is only in the last four pages of this long and complicated novel that sisterhood surfaces as a concern. Tess, knowing she will soon be hanged for Alec's murder, tells Angel to look after her younger sister, Liza-Lu: "She is so good and simple and pure. O Angel—I wish you would marry her, if you lose me, as you will do shortly. O if you would!"[14] The sudden entrance of Liza-Lu into Tess and Angel's fatal honeymoon works to foreground the relation between sisterhood, female iterability, and closure. Liza-Lu's probable/improbable marriage to Angel works, like Jane and Norah's marriages, to undo a sister's sexual fall; like Lizzie's rescue of Laura, Liza-Lu's vindication of Tess works through the principle of substitution. Hardy makes it clear, however, that the consequence of this undoing is the death of the fallen sister. In this more sinister narrative of sisterhood, one sister literally replaces the other, as both are absorbed into a narrative of progress that is finally historical rather than individual. The family, as Hardy makes clear early in the novel, is an historical construct whose rise and fall, marriages, rapes, and murders work themselves out over a larger canvas than an individual life. Hardy preserves the dimension of physical contrast in sameness that has marked the descriptions of other sisters in this study. Liza-Lu is a "spiritualized image of Tess, slighter than she, but with the same beautiful eyes.'' (Hardy, p. 506) Like the twins in Bank's and Kahn's study, Tess and Liza-Lu participate in a choreography of physical replication and contrast. One senses, with Hardy, however, that neither Tess nor her sister is the choreographer in this familial theatre; Tess' "fullness of aspect"—both cause and sign of her fall early in the novel—is a biological given, a genetic condition that shapes and is shaped by history without the assent of the body it inhabits. Hardy's abrupt ending, which can easily be read as a parody of public requirements for closure and a gesture of contempt toward his critics, makes clear the connection between the requirements of literary closure and the teleological imperative of history. Both are embodied in the relation of—that is, the difference between—the two sisters whose "endings" are so similar and so different.

The improbable replacement of Tess by Liza-Lu on the last pages of a novel whose central task is to deny the possibility of rustic innocence, is, in keeping with the dynamics of Victorian literary sisterhood, both a benign and a terrible act. By embodying principles of literary closure, Liza-Lu forces herself awkwardly, absurdly, onto the novel, undercutting the tragic dignity of Hardy's ending. Liza-Lu is not, however, merely a figure of death and diminishment. The relation between Tess and her sister, however awkwardly invoked, also acts, like the "sisterhood" of Jane and Blanche, to contain the hostility between and among women that is also a hallmark of this novel.

Once again, it is useful to turn to melodramatic adaptations of the novel to identify the sororophobic, and in this case, matrophobic underpinnings of the novel. Two adaptations are especially fruitful here: Lorimer Stoddard's *Tess of the D'Urbervilles* (1897), and Harry Mountford's *Tess*. Both Stoddard and Mountford's versions develop tensions between Tess and other women that remain sketchy in the novel. While it is clear in the novel both that Tess' fatal beauty comes to her from her mother, and that Joan Durbeyfield mistakenly opposes Tess' desire to confess her relations with Angel, the Stoddard play gives Joan a presence and an agency in Tess' affairs that make the relation between mother and daughter absolutely central to the tragedy of Tess' situation. In the play, it is not a disembodied fate, but a flamboyantly embodied Joan Durbeyfield who ensures that Tess' confessional letter to Angel never reaches him: just before the curtain of the first act, we see Joan's hand reach onto the windowsill, where Tess has left the letter and a rose, to remove the letter.

Joan Durbeyfield's hand is a synecdoche for her constant and powerful physical presence in an adaptation that opens with the Durbeyfield family's visit to Tess at Talbothays. Joan has arranged the journey specifically so that she may dissuade Tess from her confession. The family remains on stage almost throughout the first act and for the first part of the second; they intrude on

Tess with their drunkenness, their poverty, their pathos, and their slips of the tongue with a directness unmatched by the novel. Tess' competing sympathy and embarrassment are almost palpable in the initial encounter between Angel and her father, and later in a long and anxious wedding party scene in which Joan and John Durbeyfield are constantly on the brink of revealing Tess' past. Mountford takes the pressure of maternal presence even further when he has Joan act as housekeeper during Tess' and Angel's abortive honeymoon. Tess' constant anxiety that her mother will say too much, or embarrass her in some other way, adds to the tension of both plays and helps to lay the blame more squarely on the intrusive figure of the mother. Joan's speech in Stoddard's version, taken almost verbatim from the novel, in which she gloats that Tess' "trump card" is not her father's aristocratic name, but her mother's beautiful face, becomes even more sinister here, as Joan seems less hapless and more manipulative with every second she spends on stage. The name of the father has a place in Tess' undoing, but it is the maternal body, which Tess is doomed to reproduce in herself, that inscribes her fate visibly upon her.

Both the Stoddard and the Mountford adaptations also feature competition between Tess and other women her age. The dairymaids figure crucially in both plays; the Stoddard version seems especially interested in the dairymaids' relations to Tess, and gives them a great deal of time on stage as well as fairly complex biographies of their own. Mountford's version sharpens the sororophobic tensions of the novel by transforming the novel's confrontation scene between Tess and Car Darch, Alec's previous mistress, into a physical battle: in the play Car hits Tess over the head with a bottle and knocks her unconscious, just as both Alec and Angel pass from different directions. Alec rapes Tess in her stupor; she wakes up in his arms. The temporal and spatial collapsing of the confrontation with Car, the rape scene, and Angel's potential rescue of the innocent Tess (hinted at in the novel during the May dance scene where Angel fails to ask Tess to dance with him) traces Tess' fall more directly to the hands of another woman, and, more specifically, to a structure of sexual rivalry between women.

If we read these two adaptations as opening up sororophobic possibilities within Hardy's novel, we can begin to understand more clearly the function of Liza-Lu's problematic entrance into the novel. Liza-Lu's appearance on the scene establishes a relationship between women that, because it depends on a literal and corporeal sisterhood, and the corporeal death of one sister, cannot be shattered by competition for male attention. Tess' death is a necessary sacrifice to the exigencies of novel-writing, marriage, and sisterhood. In Hardy's bleak and fatalistic universe, the differences that structure and empower sisterhood are ultimately lethal. Unlike the sisters in "Goblin Market," Tess and Liza-Lu have no future together from which they can speak of a far-distant fall; in *Tess* only one sister survives, and she can live only as a ghost of the other.

Sisterhood and the Realist Tradition

Tableaux, spectacular contrasts, jealous rivalries, and fallen women belong to the theater and to the theatrical novel. The relation between sisters marked by these signs of spectacle can also be located as a structuring principle within more conventionally realist texts, as realism contains but cannot entirely repress cultural signs of theatricality. Sisters bring with them into realism echoes of a psychodrama that depends on vexed and central relations between women. *Middlemarch*, that landmark of tolerant literary realism, translates hostilities between women into its own muted but evocative lexicon, tempering the contrast between dark and light sisters into the "shade of coquetry" that distinguishes Celia Brooke's arrangement of her dress from her sister Dorothea's.

Muted as the contrast between Celia and Dorothea is, the difference between them works with and against the romance plot(s) in which Dorothea is involved to structure the novel. *Middlemarch* begins in the heart of the family with a series of disagreements between sisters and moves out into the community and into larger moral and philosophical issues that are structured in terms of encounters between women. The introduction of "Miss Brooke" into the text of the novel in the first chapter, the jewel scene, the recurrent evocation of the portrait of Will's mother and aunt that hangs in Dorothea's boudoir, the development of the Vincy/Garth plot through meetings between Rosamond and Mary, and the climactic encounter between Dorothea and Rosamond that applies closure to the moral dilemmas of the novel all take the form of physical, moral, and erotic contrast between women. The novel produces its own series of carefully elaborated and shaded tableaux where difference is read only with difficulty and understood only with pain. These spectacles of difference, some of which have as much, if not more, theatrical energy as anything I have discussed earlier, depend on intense and careful scrutiny on the part of the reader. Difference becomes a matter of intellectual or moral vision written minutely but glowingly in the folds of a dress, in the drawing off of a pair of gloves, or in a preference for emeralds.

Middlemarch begins and ends with the problem of female heroism, with the problem, in other words, of articulating the difference between a heroine and other women. The novel's "Prelude," with its resonant hagiography of St. Theresa, is tempered by its famous closing paragraph reminding us that there are no more St. Theresas or Antigones: that heroines in the age of realism "live faithfully a hidden life, and rest in unvisited tombs." Between these two framing moments, the Prelude and the final few paragraphs, Dorothea lives her remarkable life; it is against a background of other women, St. Theresa and Antigone only the most famous among them, that she comes to life as a realist heroine, "thrown into relief" in the pictorial language of the first sentence, by the women who surround her.

Dorothea is, in fact, first presented to the reader in reference to another woman and a painting: we are told that "her hand and wrist were so finely formed that she could wear sleeves not less bare of style than those in which the Blessed Virgin appeared to Italian painters."[15] The phrase "not less bare of style," which draws attention to itself through its meticulous accuracy and its awkwardness, is only the first of a long series of syntactical accommodations to other women, only the first in a series of comparisons that establish Dorothea's difference from other women in the novel and her allegiance to heroines of past times and past genres.

Dorothea's quality of difference, figured as the contrast between "a fine quotation from the Bible" and "a paragraph of today's newspaper," comes to rest, at the end of the first paragraph of the novel, in a structurally familiar comparison between Dorothea and her sister: "[Dorothea] was usually spoken of as being remarkably clever, but with the addition that her sister Celia had more common-sense. Nevertheless, Celia wore scarcely more trimmings; and it was only to close observers that her dress differed from her sister's, and had a shade of coquetry in its arrangements." (Eliot, p. 7)

The difference between Celia and Dorothea that structures both the first half of the novel and the reader's relation to it begins to take shape here. In the first sentence of the passage Celia might seem to be an addition, a supplement to Dorothea; in the second we might make the connection between supplement and ornament and dismiss Celia as a Dorothea who has stepped—however slightly—over the line of regal simplicity.

The structure of supplementarity and excess, however, is in itself an ornament to and a distraction from the powerful oppositional structure at work in this crucial first paragraph and elsewhere. The opposition is rendered visually, as it is in so many of the melodramas and sensation novels discussed earlier, but on a scale so minute as to thrust the burden of perception upon the reader. The comparison of Dorothea with her sister, like the comparisons between her and mythic heroines such as St. Theresa, allows us—indeed commands us—as readers to look closely at Dorothea's body, to scrutinize it in the name of discovering her quality of difference from other women. *Middlemarch* creates its own body of readers who learn through a series of gentle clues to read closely.

Celia and St. Theresa function in this chapter in the same way that Cleopatra does later on in the novel when Will's artist friend Naumann, coming upon that "fine bit of antithesis" (Eliot, p. 184) between Dorothea and the Cleopatra sculpture, decides to paint Dorothea as Santa Clara. The contrast between Dorothea and the other women gives us permission to gaze at and linger over the body of a woman who, for at least the first three-quarters of the novel, denies she has one; in addition, it lets Eliot resolve the literary problem of representing a heroine who is simultaneously innocent and desirable, sexually repressed and highly erotic.

The representation of Dorothea's sexuality becomes intimately involved with the characterization of Celia, whose interest in the body is betrayed in a variety of settings from her fondness for necklaces in the jewel scene, to her frank discussions of marriage and her preoccupation with Casaubon's mole and with the sounds he makes when chewing his food. These interests of Celia's, the corporeal lens through which she sees and talks about the world, are the realist novel's answer to the melodramatic trope of the fallen sister. Celia's fall, as befits a novel of "middles," is a matter of a slight shift in perception, a slight deviation from Dorothea's idealist vision. Moreover, as I will discuss later in some detail, it is a fall that makes Celia more at home in the world than her sister, a fall into, rather than out of community.

We can read in the meticulous realism of Eliot's language, however, traces of a more melodramatic opposition between sisters; if Celia's body does not undergo the process of sexual fall, her voice embodies it. Dorothea is constantly disturbed in her vision of married life by the rhythms of "Celia's pretty carnally-minded prose." (Eliot, p. 48). The point of view that frames the phrase is, of course, Dorothea's, in whom idealism seems intimately bound up with melodrama, with the large and visible gesture of self-sacrifice that bursts through, for example, in her desire, expressed to Casaubon, that the wealthy "deserve to be beaten out of our beautiful houses with a scourge of small cords." (Eliot, p. 31) It is Celia, of course, who parodies this impulse toward palpable self-denial when she explains to an assembled company that Dorothea "likes giving up." (Eliot, p. 18)

Dorothea's irritation with Celia's commentary on her actions, expressed significantly in an aversion to her voice, that "soft staccato" which periodically enters a scene to undermine Dorothea's sense of her own vision, raises larger questions about Celia's role within the novel. Celia's voice seems, at certain crucial moments, to offer itself as a principle of realism, as a voice, in other words, aligned with many of Eliot's narrative interventions in *Middlemarch* and elsewhere on the subject of her art. Celia's recognition and representation of detail make her a realist novelist within the text of *Middlemarch;* her alliance with and appreciation of the commonplace align her with the political and moral agenda of Eliot's realist enterprise. The conversation between Dorothea and Celia about Casaubon just before Dorothea announces her engagement to him establishes the two sisters as representatives of two different discourses:

> "Really, Dodo, can't you hear how he scrapes his spoon? And he always blinks before he speaks. I don't know whether Locke blinked, but I'm sure I am sorry for those who sat opposite to him, if he did."
>
> "Celia," said Dorothea with emphatic gravity, "pray don't make any more observations of that kind."
>
> "Why not? They are quite true," returned Celia, who had her reasons for persevering, though she was beginning to be a little afraid.
>
> "Many things are true which only the commonest minds observe."
>
> "Then I think the commonest minds must be rather useful. I think it is a pity Mr. Casaubon's mother had not a commoner mind; she might have taught him better." (Eliot, p. 48)

Celia's insistence on telling the truth, no matter how common, should sound familiar to readers of Eliot's authorial interventions on realism as the genre of the common person in *The Mill on the Floss* and *Adam Bede*. Her invocation of the failure of Casaubon's mother should likewise be familiar to readers of Margaret Homans' work on the multiple connections between the real, the literal, and the maternal. Celia, who consistently invokes a return to the body of the mother, first in the jewel scene, then in this first of many reconstructions of Casaubon's maternal relatives, and finally in her own devoted motherhood, seems always to align the corporeal, the material, and the common with a maternal principle. Eliot's own invocation of maternal tolerance toward the failings of her characters as a principle of realism strengthens Celia's rhetorical position within this prototypical and self-conscious novel of realist "middles." The melodramatic contrast between the fallen and unfallen sisters, has become, in the hands of George Eliot, a battle between literary genres and between modes of moral perception. Even in the potentially melodramatic "love-triangle" formed by Celia, Dorothea, and Sir James, the issue is not so much sexual jealousy between the two sisters as it is a test of their versions of reality. Dorothea insists that Sir James is courting Celia and sees her, Dorothea, only as a prospective sister-in-law; Celia, who, "compared with (Dorothea) . . . was knowing and worldly-wise" (Eliot, p. 10), knows quite well that Sir James is in love with her sister. Celia's anger at Dorothea for not recognizing the truth is couched in the language of competing visions: "Well, I am sorry for Sir James. I thought it right to tell you, because you went on as you always do, never looking just where you are, and treading in the wrong place. You always see what nobody else sees; it is impossible to satisfy you; yet you never see what is quite plain." (Eliot, p. 36)

If the battle between the sisters seems, at least on the surface, to be intellectual and moral, and not sexual, this is not to say that their relationship is free of hostility, or even of sexual rivalry. The fact that Sir James moves with such ease from Dorothea to Celia after Dorothea becomes engaged to Casaubon does not mean that the resolution of either the sexual or intellectual rivalry is simple. What Eliot has done in the opening chapters of the novel is not to repress the sexual dimension of the rivalry between sisters, but rather to eroticize moral and intellectual conflicts, to make them as psychologically resonant as quarrels over male attention. Sexual jealousy will become more explicitly the issue in Dorothea's relationship with Rosamond at the end of the novel; the relationship between sisters prepares us for the Rosamond encounters as it does in general for the importance, vitality, and painfulness of relations among women.

The jewel scene is one of the few in *Middlemarch* that has been traditionally read against the heterosexual grain of the novel as a place where women work out their relations to each other. If we read the entire novel, however, as such a place, the jewel scene becomes only the highly visible crystallization of female anxieties about women, their bodies, and their relations with other women. To say that this scene is "visible" is to participate in the visual erotics of this scene, which has to do, among other things, with the temptations of the eyes: " 'How very beautiful these gems are!' said Dorothea, under a new current of feeling, as sudden as the gleam. 'It is strange how deeply colours seem to penetrate one, like scents.' " (Eliot, p. 13)

Dorothea reframes the temptations offered by her mother's emeralds by translating sight into scent and surface into depth; the colors, in "penetrating," move beyond the surface of the body to something deeper, more private, more spiritual. Throughout the novel Dorothea will associate stimulation of the eyes with the evils of outward display; this will, of course, be thematized as Protestant aesthetics in her memory of St. Peter's and "the red drapery which was being hung for Christmas spreading itself everywhere like a disease of the retina." (Eliot, p. 188) In the very scene where Dorothea seems most resistant to and yet most tempted by the visual, she begins by differentiating herself morally from Celia in a metaphor that underscores the corporeality of their relative moral positions. Speaking of Celia's desire to wear a cross as an ornament and her own discomfort with the idea, Dorothea comforts Celia in what might be dismissed as her sister's own idiom: " 'No, dear, no,' said Dorothea, stroking her sister's cheek. 'Souls have complexions too: what will suit one will not suit another.' " (Eliot, p. 13) While on one level Dorothea is obviously translating the moral into the physical, speaking "carnally-minded prose" for the benefit of her sister, the figure of different complexions is coextensive with the series of physical comparisons that make up so much of the novel. The transfiguration of soul into complexion mimics the rhetorical work of Eliot's narrator who continually renders palpable the most minute of moral issues. The jewel scene becomes not merely a tableau of sisterly difference ironically undercut by Dorothea's capitulation to the beauty of an emerald necklace, but an exposition of Eliot's methodology of physical contrast and corporeal figuration. This methodology, which can be seen to operate on the border of melodrama and realism, can also be seen to locate itself in—that is to say, on the surface of—the bodies of the two sisters whose "complexions" become aligned not only with certain moral positions, but also with particular discourses and particular fictional genres.

Despite the vividness of the jewel scene and its persistence in *Middlemarch* criticism as the place where the relation between the Brooke sisters is discussed, Celia and her influence are by no means contained within it. Celia acts throughout as a third person, a third voice in Dorothea's and Casaubon's courtship, much as Dorothea becomes a third figure in Celia's marriage to Sir James. The fact that Dorothea's position in her sister's marriage is closer to the erotic other of melodrama does not, of course, mean that Celia's intervention in the Casaubon marriage is not in some sense profoundly sexual. Celia serves Dorothea, as indeed does Will, as a constant reminder of Casaubon's age, dryness, and impotence. Part of Celia's effectiveness in this role comes through her commitment to bodily description, her continual representation of Casaubon's repulsiveness; perhaps her most resonant moment of intervention in Dorothea's marriage is her commentary on the portrait of Will's mother and aunt that hangs in Dorothea's blue boudoir.

Celia, as usual, has only one comment during the scene where Dorothea bends closer to scrutinize the portrait of her husband's mother. It is, predictably enough, a comment that focuses on external beauty. In response to Casaubon's comment that his mother and aunt "were, like you and your sister, the only two children of their parents," she replies, "The sister is pretty." (Eliot, p. 74) This simple—and in the idiom of the text, carnal—intervention in what Dorothea must see as an important moment of personal revelation on the part of Casaubon is, like many of Celia's remarks, richer and more subversive than it might at first seem. The narrator informs us that the implication of Celia's compliment to the dead sister is that "she thought less favourably of Mr. Casaubon's mother." (Eliot, p. 74) This is certainly true, and aligns Celia's remark with her other critical reconstructions of Mrs. Casaubon, one of which was discussed in some detail above. Perhaps more important, however, the comment reenacts the structuring principle of oppositional sisterhood, transforming the portrait from an occasion of communication between Casaubon and Dorothea to yet another moment of insistence on the relationship between fallen and unfallen sisters. Casaubon himself provides the framing analogy by comparing the familial situation of his mother and aunt to "you and your sister"; Celia seems immediately to align herself, in this analogy, with the position of the sister, her comment becoming a tribute to her own beauty and to her own oppositional position as "fallen sister."

The discussion of the portrait becomes more complicated as we project it genetically and narratively into the future; the features of the pretty sister will be, as Dorothea will soon find out, repeated on Will Ladislaw's face. Celia's aesthetic choice of Will's mother over her sister would seem to suggest a future in which Celia and Will become allies. Nothing, of course, could be further from the truth. I would, however, suggest that Will's almost feminine prettiness, inherited as it is from the position of "fallen sister" that Celia herself so subtly occupies, along with his role in the novel as the reminder to Dorothea of her sexuality, indicates a similarity between Dorothea's sister and lover that allows Will to replace Celia in many of her functions as the novel proceeds. Dorothea's championship of Will in the middle sections of the novel and, indirectly, of his runaway grandmother, can be read through this grid of relations and substitutions as standing in for the union of feeling that never takes place between her and Celia.

Will's relationship with Dorothea becomes a translation into heterosexual terms of the relationship between the Brooke sisters. After the introduction of Will into the novel, Celia recedes into the background and the love triangle that disrupts the Casaubon marriage becomes more conventionally rendered as the struggle between two men for Dorothea. At this point of exchange between Celia and Will, when the impulse of disruptive sexuality is passed from sister to lover, Celia becomes frozen into an almost parodic rendition of herself. After her marriage to Sir James, Celia seems to exist only to parade her complacency and to demand that Dorothea visit her baby at his bath. It is clear, even from her cameo appearances in the rest of the novel, that Celia wants Dorothea to return to her and to a reframed tableau of sisterly contrast in which Celia can play the mother, and Dorothea the widow. Dorothea's visits with her sister are predictably described in terms of such tableaux: "It was a pretty picture to see this little lady in white muslin unfastening the widow's cap from her more majestic sister, and tossing it on to a chair. Just as the coils and braids of dark-brown hair had been set free, Sir James entered the room. He looked at the released head, and said, 'Ah!' in a tone of satisfaction." (Eliot, p. 535)

As the appropriate audience for this domestic picture, arriving at the climactic moment whose capture forms the essence of the tableau, Sir James might well exclaim in satisfaction. Celia, it seems, has harnessed and rearranged the eroticism of her husband's attachment to her sister by redirecting it to a safely eroticized contrast between the two sisters he loves. Dorothea resists domestic pictures as she resists having to "sit like a model for Saint Catherine" at Freshitt. (Eliot, p. 523) After Casaubon's death she is happiest away from her sister in her own home at Lowick.

If, toward the end of the novel, Celia is frozen into the background of Dorothea's life, another woman emerges to weave herself into the pattern of Dorothea's moral and erotic development: the woman who takes on the burden of difference from Dorothea is, of course, Rosamond Lydgate. If Will assumes certain of Celia's positions vis-à-vis Dorothea, Rosamond begins to occupy the more traditional position of the unscrupulous sexual rival so muted and yet so important in the relation between the Brooke sisters. The more dramatic coloring of the contrast between Dorothea and Rosamond seems partially to be a function of the shift in the novel's narrative point of view: as the novel progresses inexorably toward its romantic ending, the position from which the reader is persistently asked to gaze at Dorothea seems more and more closely identified with Will's. While Celia's voice always served in the first half of the novel as a counter to the appropriative and idealizing male gaze of Naumann, Sir James, or even Will himself, the doubleness of the novel's vision in looking at Dorothea becomes contracted into an account of Will's loving gaze. Rosamond certainly resists aligning herself with Will's gaze as long as she can, but, in the climactic encounter between them that produces Rosamond's confession of having forced her own romantic fantasies on Will, Rosamond learns, as it were, to see Dorothea through Will's eyes.

Indeed, the encounter between Rosamond and Dorothea, evocative and intensely written as it is, is not nearly as complex as the earlier scenes with Celia in which the narrative moves repeatedly from one sister's moral vision to the other's. Rosamond becomes an embodiment of all other women's essential difference from Dorothea, a foil for Dorothea's moral superiority, perhaps predictably described by Will in the idiom of Dorothea's difference from all others of her sex. From his first encounters with Dorothea he notes her lack of ostentation, the simplicity of her dress, "as if she had taken a vow to be different from all other women." Many pages later, as he tries to explain to Rosamond the harm that Dorothea's misinterpretation of their relationship might occasion, he struggles to explain why the word "preference" cannot begin to describe his feelings for Dorothea: "Explain my preference! I never had a *preference* for her, any more than I have a preference for breathing. No other woman exists by the side of her. I would rather touch her hand if it were dead, than I would touch any other woman's living." (Eliot, pp. 767–68) The romantic rhetoric Will falls back upon as the most adequate way to explain his feelings is structured by the most fundamental of binary oppositions: life and death, existence and non-existence. Will is struggling throughout this passage, and throughout his conversation with Rosamond, to make *distinctions;* he can only do so as definitively as he would like by appealing to the figure of different worlds. Rosamond and Dorothea become, under the savage separation of Will's imagery, distinct states of being referable to an idiom of a world outside language and human understanding. We may well mistrust Will's rhetoric here, and perhaps even begin to doubt the narrative point of view that so increasingly aligns itself with his. If Celia has dropped from the picture, so perhaps has the voice of realism so acutely aligned with her own ironic observations.

On the surface, the encounter between Dorothea and Rosamond resists irony; throughout the scene Dorothea enacts her difference, her specialness, Will's vision. By the end of Dorothea's visit, Rosamond can only echo Will's words about Dorothea: she tells her husband "I think she (Dorothea) must be better than any one." (Eliot, p. 788) The encounter might simply be seen to move teleologically toward an affirmation of Dorothea's difference.

The structure of difference, however, is subtly undermined in this scene by the process of echoing itself. Each woman, in this attenuated and beautifully choreographed scene, takes on a series of roles and positions that are themselves echoes of others earlier in the novel. Echoing, as a structuring trope that plays with identity and repetition, foregrounds the oscillation between sameness and difference that makes this scene so important.

Rosamond's first thought in the encounter is to judge Dorothea by herself; she assumes that Dorothea has come to make reproaches, to display a "jealous hatred." Instead, Rosamond realizes from a scrutiny of Dorothea's face that "Mrs. Casaubon's state of mind must be something quite different than what she had imagined." (Eliot, p. 781) The scene at this point becomes a test of Rosamond's ability to imagine otherness: in order for the relationship to progress, Rosamond must move beyond her own elaborate egotism to imagine the psychological state of the other woman. As the scene progresses, however, Rosamond must bridge that otherness and become—if only temporarily—more like Dorothea; indeed she must suspend her own agency in the encounter and become absorbed in Dorothea's moral energy. Rosamond's confession that Will loves Dorothea and not herself is remarkably attributed to Dorothea: "With her usual tendency to over-estimate the good in others, she [Dorothea] felt a great outgoing of her heart towards Rosamond for the generous effort which had redeemed her from suffering, not counting that the effort was a reflex of her own energy." (Eliot, p. 787)

Dorothea's inability to imagine otherness gets translated as a "tendency to over-estimate the good in others"; Rosamond's has, throughout the novel, been figured in parables of egotism like the famous scratched mirror. Dorothea's triumph in this scene is not so much the discovery of Will's love for her, but the incorporation of Rosamond into her own moral vision. Dorothea, whose difference from other women carries her to and through the scene, emerges from it physically changed by the incorporation of Rosamond. In the final love scene with Will, Dorothea's body takes on an almost eerie similarity to Rosamond's; she is described in the language of flowers hitherto specifically reserved for Rosamond, as her head, in an echo of Rosamond's earlier in the novel, "becom(es) a little more erect on its beautiful stem." (Eliot, p. 797) The absorption of Rosamond's body into Dorothea's is foreshadowed in the very beginning of their encounter when Dorothea encloses Rosamond's hand in hers: "Rosamond . . . could not avoid putting her small hand into Dorothea's, which clasped it with gentle motherliness." (Eliot, p. 781) The "gentle motherliness" of Dorothea's enclosing ungloved hand attests to the assimilative power of her moral vision, its ability to absorb difference. Like the maternal body itself, Dorothea's motherly hand temporarily represses and contains differences among women. Dorothea, as a figure for difference, ironically triumphs by transforming difference into a powerful series of identifying gestures.

If Dorothea and Rosamond begin to echo each other powerfully, the power of the echo reaches beyond the two women to include other scenes, other characters, other positions in the novel. The climactic moment in this scene where Rosamond discards artifice to look up, crying, into Dorothea's face, is almost identical to her one earlier moment of naturalness when she unintentionally tells the story of her love to Lydgate. When Rosamond turns to Dorothea: "she withdrew the handkerchief with which she had been hiding her face, her eyes met Dorothea's as helplessly as if they had been blue flowers. What was the use of thinking about behaviour after this crying? And Dorothea looked almost as childish." (Eliot, pp. 784–85) When Rosamond, many chapters earlier, turns to Lydgate: "At this moment she was as natural as she had ever been when she was five years old: she felt that her tears had risen, and it was no use to try to do anything else than let them stay like water on a blue flower or let them fall over her cheeks, even as they would." (Eliot, p. 294) If there is a difference between these two scenes it is a sexual difference; Dorothea cries with Rosamond while Lydgate of course does not. The difference that is always a part of Dorothea's character asserts itself, however, in the "almost" and in the related suggestion of Dorothea's greater maturity. Again, as behooves a maternal figure, Dorothea disguises any attempts to transcend difference with the power of empathy.

The juxtaposition of the two passages suggests once again the relation between what I am calling the heterosexual or romance plot and the sister plot of *Middlemarch*. Each plot creates a series of analogous positions: Will and Celia, and, in this case, Dorothea and Lydgate, are linked in terms of the positions they occupy with regard to other characters and to the narrative stance of the novel. "Sexual difference" describes both the relation of a character in a particular position with specific other characters, and with the character who occupies the analogous position in the "other" plot of the novel. Dorothea's encounter with Rosamond marks the sexual difference between them; her relationship with Lydgate opens up the question of nonsexual friendship between men and women and hence the question of sexual difference between them. As Rosamond realizes, "Lydgate might have said anything to Mrs. Casaubon . . . she was certainly different from other women." (Eliot, p. 788)

The sororophobic elements of *Middlemarch* are not limited to the novel's thematics; read carefully they form a submerged counter-narrative—the sister plot—which interacts in complex ways with the dominant romance plot. The sister plot, embodied most visibly in the relations between Celia and Dorothea, and replicated with a difference in the relations between Dorothea and Rosamond, and Rosamond and Mary Garth, delays, defers, challenges, and ultimately defers *to* the romance plot, as Will's point of view overtakes and replaces first Celia's, then Rosamond's, and, finally, becomes coterminous with the narrative voice. One can speak not only of sororophobic moments in a novel as they are expressed and contained by the relationship between sisters, but also of a sororophobic narrative that, at certain moments, runs counter to the hegemony of the Victorian marriage plot.

Inter-Chapter 1

"That Stormy Sisterhood": Portrait of the Brontës

This, the only surviving portrait of the three of them, groups them forever around phallic absence, the organizing principle, the painter, their brother. Branwell's decision to erase himself from this painting of his sisters only draws attention to the figure that once represented him, now alluded to by a vertical swath of yellowish paint. In so vividly depicting his own absence, he turns himself—hesitantly—into a phallic presence, into the column that comes to stand, in Charlotte's portraits of Brocklehurst and St. John, for the sin of male arrogance. Branwell under erasure reminds us in a way no signature could that he is the painter, that his sisters sit in reference to him. Branwell's arrogance, however, is no simple thing; his sisters will leave their mark, and he will leave his through scarring them; Emily's biography is especially marked by Branwell's entrances and exits, his delirium tremens, his drunkenness, his genius, and his shameful death that some say showed the way for Emily's own.

This sisterhood stands in the shadow of the brother. Branwell arranges his sisters, flattens their faces, their differences; it is hard to tell Anne from Emily. The portrait reminds us eerily of an earlier effort by Branwell to capture his sisters' likenesses: the so-called "gun group." In this sketch Branwell does not erase himself; he sits again between two sisters, the third figure to the right of center, holding a gun. In this sketch Brontë scholars can literally not tell Anne from Emily; the argument over the sisters' identity rages today. There is no doubt over the identity of Branwell; he is the one with the gun on his knee. In the finished portrait there is also no room for debate; Branwell is the one who isn't there. The gun, like Branwell, suggests itself through its absence, through the

51

Figure 1. Branwell Brontë's painting of his sisters, c. 1835. *Courtesy of the National Portrait Gallery, London.*

juxtaposition of painting with sketch; like Branwell, the gun speaks more loudly through its absence. The painting becomes the portrait without the gun. The gun in the sketch, the gun that perhaps never was in the painting, marks Branwell off from his sisters, cuts Charlotte, to the right of her brother, off from Emily and Anne to his left. Both the column of yellow paint and the gun draw the viewer's eye to Branwell and up along a vertical plane. The gun adds mass to his body; the vertical swath of paint makes him taller, the tallest, taller than all of his sisters although we are told by Mrs. Gaskell that Emily was the "tallest person in the house except her father."[1]

The painting plays—perhaps it would be better to say works—with difference, sameness, and opposition. It allows for very little difference between Emily and Anne; their faces point solemnly, almost sullenly, in the same direction; their linked gazes remind us of Ellen Nussey's observation that the two sisters were like twins. Across the painting, across the obliterated body of Branwell, Charlotte sits plump and square. The painting has cracked along the lines where it was once folded; the sisters look out to the spectator from behind a grid of cracks that cuts Emily and Anne off from Charlotte and severs Anne's chin. The isolation is prophetic; Charlotte alone will survive—for a few important years. She will represent the Brontës, tell the stories of her sisters. She will never intrude upon the twinning of her two younger sisters, will never fully understand their need for each other. If there is a place for difference within this sisterhood, which does not reside in the figure of the brother, it is in the face and body of Charlotte. If we look below the grid, to where the sisters' bodies disappear into the textured darkness of their dresses, we see only one hand. It is Charlotte's: the hand that will, after the deaths of Anne and Emily, destroy manuscripts, add prefaces to published works, choose from among their possessions and their writings those that will survive into what will quickly become the cult of the Brontës.

Figure 2. Branwell Brontë, "The Gun Group" portrait of the Brontës. *Courtesy of the Brontë Parsonage Museum.*

If the painting inscribes for posterity the difference between the Brontë sisters and their brother, and the difference between Charlotte on the one hand, and Emily and Anne on the other, it only echoes and foreshadows a litany of verbal portraits handed down to us from friends, pupils, enemies, and biographers of the sisters who were simultaneously so startlingly alike and so spectacularly different. To remove Branwell from the picture, to repress his maleness, his paintbrush, and his gun is still to have to face difference. The voices that speak to us of the Brontë sisters speak in comparatives; it is against and across each others' bodies that each sister really begins to take shape. Emily was the tallest, Anne, the most delicate looking, Charlotte the plainest, Emily the prettiest,[2] Emily, or perhaps Charlotte, the practical one. These sisters come in degrees, can be ranked: Emily was taller than Anne who was taller than Charlotte; we must resort here to superlative as well as comparative forms. Charlotte died young, Anne died younger, Emily died youngest of all—except for those who would not enter the picture if it were not for "the Brontë sisters" as institution: Branwell, Maria, and Elizabeth, and, of course, first of all, the mother of these famous children.

> Winifred Gerin on Charlotte: "[She was] admittedly the least attractive of the three Miss Brontës." (Gerin, p. 106)
>
> Pupil Laetitia Wheelwright comparing Emily to Charlotte: "I simply disliked her from the first; her tallish, ungainly ill-dressed figure contrasting so strongly with Charlotte's small, neat, trim person, although their dresses were alike." (Gerin, p. 130)
>
> Pupil Louise de Bassompierre comparing Emily to Charlotte: "Miss Emily était beaucoup moins brillante que sa soeur mais bien plus sympathique." (Gerin, p. 131)
>
> Elizabeth Gaskell on the question of relative genius: "[M. Heger] rated Emily's genius as something even higher than Charlotte's." (Gaskell, p. 230)
>
> Winifred Gerin on Emily's and Anne's poetry: "It would be unfair to Anne to make a literary comparison." (Gerin, p. 173)
>
> Elizabeth Gaskell on Anne's "shyness" and Emily's "reserve": "I distinguish reserve from shyness, because I imagine shyness would please, if it knew how, whereas reserve is indifferent whether it pleases or not." (Gaskell, p. 162)

Locked together in their infancy, the sisters and their brother lived out Victorian strictures on family closeness. They collaborated on the creation and articulation of imaginary kingdoms. When they were forced to separate, they continued to tell each other stories of their kingdoms in letters. As adults, the sisters and the brother diverged, took different routes to fame and—famously—to the grave. The sisters planned to open a school together; the brother went to London to become a painter and ran immediately back home. He took up drinking and drugs, his sisters renamed themselves, and published—again together—a volume of poetry. Their first pieces of adult fiction were written side by side, came into the world together as productions of a sisterhood at once meek and powerful. The writing of the first round of Brontë novels was an experiment in sisterly unity; the publication of the novels made visible the cracks in that sisterhood. Public reactions to the novels officially inscribed the language of sisterly difference. We must now begin to speak differently of the sisters.

Charlotte's first novel, *The Professor,* was rejected, while *Wuthering Heights* and *Agnes Grey* were eventually accepted. Charlotte wrote most of her second novel, *Jane Eyre,* alone, away from the parsonage, in Manchester, where Elizabeth Gaskell, unknown to her, was writing *Mary Barton.* Charlotte was in Manchester in the first place because she had been, in this instance favorably, compared to her sisters; she was chosen to nurse her father through an eye operation, to obtain lodgings in an unfamiliar city, and to talk to the doctor in attendance, because she was considered to be the most social of the three painfully antisocial sisters. *Jane Eyre* was published in six weeks, long before her sisters' novels, which had been accepted earlier, came out. When Anne's and Emily's unscrupulous publisher rushed to publish *Wuthering Heights* and *Agnes Grey* to take advantage of *Jane Eyre*'s immense success, the two novels were thought to be immature productions of the author of *Jane Eyre. Wuthering Heights* was dismissed as unspeakably coarse; *Agnes Grey* was dismissed with very little notice. The official verdict on both novels, as well as on her sisters' other works, was Charlotte's.

Charlotte on *Wuthering Heights:* "Whether it is right or advisable to create beings like Heathcliff, I do not know: I scarcely think it is."[3]

Charlotte on *The Tenant of Wildfell Hall:* "The choice of subject was an entire mistake."[4]

Charlotte on whether to publish a posthumous edition of her sisters' poems: "an influence stronger than could be exercised by any motive of expediency, necessarily regulated the selection. I have, then, culled from the mass only a little poem here and there. The whole makes but a tiny nosegay, and the colour and perfume of the flowers are not such as fit them for festal uses."[5]

We read Emily's and Anne's works through Charlotte's painstaking comparisons, through her letters, remarks, and prefaces—through the first Brontë biography, Elizabeth Gaskell's memorial to the surviving sister, Charlotte. We read Emily's and Anne's corpus as we read their bodies, through Charlotte's disfiguring spectacles, through her excisions, omissions, and silences. What happened to Emily's second novel, already well in progress by the time of her death? Was it Charlotte or Emily who destroyed it, who made us read *Wuthering Heights* as a single burst of novelistic genius? Charlotte silences Emily's genius as a writer in the very novel that serves as a memorial to her; in *Shirley,* Charlotte has the narrator claim that the heroine, based by Charlotte's own admission on her sister Emily, will never be a writer.

Who can resist comparing the sisters to each other? Who can resist the structure of opposition, the grid of difference and sameness? We feast on the differences between the sisters, on the arguments and differences that arose among them. Biographers chart their shifting alliances: Emily and Anne were spiritual "twins," Branwell initially preferred Charlotte to his other sisters, but Charlotte turned away from her brother and toward Emily when Branwell turned to drink. Emily defended Branwell; Anne tried to reform him. Charlotte preferred Emily's company to Anne's and brought Emily with her to Belgium in spite of Emily's history of excruciating homesickness. Emily could not forgive Charlotte for "happening" upon a manuscript of her poems or betraying her real identity to publisher George Smith. Emily and Anne refused to take their work to Charlotte's publisher even when it became clear that Newby, who published *Wuthering Heights* and *Agnes Grey,* was dishonest and stingy. Charlotte betrayed her preference for Emily in a final comparison between her sisters' deaths: "(Anne's) quiet, Christian death did not rend my heart as Emily's stern, simple, undemonstrative end did. I let Anne go to God, and felt He had a right to her. I could hardly let Emily go." (Gerin, p. 261)

These sisters internalize the idiom of comparison; they come to life with respect to each other, sometimes without respect for each other. Women in their books take their lives from other women: Jane triumphs because she is not Blanche, not Georgiana, not Eliza. Lucy Snowe triumphs because she is not the Cleopatra or the women portrayed in that series of lifeless domestic pictures, "La Vie D'Une Femme." Cathy Linton is born on the deathbed of her mother, that other Cathy Linton, who died struggling against the name they both share. Sisterhood is powerful but not easy: sisters are exaggerated and parodic opposites like the flirtatious Georgiana and the sanctimonious Eliza, indistinguishable from each other, like Diana and Mary Rivers, or jealous rivals like Isabella and Cathy, sisters in and under Edgar Linton's law—and again under the equally powerful and perhaps more demonic law of Heathcliff.

Is it enough, with Virginia Woolf, to say "Jane liked Chloe" or even "Charlotte loved Emily"? Surely even without the specter of Branwell it is more complicated than that. But the specter of Branwell intrudes anyway; these sisters are not alone; they do not represent themselves, their bodies, and their faces to us. They stare out of the portrait in different directions, their bodies held a little awkwardly: is this a failure of physical grace? Of sister love? Of brotherly loyalty? Or is it—simply—a failure of genius on the part of the painter that these sisters look so wooden, so separate? Certainly it is not Branwell's fault that the paint cracked, producing scars that run along his sisters' faces. Or could he, who was so inept at preserving his own dignity, his own life, have done better at preserving his sisters for immortality? Perhaps more important, could Charlotte, into whose capable hands the painting probably fell—again, we do not know what those hands were doing with the documents in the case— have made with those same hands a sisterhood less cracked, less stormy? Could she have given us another Emily, another Anne, another series of portraits in words?

We cannot hope to reconstruct the Brontë sisterhood as it was, but we can hope not to simplify its energies, its allegiances, its passions. It is perhaps worth noting that Charlotte Brontë conceived of passion itself in a sororal idiom. Speaking of a literary ''sister'' about whom she had mixed feelings, Charlotte once wrote that in *Emma* (Charlotte's last piece of work, a fragment of a novel, was to bear the same name), Jane Austen ''ruffles her reader by nothing vehement, disturbs him by nothing profound: the Passions are perfectly unknown to her; she rejects even a speaking acquaintance with that stormy Sisterhood.'' (Peters, p. 285) Charlotte's acquaintance with passion and with sisterhood pervades her novels, her letters, and her life; it is the complex relation between passion and sisterhood that must be understood before her readers, and before feminist critics in particular, can appreciate the full complexity of her legacy.

Chapter 2

"Another Woman in Your Shape": Sexual and Class Duplicity in Sensation Fiction

Wilkie Collins' *The Woman in White* is, famously, about two white-draped women, the serene and beautiful heiress Laura Fairlie, and her pallid and sinister double, the feeble-witted escapee from a mental institution, Anne Catherick. The novel, fuelled by both the similarities and differences between the two, traces the process of abuse and misfortune that turns Laura into a ghost of herself and an exact double of Anne. When we realize at the end of the novel that Anne is probably Laura's illegitimate half-sister, *The Woman in White* becomes a text book sororophobic text, playing out sameness and difference between sisters in the idiom of madness.

If we focus, as the title directs us to, only on the sensational Anne Catherick/ Laura Fairlie plot, we can, however, miss out on another kind of female doubling that haunts the novel and also emanates from the obsessively reiterated body of Laura Fairlie; this is a doubling which, according to Victorian norms, *should* take place but does not: the transformation of a young girl into another person after marriage. Laura Fairlie's marriage to the sinister baronet, Sir Percival Glyde, fails to transform her entirely into his wife, partly because she is in love with another man. We watch Laura's marriage through the eyes of her cousin, Marian Halcombe, who serves as witness, detective, and, not incidentally, as herself a sororophobic foil to Laura's beauty and passivity. Marian reads Laura's letters from her wedding trip, looking with contradictory feelings for evidence that her cousin has become someone else:

> I cannot find that (Sir Percival Glyde's) habits and opinions have changed and coloured hers in any single particular. The usual moral transformation which is

insensibly wrought in a young, fresh, sensitive woman by her marriage, seems never to have taken place in Laura. . . . I only see a sad torpor, an unchangeable indifference, when I turn my mind from her in the old character of a sister, and look at her, through the medium of her letters, in the new character of a wife. In other words, it is always Laura Fairlie who has been writing to me for the last six months, and never Lady Glyde.[1]

A successful marriage should replace an "old character" with a new, transforming the sister into the wife. In a novel in which Laura Fairlie's identity is always subject to the criminal manipulations of others—Sir Percival and the villainous Count Fosco kill Anne Catherick and bury her as Lady Glyde while they imprison Laura in a madhouse as Anne Catherick so that Sir Percival can gain access to his wife's money—marriage might at first seem like a benign version of this transformation, one explicitly opposed to the criminal manipulations of identity on which the mystery plot is based. Like all sensation novels, however, *The Woman in White* brings the criminal into the domestic, obscuring safe distinctions between them. Every act of immorality or criminality has its double within what seems to be the safe haven of Victorian marriage: Anne Catherick appears in the book as Laura's double both because Laura's father committed adultery and fathered a child who looks so much like his legitimate daughter, and because Laura's saintly and domestic mother was so trusting that she took a fancy to Anne and dressed her in her daughter's own cast-offs; Laura marries the evil and dissolute Sir Percival in the first place both because of his machinations and her cousin's well-intentioned pressure. Legitimacy and illegitimacy become confounded as marriage, bigamy, and adultery all partake of the idiom of doubling.

The Woman in White is, of course, not the only sensation novel to be preoccupied with female doubling. Sensation novels abound with women who disguise, transform, and replicate themselves, who diffuse their identities and scatter clues to them over the surface of their parent texts: Lady Audley of Mary Elizabeth Braddon's *Lady Audley's Secret,* and Isabel Vane of Mrs. Henry Wood's *East Lynne,* are just two sensational heroines who deliberately produce multiple identities for themselves in the course of the novels in which they appear and disappear.

In the cases of Lady Audley and Isabel Vane this duplicity, this multiplicity of identity, is explicitly marked by the text as criminal; it is the job of the reader and/or the detective figure of each novel to sort through the multiple identities offered by each heroine, to work against her self-reproduction, and to close the novel with a woman confined to a single identity, a single name, and a single place—in both cases, the grave.

It is easy to see Lady Audley and Isabel Vane as special cases; indeed the idiom of sensation fiction is exceptionality, improbability, and excess. It would perhaps be more useful, however, to see them as somehow representative of Victorian anxieties about all women, as embodying in their many bodies cultural fears about female duplicity. In the same way, while these novels can be and have been categorized as novels about bigamy and adultery, they can also be read as novels about marriage and the changes of identity contained and displayed within marriage as an institution.

Any reading that grants to Lady Audley and Isabel Vane the status of representative women can take strength from at least two discourses: psychoanalysis and history. Much contemporary psychodynamic theory of female subjectivity depends precisely on figures of female doubleness, fluidity, or multiplicity, from Luce Irigaray's contradictory "two lips," to Nancy Chodorow's "permeability" of ego boundaries, to Helene Cixous' multiple and multiplying erogenous zones. Luce Irigaray proposes and explores an erotics of female multiplicity that undermines what she calls "the *one* of form, of the individual, of the (male) sexual organ, of the proper name, of the proper meaning."[2] She imagines a female sexuality that depends on and reproduces itself through difference:

> But *woman has sex organs more or less everywhere*. She finds pleasure almost anywhere. Even if we refrain from invoking the hystericization of her entire body, the geography of her pleasure is far more diversified, more multiple in its differences, more complex, more subtle, than is commonly imagined—in an imaginary rather too narrowly focused on sameness. (*Sex*, p. 280)

Irigaray's task in *Speculum of the Other Woman*, is to identify and describe that imaginary of the same, that "phallomorphic" economy based on oneness, that tradition of logic that we might call unitary thinking. In *This Sex Which Is Not One*, particularly in the title essay and in "When Our Two Lips Speak Together," and "The Mechanics of Fluids," she attempts the even more difficult task of imagining beyond the imaginary of the same to describe a(?) contradictory, shifting, and largely pre- or extraverbal female sexuality in a language she claims is constituted by unity, singularity, and imposed coherence.

One can choose of course either to mourn women's supposed inability to construct and sustain a stable self, or to celebrate the empathy and fluidity that can be read as a psychic refusal to separate from others; one can correlate doubleness with ethical duplicity or see in it the seeds of a new and more productive ethics. The sensation novels I discuss below struggle with these contradictory possibilities as they dramatize the journey of multiple female selves in a world that punishes women for their supposed duplicity by assigning them a single and confined place. Like Irigaray, Braddon and Wood seem convinced of the multiplicity of the female self; unlike Irigaray, they are obviously deeply conflicted about the consequences of such multiplicity as they struggle both to represent their heroines sympathetically and to produce literary forms that punish and contain them.

One need not turn to psychoanalysis for an account of the fluidity of the female self; one can also, of course, turn to historical formations as ways of thinking about the topic. Central to any historical account would be the institution most commonly supposed to define female subjectivity in the nineteenth century: the strangely contradictory institution of marriage. Marriage demanded, and indeed imposed, a certain stability on the part of women; loyalty, constancy, and fidelity operated within Victorian marriage as marks and guarantors of changelessness. Nonetheless, marriage itself, as it was configured in Victorian culture, assumed a fundamental change of self on the part of the woman, most overtly marked by the change in name and status conferred upon her by the act of marrying. The change described by marriage was of course deeper than a nominal one; in a culture that equated singleness with virginity and virginity with innocence, marriage could only produce a radical realignment of subjectivity, a completely changed relation to body, to culture, and to notions of self-identity. The duplicity at the heart of Victorian marriage allows us to talk simultaneously about two categories often submerged in or obfuscated by feminist notions of gender: sexuality and class.[3] Victorian marriage, of course, called for a radical transformation of sexual status; Victorian conduct books repeatedly enjoined young women to make the rupture between a previous, supposedly nonsexual self and a married self complete by claiming that young women should have no thoughts of sex or love until *after* they had been proposed to by a suitable man. *East Lynne* investigates the difference between that sanctioned doubleness and more potentially subversive forms of sexual duplicity as Isabel struggles to explain to herself and to her uncle the difference between her feelings for her new husband, Archibald Carlyle, which she calls "liking," and something else which she calls "love." Lord Mount Severn sees such a distinction as a sign that Isabel already knows too much. "If you do not love Mr. Carlyle, how comes it that you are so wise in the distinction between 'liking' and 'love'? It cannot be that you love anybody else!"[4] Isabel's problem, of course, is that she does "love" somebody else, her rake of a cousin Francis Levinson, and that she is at this point already duplicitous in a sexual economy that allows women only one kind of feeling. The transformation of Isabel Vane into Isabel Carlyle is incomplete, insufficiently double, because she has already created, for herself and by herself, a sexual self unsanctioned and uncontained by marriage.

The ideal Victorian marriage also served as one of the few appropriate vehicles for female class mobility; if marriage was supposed to produce in the wife a sexual double of the young girl, it could also—since, as conduct books repeatedly admonished, a woman inevitably took on the class status of her husband—produce a double of a different class. A woman's class identity, like her sexuality, could, and indeed in the common cultural fantasy of progressivist marriage, should change with the change of her name. Again, as in the case of sexual transformation, change of class, although in one sense radical and life-changing, was also not supposed to go too far; modest class advancement was one thing, the crossing of major class boundaries through marriage was another. Marriage was supposed simultaneously to produce, contain, and display class as well as sexual change: to produce, display, and contain sexual and class doubleness.

The complex relations between marriage, doubleness, and class is perhaps best explored in *Lady Audley's Secret,* in which Lady Audley, née Helen Malden, moves through a series of identities and transformations—some legal, some fraudulent—on her way to the aristocratic marriage that gives her and the book their titles. In moving from the daughter of a drunken and impoverished naval officer to the wife of Sir Michael Audley, Lady Audley—I use this name as opposed to her many others both for convenience and as a marker of the staus she achieves—only does what it is incumbent upon all Victorian heroines to do: she makes a marriage that raises her class status. Lady Audley's involvement in the marriage plot differs from that of the conventional heroine in only two respects: first she marries bigamously and fakes her own death to hide her bigamy, and second, she, and not a maternal or other beneficent figure, takes control over the plotting of her marriages. In this second respect she is in a direct line of descent from Thackeray's Becky Sharp, who, in the absence of a mother to plot for her, must mold the marriage plot to her own ends. Lady Audley, like Becky Sharp, lives out the teleology of class advancement in the fertility of her own mind.

Sensation novels seem, through the multiple identities of their central characters, to be displaying an anxiety about the sexual and class doubleness that might potentially inhabit all women. It is, of course, through marriage and its attendant transformations in sex and class that doubleness is simultaneously expressed and contained; if a woman takes on the class status of her husband and is marked by his last name as—officially—a sexual being, marriage becomes itself already a source of transformation and doubleness, one that bigamy and adultery can only amplify, underscore, or parody. Lady Audley's two marriages, one legal and one bigamous, which turn her in the one case from Helen Malden to Helen Talboys and in the other from Lucy Graham to Lucy, Lady Audley, are in many ways continuous with her parthenogenic name change from Helen Talboys to her alias, Lucy Graham. Marriage, bigamy, and forgery act together as transformers of identity, as *Lady Audley's Secret* reproduces and parodies the conventional marriage plot.

This chapter focuses on the problem of the multiple female self and on the convergence of class and sexuality as locations of that multiplicity. I begin, as I did in the previous chapter, with non-canonical texts from a Victorian sub-genre: in this case with *Lady Audley's Secret* and *East Lynne*. I then move, again as I did in my discussion of sisterhood, to a more canonical text, and to a consideration of how anxieties about class and sexuality get figured as concerns about female duplicity in Thomas Hardy's *Tess of the D'Urbervilles*. All three novels are structured, in their different ways, by the competition between men and women for the control of female doubleness figured both as literal and metaphorical reproduction.

Lady Audley's Secret

In a novel that belies the singularity of the final word of its title with the plurality of its secrets—hidden drawers, chambers, rooms, passageways, crimes, and dreams—the heroine of Mary Elizabeth Braddon's *Lady Audley's Secret* explains early on what may be the novel's most important secret of all: the workings of masculine power over female reproduction and the strategies women must use to subvert that power. In the scene immediately following George Talboys' disappearance, Robert Audley meets his aunt by marriage, Lucy, Lady Audley, face to face for the first time. He expresses worry over George's whereabouts, confiding to his aunt that George has not been himself since the death of his young wife a year ago. Lady Audley responds with a flippant and general statement about masculine infidelity, although as the reader probably already suspects, the fate of George Talboys and his bride hits precariously close to home: "I did not think men were capable of these deep and lasting affections. I thought that one pretty face was as good as another pretty face to them; and that when number one with blue eyes and fair hair died, they had only to look out for number two, with dark eyes and black hair, by way of variety."[5]

Lady Audley's dismissal of George's pain and of the mystery surrounding his disappearance takes the form of an insight into a system of reproduction I have called female iterability: the inevitable replacement of one woman by another in the sexual and economic system of Victorian marriage. And, indeed, the struggle for the control of the female iterability makes for the "secret" at the heart of the novel. Lady Audley has, by the time of her confrontation with Robert, repeatedly replaced old versions of herself with new ones; she has been, at various moments, Helen Malden, Helen Talboys, Lucy Graham, and Lucy Audley. Rather than allow herself to be replaced by "number two with dark eyes and black hair," she has made sure that she, with her signature golden curls, has been the only one to replace herself.

Just as Lady Audley has taken over and incorporated the power of replacement and reiteration, so she takes over that other crucial aspect of the marital economy: reproduction. Lady Audley had one child as Helen Talboys; it is as a mother that she becomes not only financially dependent on her husband but vulnerable in other ways as well. In her final confession scene, Lady Audley explains that she inherited from her mother a "taint of madness" activated by childbirth and early child rearing. Caught between the legacy of her mother and the economic and psychological problems of becoming one, Lady Audley simultaneously eschews her maternal origins and her own maternality by reproducing only versions of herself. As her own mother and her own daughter, Lady Audley assumes tentative control over her body and her fate. For this reason, Lady Audley, however beautiful and however erotic, is in some sense sexless; like many Victorian feminists who focused on the rights of women to refuse sex, and like her literary successor, Gwendolyn Harleth, Lady Audley is deeply invested in her ability to control access to her body in the form of lovemaking or detection: it is no coincidence that she and the elderly Sir Michael have no children and that she instinctively and obsessively locks her doors, drawers, and jewelry boxes against the men in the novel.

The structure of the detective novel legitimizes penetration into Lady Audley's sexual past, her chambers, and even her body as detective and reader move through a series of smaller and smaller spaces to get to the secret promised by the title. Robert's deductive project is to inhabit and open all those spaces, to get to a single identity, a single answer, which will, in the obsessive idiom of the novel, unlock the mystery of the text. He must produce "links of iron in the wonderful chain forged by the science of the detective officer" (Braddon, p. 81): he must "forge"—and the word is doubly important given Lady Audley's own crimes—connections between Lady Audley's various selves through producing a coherent narrative of her life, and ultimately reduce her to the single identity of criminal and exile her, under this identity, from his family. Lady Audley's goal is to move in an opposite direction along the metaphoric chain of self-substitution: it is up to her to keep her identities discrete, multiple, and fluid. It is up to her, in other words, to keep the identity of George Talboys' young bride separate from the identity of Lady Audley; to insist, in the lexicon of duplicity and madness, that she is somehow not herself.

Throughout much of the novel Lady Audley's powers of self-reproduction are such that they overflow the confines of her own body and produce in the novel a series of textual doubles by no means confined to the official identities marked by her changes in name. The novel is filled with Lady Audley's doubles in the form of other characters, dream-visions, and metaphoric representations.

Perhaps the most troubling of these doubles from a literary point of view is Lady Audley's maid, Phoebe, who is described as looking almost exactly like Lady Audley, but without her coloring. Early in the novel it seems as though it will be part of Lady Audley's scheme of self-defense to get Phoebe to impersonate her. In a scene that seems to suggest such an impersonation, Lady Audley tells Phoebe:

> You *are* like me, and your features are very nice; it is only color that you want. My hair is pale yellow shot with gold, and yours is drab; my eyebrows and eyelashes are dark brown, and yours are almost—I scarcely like to say it, but they're almost white, my dear Phoebe. Your complexion is sallow, and mine is pink and rosy. Why, with a bottle of hair-dye, such as we see advertised in the papers, and a pot of rouge, you'd be as good-looking as I, any day, Phoebe. (Braddon, p. 39)

The hair dye and the pot of rouge never surface, however, and Lady Audley chooses other means to avoid an encounter with George Talboys, who is planning to visit Audley Court with Robert. One could, especially given the fact that *Lady Audley's Secret* was written by Braddon in a few weeks under tremendous financial pressure, dismiss the Phoebe incident as the trace of a previous idea for the plot. It seems equally possible, however, given the novel's insistent thematization of doubling, that the double without a function is precisely a sign of duplicitous excess: a self-reproduction with no explicit purpose in the economy of the novel, a reproduction, as it were, with no real reproductive function. Such a reading might on the one hand emphasize Lady Audley's power to replicate herself; on the other, it might point away from reproduction of and through other characters to her more unique and dangerous interest in producing a series of others within herself.

If Phoebe is a textual double without color, the novel is populated by a series of Lady Audley's doubles even more colorful than the original. The most famous of these is the pre-Raphaelite portrait of Lady Audley that hangs in her bedroom. The portrait works simultaneously in two linked but opposite ways: as a symbol of Lady Audley's duplicity, and as a tantalizing figure for a single "truth." Robert and George are led to the portrait by Alicia Audley, Sir Michael's daughter who instinctively distrusts and despises her stepmother, and who is in love with Robert. Finding the door to Lady Audley's room, where the portrait hangs, locked, Alicia remembers a secret passage she and Robert used to explore as children that leads to Lady Audley's rooms. Both the passage and the room are filled with discarded clothing; in the passage is a trunk filled with priest's clothes dating back to the era of priest holes and Catholic persecution, while Lady Audley's own chamber is piled high with dresses she has tried on and taken off. The clothing, of course, suggests disguise and forms one of the many material links between the secrets of Catholicism and the confessional and Lady Audley's crimes.[6] They also tantalize, however, with the specter of a real body, the naked truth, the possibility of penetrating beneath the surface to an essential identity.

This is a promise held out and denied by the actual portrait to which the two men finally gain access after passing through Lady Audley's dressing room to her bedroom. A masterpiece of pre-Raphaelite exaggeration, the portrait plays with its own difference from the public Lady Audley:

> It was so like, and yet so unalike. It was as if you had burned strange-colored fires before my lady's face, and by their influence brought out new lines and new expressions never seen in it before. The perfection of feature, the brilliancy of coloring, were there; but I suppose the painter had copied quaint mediaeval monstrosities until his brain had grown bewildered, for my lady, in his portrait of her, had something of the aspect of a beautiful fiend. (Braddon, p. 46)

In the complex economy of female iteration, the portrait serves as a mirror-opposite of Phoebe's doubling of Lady Audley whose body can be more easily accessed and read when projected onto characters and textual places outside herself. Lady Audley's body remains a constant, however, despite its constant movement from character to character, room to room, frame to frame.

It is easy to see the portrait as the "true" Lady Audley; indeed the portrait, more than any other of her doubles, offers a permanent inscription of her evil. It is through the portrait that George Talboys recognizes his wife and goes into the shock that will lead him to his quasi-fatal confrontation with her the next day. Alicia certainly sees the portrait as simply revelatory of the real Lady Audley. When Robert rejoins Alicia in the passage—significantly it is only the two men who actually penetrate her chamber—she explains her feelings about the painting to Robert:

> I've a strange fancy. . . . I think that sometimes a painter is in manner inspired, and is able to see, through the normal expression of the face, another expression that is equally a part of it, though not to be perceived by common eyes. *We* have never seen my lady look as she does in that picture; but I think that she *could* look so. (Braddon, p. 48)

Alicia reads Lady Audley's duplicity more accurately, at this point, than does her cousin. Robert insists, in the idiom of singularity that is to dominate his detective enterprise: "Don't be German, Alicia, if you love me. The picture is—the picture: and my lady is—my lady. That's my way of taking things, and I'm not metaphysical; don't unsettle me." (Braddon, p. 48) Robert's insistence that he is not "metaphysical," his nervousness about all things "German," suggests a very real anxiety about the possibility of doubleness, a possibility he exiles to the continent as neatly as does Henry Tilney in his famous consolatory speech to Catherine Moreland in *Northanger Abbey*. It is as if Alicia knows, however, that this is not a Gothic but a sensation novel where duplicity penetrates into English homes, the English countryside, and the English family, often in the person of the angelic heroine.

The problem with Alicia's more intuitive diagnosis, however—that the portrait is the "real" Lady Audley—is that it too fails to take into account the fluidity of the female self in this novel. Lady Audley might be framed within a portrait or a confession, but she inhabits a series of textual and geographical spaces in the novel simultaneously, appearing in London when she is presumed to be at Audley Court, in Robert's dreams, and in the series of clues that she scatters throughout the novel with her typically generous and sinister excess.

Most of Lady Audley's other textual doublings occur as moments, almost literally as flashpoints, as Lady Audley's face is lighted up a certain way to reveal duplicity beneath the surface. Perhaps the most compelling of these transient moments takes place in Lady Audley's bed as she crouches under the covers during a storm the night before she attempts to murder George. The account we get of this night is retrospective and from the point of view of Sir Michael, who is relieved when his wife comes down to breakfast with pink cheeks looking like her "merry self again." Sir Michael contrasts the woman he saw the night before with this morning vision of health and beauty:

> Do you know, Lucy, that once last night, when you looked out through the dark-green bed-curtains, with your poor, white face, and the purple rims round your hollow eyes, I had almost a difficulty to recognize my little wife in that terrified, agonized-looking creature, crying out about the storm. Thank God for the morning sun, which has brought back the rosy cheeks and bright smile! I hope to heaven, Lucy, I shall never again see you look as you did last night. (Braddon, p. 51)

The purple around Lady Audley's eyes reminds us both of the portrait and of a scene later in the novel in which her face is sinisterly marked by the reds and blues of a stained glass window behind her. The colors can be simply read as "strange-colored fires," as nothing short of the flames of hell; they also suggest, of course, Lady Audley's ability to take on any and all colors, including the pink and white of beautiful young womanhood. Again, through the play of rose and purple in this passage, the distinction between the angelic and its opposite becomes itself suspect.

As the novel moves inexorably toward Lady Audley's capture, the images of duplicity grow more troubling and more murderous. Perhaps most sinister of all, however, is the movement of the text to refuse Lady Audley her potential doubleness, to rewrite her as single or absent. Late in the novel, a series of images in which Lady Audley obsessively looks at herself and poses in the mirror comes to a climax that simultaneously turns the mirror-image outward in the form of attempted murder and inward in the form of the dissolution and disappearance of Lady Audley's body. Her back to the wall, Lady Audley decides toward the end of the novel to murder Robert in his bed at the Castle Inn where Phoebe and her blackmailing husband are proprietors. Lady Audley goes upstairs to what she thinks is the bedroom adjoining Robert's, supposedly to comb her hair. As she "smooth(s) her wet hair before the looking-glass," she places her candle "very close to the lace furbelows about the glass; so close that the starched muslin seemed to draw the flame toward it by some power of attraction in its fragile tissue." (Braddon, p. 213) The "power of attraction" of the looking-glass suggests the magnetism of Lady Audley's own beauty, a beauty that, for once, we do not see reflected in textual description. For once, Braddon is content to use the phrase "wet hair"; for once we do not hear of the feathery golden ringlets, the halo of blonde curls parodied in the famous *North British Review* article on sensation novels[7] and whose exuberance and textual dispersal I discuss below. Indeed, the mirror seems to function as an empty center, a blankness, in this scene, as Lady Audley turns from the mirror with a singular purpose. In this almost vampyric scene, which refuses to reflect Lady Audley back to the reader, the decorations around the mirror and not the mirror itself are potentially fatal; it is as if the muslin curtains, like the empty dresses in the portrait scene, are in fact the real Lady Audley. The metonymic shift from body to fabric simultaneously undermines Lady Audley's agency and suggests the complexity of her position as murderess, bigamist, and subject. One of the factors, of course, that makes Lady Audley's duplicity so pervasive, so much a matter of multiplying surfaces, so hard to untangle, is the doubleness of marriage itself. In a wonderful rewriting of the scene in *Jane Eyre* in which Jane, on the night before her abortive wedding, looks unbelievingly at her trunk labelled "Mrs. Rochester," Robert finally discovers an old hatbox of Lady Audley's from which he slowly peels the label bearing the name Lucy Graham to reveal the "Helen Talboys" beneath. This moment, like so many others in the text, is invested in the detective idiom of peeling back, stripping away, forging a chain; this pair of names, however, read with names of Jane Eyre's ("Mrs. Rochester") trunk, once again works to collapse distinctions among marriage, bigamy, and self-replication: Jane Eyre is uncomfortable with the specter of Mrs. Rochester both because she inhabits the body of another woman (Bertha) and because the marriage that Rochester promises is, like most Victorian marriages, a sacrifice of female identity. Lucy's hatbox parodies the transformation at the heart of Victorian marriage and claims the power of that transformation for women outside marriage. In a familiar gesture, Lady Audley is moving backward along the chain of transformation that leads to marriage; by calling herself Lucy Graham instead of Helen Talboys she is unmarrying George and replacing marriage with self-generation.

Ultimately, of course, the form of the detective novel and the power of the detective idiom get the best of Lady Audley, freezing her into place. Significantly in this novel of many identities, it is Lady Audley's body that repeatedly betrays her, appearing as it does as a series of fragments in the form of clues. The novel and Robert repeatedly focus in on two parts of Lady Audley's body: her curls and her handwriting. Her curls appear in her lockets, curled up between the pages of an annual, and in the possession of various characters, and transform themselves metaphorically into the novel's repeated invocation of locks to doors, boxes, and trunks. The novel performs a similar metaphoric operation on her hands: while her tiny hands, their rings, their bruises, and their fingers appear repeatedly, they also get transformed into the motif of handwriting, as a close examination of both proves Lady Audley and Helen Talboys to be the same person. The bodily fragments that ultimately betray Lady Audley can be read either as signs of incomplete or excessive doubling, or, more poignantly, as doubling's double or as its opposite, as the fragmentation that renders Lady Audley less, not more, than one. The detective idiom particularizes, fetishizes, and fragments, putting an end to the possibility of reproduction.

Lady Audley's final confession becomes, finally, an attempt to impose and live through doubleness. Even when she is identified, captured, and accused, she retains her duplicity through the invocation of her mother and more particularly of her mother's madness. The text does not allow us—or for that matter, Robert—to decide whether Lady Audley is "really" mad or "simply" criminal; this is a secret Lady Audley—if she herself knows the answer—takes to the grave with her. Ironically, as Robert decides to send her to the madhouse, he is forced to accede to her idiom of doubleness by changing her name to Mme. Taylor to protect the reputation of his family. This name change is simultaneously a final gesture of control—Robert is ultimately restored to the Adamic power of naming as Lady Audley's power of self-naming comes pathetically to an end—and an acknowledgment that he and the medical experts cannot come to a conclusion about a stable identity for this woman who has occupied so many names and places.

If the detective plot of this novel depends on singularity, its sexual politics finally depend on female iterability, on the replacement of one woman by another within a masculine economy. Robert's participation in the love plot depends precisely on his own notion of female iterability; his periodic misogynist outbursts take the form of blaming women for the disturbances in his hitherto peaceful life. After visiting Clara Talboys, who persuades him to go on with his investigations into the disappearance of his brother, he complains:

> "I hate women. . . . They're bold, brazen, abominable creatures, invented for the annoyance and destruction of their superiors. Look at this business of poor George's! It is all woman's work from one end to the other. He marries a woman, and his father casts him off penniless and professionless. He hears of the woman's death and he breaks his heart—his good honest, manly heart. . . . He goes to a woman's house and he is never seen alive again. And now I find myself driven into a corner by another woman, of whose existence I had never thought until this day. And—and then," mused Mr. Audley rather irrelevantly, "there's Alicia, too; *she's* another nuisance. She'd like me to marry her I know." (Braddon, p. 137)

Robert's litany of female nuisances does not discriminate between the criminal and the domestic; women seem equally problematic for wanting to marry him or murder his friend, as once again the discourses of the legal and the illegal get confounded. Later on in the novel, Robert makes a more succinct list of women who annoy him: it is, significantly, only a list of names: "Helen Malden, Lady Audley, Clara Talboys, and now Miss Tonks." (Braddon, p. 156) Once again there is a total disregard for distinctions among the women; Helen Talboys and Lady Audley are after all, as he now knows, the same person; Clara Talboys is the woman with whom he is in love, and Miss Tonks is only a minor witness to Lady Audley's identity, who has actually helped him on with the case. One cannot help recalling Lady Audley's bitter testimony to the replacement of one woman by another in the male psyche.

For the purposes of the love plot, however, Robert must make a distinction among the women with whom he is in some way erotically entangled. The distinction is both corporeal and succinct; the minute Clara Talboys enters the text, the narrator provides the answer to the mystery of the marriage plot: "She was different to (sic) all other women that he had ever seen. His cousin was pretty, his uncle's wife was lovely, but Clara Talboys was beautiful." (Braddon, p. 132) The comparison proffered by the narrator takes us into a system of difference within the sameness in which Clara belatedly triumphs as the novel's heroine. There is, however, another side to that difference, another economy in which Clara participates. The text makes no secret of the fact that Clara looks exactly like her brother George, and that much of Robert's fascination with her stems from the fact that when she gazes at him, he feels as if George's eyes are upon him. Clara forms a bridge to, a compromise with, the homosocial economy of the text in which, as Eve Sedgwick and her structuralist predecessors suggest, women operate only as gifts or tokens of exchange between men. Clara breaks the chain of reiterability by being "different to all other women," by being more like her brother than she is like Lady Audley. By deciding to marry Clara and not Alicia, Robert can simultaneously hold on to his belief that all women are the same and that his wife is different from all others.

In this way, the control over female doubling passes from Lady Audley to Robert, from the criminal to the detective, as the novel leaves her erotic life to close with his. In the end, Lady Audley is exiled from the marriage plot that is her milieu, the place among many places where she operates with the most confidence. The name "Mme. Taylor" ambiguously offers her an imaginary husband while relieving her of two others. Locked in a place topographically similar to those in which she defended herself throughout the novel, she can no longer reproduce herself; instead the novel turns in the final chapter to Robert and Clara's infant son, who seems to have borrowed two key terms from Lady Audley's lexicon. The baby, eerily enough, "peers wonderingly from his nurse's arms at that other baby in the purple depth of the quiet water." The "purple" and the "other baby" suggest Lady Audley; the child's carefully remarked maleness, however, suggests the appropriateness of such colorful doubling in a household where the baby's father lives both with a homosocial double of himself and with a woman who is a double of his double.

The ending of the novel also reestablishes middle-class life and middle-class morality at the expense of the two extremes. Sir Michael abandons Audley Court with its aristocratic associations to share the "fairy cottage" on the Thames with George, Clara, Robert, and their children, as little Georgy moves from his grandfather's home to join the rest of the family. Lady Audley, marked by the sexually and socially ambiguous "Mme." is exiled from the class system she has worked as she has worked the marriage plot, her fantasy of class transcendence and asexual reproduction denied to her by the reformation of an appropriately fertile middle-class suburban family.

East Lynne

If in *Lady Audley's Secret* the battle over the terms of female identity occurs between Lady Audley and Robert, the battle in *East Lynne* is waged primarily in the even more intimate domestic theater of the relation between husband and wife. Archibald Carlyle, like Robert Audley, functions both as a relative to the duplicitous antiheroine and as an amateur detective. In his position as lawyer, Carlyle embodies in the community and in the novel the virtues of logic, reason, and plain-speaking; in his position as husband he has continual access to the lexicon of reason in his dealings with his wife who, throughout the first half of the novel, is subject to dreams, jealous nightmares, and sexual fantasies.

These moments of fantasy, shared by Isabel with other female characters, are the first clues to an inherent female duplicity that will erupt, as the novel goes on, from the level of character into the level of sensational plotting. Isabel's jealous imaginings get translated into action as her panic about her husband's interest in another woman causes her to elope with Sir Francis Levinson; the elopement, in turn, marks and transforms her body, first through pregnancy, illness, and remorse, and finally through the disfigurement that makes Isabel's doubleness visible and complete, allowing her to reenter her own home as governess to her children. If Lady Audley's doubleness gets projected onto a series of places and faces outside herself, allowing her body to remain unchanged, Isabel Vane's takes a visible toll. If Lady Audley is ultimately "identified" by the fact that her body remains the same through a series of personae, Isabel's punishment is made manifest in the disfigurement, crippling, and scarring which make her painfully unrecognizable in her own home.

Although Isabel bears the visible burden of duplicity, serving as the scapegoat for the novel's anxieties about doubleness, she is by no means the only character working through the problem of duplicity. Whereas in *Lady Audley's Secret* duplicity is relatively easily confined in Lady Audley's (admittedly unconfinable) body, in *East Lynne* almost every character, almost every gesture, has its double. Structurally, the novel depends on two crucial mirrorings: Carlyle's two marriages—first to Isabel and then, when Isabel is presumed dead after the train wreck, to her rival, Barbara Hare—and the close relation between the marriage and detective plots, with Francis Levinson turning out to be the villain of both.

East Lynne manages, displays, and explores doubleness on three levels, each potentially more dangerous than the last. Perhaps the safest form is male and homosocial. Just as in *Lady Audley's Secret,* where the doubling of George and Robert serves as a moral center to a novel in danger of being sucked into a whirlpool of female desire, in *East Lynne* male doubling of a slightly different kind works to structure and contain female desire. Very early in the novel, Isabel is introduced to Carlyle at dinner and Francis Levinson at tea. Soon after the introduction of Levinson into the text and into Isabel's life, the occasion is marked by a speculative narrative intrusion: "Strange—strange that she (Isabel) should make the acquaintance of those two men in the same day, almost in the same hour: the two, of all the human race, who were to exercise so powerful an influence over her future life!" (Wood, p. 11) The intrusion posits a heroine caught between two men with the power to shape her life; like Alec D'Urberville and Angel Clare in *Tess of the D'Urbervilles,* these two men represent different fates, different stories the heroine can live out. Again like Alec and Angel, Carlyle and Levinson meet, as it were, across the body of the heroine as it is poised on the verge of womanhood: their alternate notions of sexuality will be written upon it and will become, in effect, her sexuality, her story. Carlyle and Levinson come together at what the text asserts as an originary moment, a transition into sexuality and into narrative that is already proleptically marked by the text's knowledge of the heroine's inevitable sexual fall.

The alternatives Isabel faces at this crucial moment are designed of course to be quite distinct; unlike Isabel and Barbara Hare, this pair of male doubles is easily readable in moral terms. Isabel, unlike Tess, is allowed to make what seems to be the right "choice"; Levinson warns her that he must marry money, Carlyle proposes marriage, and Isabel is forced into what seems like safety and security. The neat opposition between the good man and the bad, between the two possible marriages, breaks down, however, first because Carlyle, like Angel Clare, begins through his own blindness to slip from the position of perfect husband, and, second, because in this novel, which begins with a marriage, the "resolution" of the marriage plot in no way provides closure for the novel's vexing questions about sexuality. Isabel's "choice" must constantly be remade, reaffirmed, and ultimately called into question as the narrative moves beyond the happy ending into the life of marriage itself.

If the novel opens with a romantic choice between men that is not a choice at all, it closes with a political choice that is both clear and permanent. Levinson and Carlyle are transformed from rivals for Isabel's hand into candidates for public office as, after Levinson returns from the continent where he had abandoned Isabel to claim his title and estate, they compete for the parliamentary seat at West Lynne. The voters of West Lynne represent not only their village but the reader as well in their astonishment that Francis Levinson should dare to run against the man he has cuckolded; the reader adds her incredulity because she knows what the villagers do not, that Levinson in coming back to West Lynne is returning not only to the place where he has absconded with the squire's wife, but also to the scene of his murder of Hallijohn. Only Carlyle seems unmoved by the insult of Levinson's return.

Carlyle's stoicism is a form of accession to the narrative teleology of the novel in which private life—necessarily messy, double, uncomfortable, and feminine—gets translated into the relatively safe and masculine space of the public and the political. The election is an airing out, a purification of private difficulties; the contest for the seat is not merely a chance for Carlyle to win against his rival but a chance to make that victory clearer, simpler, cleaner.

The election allows not only the public working out of private matters, but, on the level of narrative structure, the translation of the marriage or private plot into the detective or public plot. It is while making a speech to the electorate that Levinson is eventually arrested for the murder of Hallijohn; his public entrance into West Lynne, his transformation into a public figure allows him to be identified not only as an adulterer but as a murderer. Thus the political plot and the political competition, however small a space they take up in the novel, allow for that translation, making possible Carlyle's public revenge. Levinson's own doubling—his identity with and as the mysterious Captain Thorne who left West Lynne on the night of the murder—is quickly and publicly cleared up once he becomes a candidate. Neither the detective nor the political plot leaves a remainder: all questions are solved, all problems resolved as Levinson's two identities collapse into one and one man wins easily and spectacularly over the other.

Levinson's propensity for doubleness is explicitly aligned throughout the novel to his class and sexual status. The novel's uneasy feelings about the aristocracy and about female sexuality come together, ironically, in the gesture that gives Levinson's identity away: his habit, in both his personae, of brushing curls back from his forehead with what witnesses describe as a "white" hand emblazoned with a large diamond ring. The whiteness of the hand and the prominence of the ring suggest an effeminacy and effeteness foreign to the middle-class norms of the novel; aristocracy is dangerous in men and women alike, while female sexuality can even insidiously write itself on the male body. Like Lady Audley's, Levinson's curls and ring, signs of his duplicity, betray him into a single criminal identity.

While Carlyle allows and indeed thrives on doubling in the public arena, he literally cannot bear it in his private life. From his first entrance into the text where he is aligned with middle-class business principles and with plain-speaking, he acts as a spokesman for the singular, the legalistic, and the literal. When Isabel, half-delirious after the birth of a child, hears the servants gossiping about Barbara's notorious infatuation with Carlyle, she becomes anxious and depressed, explaining to Carlyle that she has had a "dream" that he really loves Barbara. Carlyle ends the discussion with an appeal to the legal status of their marriage: "Don't have any more of these dreams if you can help it. . . . Regard them for what they are—illusions, neither pleasant for you, nor fair to me. I am bound to you by fond ties as well as legal ones, remember, Isabel; and it is out of Barbara Hare's power to step between us." (Wood, p. 153) Carlyle's "don't have any more of these dreams if you can help it" will become, as we shall see, a marker of the clash between male and female, legalistic and emotional discourses in *East Lynne*. The paradoxical injunction to women not to dream will be repeated in less benign form in one of the novel's subplots where the domineering Judge Hare becomes violent whenever his wife admits she has dreamt about their son. Carlyle's gentle admonitions, juxtaposed with Judge Hare's abuse, suggest a pattern of male resistance to female fantasy. Carlyle's judicious balance between "fond ties" and "legal ones" in his attempt to console Isabel is somewhat undermined by the word "power" in the final clause of his speech: the subtle victory of public over private discourse marked by the word "power" suggests Carlyle's sense of marriage as a legal and political entity free from ambiguities of fantasy or desire. Carlyle's definition of marriage is invested in a discourse even more authoritative than the law; even after he is legally divorced from Isabel, he explains to Barbara that he cannot remarry as long as "She—who was my wife—lives." He puts an end to the discussion with a quotation from the Hebrew Bible: "Whosoever putteth away his wife, and marrieth another, committeth adultery." (Wood, p. 267) It is, of course, typical of Carlyle that in a question of biblical hermeneutics, he should choose the most literal interpretation, and that his position should be one that puts as much distance as possible between adultery, bigamy, and marriage, concepts with whose boundaries sensation fiction so frequently flirts. In living according to a literalist hermeneutics, Carlyle attempts to banish the specter of female doubleness from his home.

The irony of Carlyle's situation is of course that he does, despite himself, end up marrying in a way he would consider to be bigamous, that his attempts to control female duplicity through marriage are spectacular and improbable failures. This is because, throughout the novel, female desire is systematically portrayed as both duplicitous and ungovernable, female discourse as a polymorphous and polyvocal challenge to law, order, and institutional power.

This challenge, as I have suggested earlier, takes on two forms, as female doubleness inhabits two primary textual places, two powerful discourses that might be called the characterological and the psychological. Doubling on the level of character itself takes two primary forms—the maternal and the sororal—as anxieties about female sexuality become embedded in the idiom of the matrophobic and the sororophobic.

Maternal doubleness takes many forms in *East Lynne,* infecting Isabel's relation to both her mother and her daughter, as well as the other important maternal relation in the novel: that of Mrs. Hare to her two children. Like *Lady Audley's Secret, East Lynne* works with the metaphor of maternal inheritance; Isabel, who looks, predictably enough, exactly like her dead mother, inherits from that mother something more nebulous but at least as dangerous as the madness that passes from Mrs. Malden to Lady Audley: an impulsive sexuality strangely at odds with a character generally presented as innocent and pure. Isabel's mother committed, as her husband explains, only one "mad act": she ran away with him to Gretna Green. Otherwise, he tells Carlyle, she was "all goodness and refinement," and reared her daughter as "an English girl should be, not to frivolity and foppery." (Wood, p. 7) Lady Mount Severn's careful rearing is not enough to counteract the power of her example; her single "mad act" has a predictive and reproductive power in shaping her daughter's sexuality. Isabel too commits one such act; in running to the Continent with

Francis Levinson, in leaving England, her husband, and her children behind, she amplifies and embodies her mother's sexual legacy.

The ambivalence of Isabel's maternal inheritance takes a concrete and readable shape in the symbolic cross, also a legacy from her mother, which she wears around her neck early in the novel as her only ornament.[8] In an overdetermined prefigurative gesture, Francis Levinson steps on the cross, breaking it in two. It is easy—too easy—to read this moment as a severing of Isabel from her mother; Isabel herself, as alive to omens as any avid reader of sensation fiction, certainly reads it this way. The matrix of maternal doubling and duplicity in which Isabel's sexuality is embedded, however, forces us to read more suspiciously as the broken cross signals not so much separation from as reiteration of the mother. The mother's jewel is always already broken; it is the very brokenness of the cross and not the cross itself that serves as Isabel's true inheritance from her mother.

Isabel's replication of her mother's fate is only one link of the chain of maternal replication figured by the broken necklace; Isabel's own daughter Isabel Lucy, again a perfect likeness of her own mother, is constantly in danger of repeating her mother's fate. It is for this reason that Carlyle eradicates his daughter's first name; after her mother's elopement he orders that she be called only "Lucy." Carlyle's instinctive attempt to interrupt female sexual doubling is undercut by Isabel's equally instinctive desire to return to the past in her return as her children's governess in the second half of the book. Isabel repeatedly slips and calls her daughter "Isabel," in a sign both of her own immediate past and of the larger narrative past that begins with Lucy's grandmother's decision to elope.

If, on the level of character, Isabel carries on and within her body signs of matrophobic reiteration, the novel's structure depends on sororophobia and on an almost endless series of sororophobic repetitions and replacements. Barbara Hare is replaced in Carlyle's affection by Isabel in the first twenty pages of the novel; after her marriage, Isabel is haunted by the idea that she will be replaced before or after her death by Barbara. Despite Carlyle's protests that he has never thought of Barbara as anything other than a friend, he does of course marry her as soon as Isabel is assumed to be dead. Finally, Isabel's return in the guise of governess to East Lynne, and to the house where she was first married, opens the way for an excruciating litany of doubled scenes in which Isabel is forced to see Barbara occupying a series of positions—at the piano, in Carlyle's arms—and in possession of an endless series of things—a bracelet, a hairbrush, the respect of Isabel's own children, Carlyle's affections—which she once enjoyed herself. Indeed the whole idiom of the second half of the novel is repetition: Barbara repeats Isabel's actions by singing the same songs, occupying the same rooms, saying the same loving words to the same husband. The position of wife—once Isabel's, now Barbara's—gets translated into a series of physical positions and gestures whose symmetry tortures Isabel throughout the novel's second half:

> Lady Isabel stole across the drawing-room to the other door, which was ajar. Barbara was seated at the piano, and Mr. Carlyle stood by her, his arm on her chair, and bending his face on a level with hers, possibly to look at the music. So once had stolen, so once had peeped the unhappy Barbara, to hear this self-same song. *She* had been his wife then; she had received his kisses when it was over. Their positions were reversed. (Wood, p. 362)

The ambiguous "she," the grammatical shifter of the last sentence, marks the path of female reiteration and replication. Isabel's internal monologue becomes itself confused and confusing as to the identity of the words "wife" and "she."

To say that Barbara has replaced Isabel—or even that Isabel, in looking in from the outside has replaced Barbara—is to underestimate the complexity of the novel and its structuring sororophobia. The problem is precisely that one woman has not in any linear way replaced the other, that both occupy the same place, that both live, love, and desire at once.

Despite Carlyle's repeated attempts to prevent the possibility of Isabel and Barbara's coexistence in his world, the novel's wonderfully melodramatic final scene, where Carlyle finally recognizes Isabel on her deathbed in the governess' room at East Lynne, is a testament to the power of female iteration. Isabel's version of the afterlife is one in which she and Carlyle can "meet again . . . and live together for ever and for ever" without sin. She assures Carlyle that her vision is a Christian one based on Christ's own promise that there will be no marrying or giving in marriage in heaven. By invoking Christianity in defense of sexual doubleness, Isabel aligns herself with a power that overrides Carlyle's legalism. She admits that she does not know "how it will be," how their relationship will be arranged, but she places her faith in a non-unitary God. It is, of course, significant that Isabel does not mention Barbara in this fantasy of the afterlife; her implicit acknowledgment of her rival and replacement comes only in the form of uncertainty about the specifics of God's plan. Barbara is present, but her presence does not have the power to change or to alter Isabel's love for Carlyle.

Carlyle's legalism, his uneasiness with the double and the multiple, runs counter to Isabel's ecstatic vision throughout the entire final scene. When he first recognizes Isabel, the "first clear thought that came thumping through his brain was, that he must be a man of two wives." (Wood, p. 516) If Barbara can be simultaneously present and absent for Isabel, she acts for Carlyle as a barrier between himself and the (former?) wife who insists she is speaking as if from the grave. Carlyle stoops as if to kiss Isabel goodbye, but a something—someone—intervenes:

Lower and lower bent he his head, until his breath nearly mingled with hers. But, suddenly, his face grew red with a scarlet flush, and he lifted it again. Did the form of one, then in a felon's cell at Lynneborough, thrust itself before him? or that of his absent and unconscious wife? (Wood, p. 518)

Even at the moment of Carlyle's resistance Barbara appears only as one alternative, as one possible explanation for his behavior. She first enters this passage, strangely enough, as a double for Francis Levinson, not for Isabel. Levinson, designated here as "one," is in some sense responsible for the obfuscation of "one" and "two," for the undoing of the referentiality of language and the power of marriage to work within it. By the end of the passage, Barbara has become the "unconscious wife," her unconsciousness a property she shares or is about to share with Isabel, who slips blissfully into unconsciousness after her interview with Carlyle. Both "unconscious" and "wife" become shifters as Carlyle desperately struggles to achieve some control over the situation.

Control is of course easier—if by no means simple—after Isabel's death. Like Lady Audley, Lady Isabel is disposed of and renamed by a group of men who apply closure to the novel and her powers within it. Interestingly, while Lady Audley is given a new francophone name, Lady Isabel—the self-styled "Madame Vine"—is stripped of hers and returned to the name of her childhood. She is buried not under a name, but under a series of initials: "I.M.V.," as if the reduction from name to initials were a talisman against the power of her self-naming. Perhaps even more interesting than the reduction from name to initial is the question of the referentiality of the carceral "I. M. V."; the initials, although monumental, are in some sense unreadable. Do they stand for "Isabel Mount Severn Vane" with the "Severn" left out? For "Isabel, Madame Vine?" For "Isabel Mary Vane?" For some other condensation or combination of Isabel's many identities? The letters which seem initially to provide closure open up instead a series of questions, a series of identities that resist any ending to the problem of who Isabel is or is not.[9]

If the inter-generational doubling of maternal inheritance and the intra-generational doubling of sexual rivalry are both presented as challenges to the legal, the literal, and the masculine, doubling within the feminine psyche is still more dangerous. The duplicity within Isabel herself, which begins with her innocent confusion about liking and love and ends with her Lady Audley-like faked death and disguise, is all the more frightening because Isabel, unlike her sensational predecessor, is by no means a villainess. Indeed in order to account for Isabel's doubleness one must begin to posit something as general as a Victorian fear of doubling in all women, even those who commit only "one mad act."

East Lynne, unlike *Lady Audley's Secret,* is the story of the "one mad act," the singular moment of weakness that makes all women duplicitous in the sexually and spiritually monogamous economy of Victorian marriage. Isabel's adulterous feelings for Levinson coexist with a sense of her own sexual and class security. In a passage remarkable for its openness and complexity, Wood gives us a glimpse of Isabel's mind as she discovers, or rather, rediscovers, her attraction to her cousin:

> She was aware that a sensation all too warm, a feeling of attraction towards Francis Levinson, was working within her; not a voluntary one; she could no more repress it than she could repress her own sense of being: and, mixed with it was the stern voice of conscience, overwhelming her with the most lively terror. . . . But, do not mistake the word terror; or suppose that Lady Isabel Carlyle applied it here in the vulgar acceptation of the term. She did not fear for herself . . . she would have believed it as impossible for her ever to forsake her duty as a wife, a gentlewoman, and a Christian, as for the sun to turn around from the west to the east. (Wood, p. 177)

Bifurcated by the "but," this passage is split between a frank avowal of sexuality in the first half and an attempt to contain that sexuality in the second. "Wife," "gentlewoman," and "Christian" serve as talismans against "terror" and "attraction." More sinisterly symmetrical, however, are the twin invocations of ontology and subjectivity: "she could no more repress it than she could repress her own sense of being," and "she did not fear for herself." The battleground here is, of course, the self, Isabel's own sense of her identity, and here we might oppose the phrase "her own sense of being" to the suddenly hollow litany "wife," "gentlewoman," "Christian."

I would argue that the contradiction at the heart of this passage is not only between Isabel's "sense of being" and the roles she is forced to play, but already inscribed in those roles. Although the novel does not spend much time on Isabel's religious feelings or opinions, it does offer a scrupulous account of the contradictory desires and decisions that shaped her class and marital positions; Isabel becomes Carlyle's wife for a variety of reasons, from fear of losing her home to fear of her love for Francis Levinson. The marriage involves a complicated class adjustment when Isabel returns as a wife to the aristocratic home her father sold to a middle-class lawyer in order to pay his—also aristocratic—debts. The opening of the novel, with the sale of East Lynne, signals a passage of power from the aristocracy to the professional middle class; it does so through a series of attacks on aristocratic profligacy and privilege; Lord Mount Severn even dies of the archetypal disease of spendthrift aristocrats—the gout—while Isabel's initial unhappiness in the marriage is blamed on her aristocratic scorn for domestic work: she balks haughtily, for example, at her sister-in-law's suggestion that she fold a pile of napkins. Caught in this homosocial reordering of society and between the two men who, each in his different way, try and fail to make a home for her at East Lynne, Isabel accedes to a marriage that exposes the novel's sense of sex and class contradictions. Isabel's dependence on her social position to help her resist Levinson's advances is pitiable since that very social position is profoundly unstable, radically double.

Isabel's final decision to elope with Levinson is both an inevitable result of her earliest sexual feelings and a radical break from her self and her past. The narrator repeatedly intrudes upon the elopement scene with what are not so much explanations as reiterations of the same point: that Isabel hardly knew what she was doing. If we can locate a moment in the text that provides what we might call motivation, it is in the form of a universal, gendered, truth: "A jealous woman is mad; an outraged woman is doubly mad." (Wood, p. 227) Here, Isabel explicitly becomes a representative woman; here we have the language of madness and doubleness that so permeates *Lady Audley's Secret*. The narrator, in imagining and sympathizing with Isabel's state of mind, normalizes her experience.

This normalizing is taken a step further, when, many pages later, Isabel receives sympathy from an unexpected source. As Mrs. Hare tells the excruciatingly familiar and all-too-often repeated "secret" of Lady Isabel's elopement to Isabel in her disguise as the governess, Mme. Vine, Barbara's mother states firmly that she believes Isabel, "refined, modest, with every feeling of an English gentlewoman," must "have gone away in a dream, not knowing what she was doing." (Wood, p. 360) Mrs. Hare not only rearticulates her class alliance with Isabel, but in suggesting that Isabel must have eloped in a "dream," she connects Isabel's jealous fantasies with her own prophetic dreams, a connection made explicitly female, explicitly maternal, in the text. Isabel elopes because she is a woman, and because, in this text, all women dream. The community of female dreamers suggests that *East Lynne*'s position of female fantasy is more sympathetic than the one articulated by *Lady Audley's Secret;* Lady Audley operates alone with only her doubles for company; Isabel's desires, Isabel's doubling, are part of a larger world of female fantasy.

The doubleness that constitutes female subjectivity through dreaming and desire is made manifest and translated into class terms through the image of the governess. By disguising herself as a governess, already a figure of class and sexual duality in Victorian fiction and culture, Isabel is doubly double.[10] Isabel's status as governess is mined throughout the novel for images of Isabel's ambiguous status, as we see, for example, when Barbara chooses to confide in "Mme. Vine" about her husband's first wife. She ends her story with an appeal to the governess' sense of familial loyalty to the Carlyles: "'You will understand, Madame Vine, that this history has been given you in confidence. I look upon you as one of ourselves.' There was no answer. Madame Vine sat on, with her white face. It wore altogether a ghastly look.'' (Wood, p. 417) Barbara's assurance that Isabel, as Mme. Vine, is ''one of ourselves'' is ironic in at least two registers: Isabel is, in a complicated sense that only the final deathbed vision of the novel will make room for, actually a member of Barbara's family, but the phrase also suggests the hollow assurances of an employer to a semi-privileged employee. As adulterous wife and as governess, Isabel must be exiled from the family; her presence in both capacities serves to demarcate familial boundaries.

As wife, mother, and governess, Isabel embodies the three most sanctioned life possibilities for Victorian leisure-class women; each of these roles is itself double in terms of sexuality and class: by becoming all of them simultaneously, Isabel contains within her scarred body the contradictions of all three roles with themselves and with each other. Isabel, even more than Lady Audley, brings to light the doubleness at the heart of Victorian constructions of proper womanhood.

Tess

For reasons of genre and of thematics, *Tess of the D'Urbervilles* might seem in many ways to be a different case from either *Lady Audley's Secret* or *East Lynne. Tess,* is, of course, not usually classified as a sensation novel, although with its violent and erotic plot twists, its villainous angel-heroine, its constant visual return to the female body and to the secrets it carries into the text, it has much in common with novels more usually associated with the genre.[11] *Tess* is also, of course, an exploration of female agency, although from a different, perhaps opposite angle; despite their different degrees of culpability, both Isabel Vane and Lady Audley try to work doubleness to their advantage, while Tess, canonically constructed as a passive heroine, has doubling thrust upon her in a series of forms from historical repetition to the double standard. Doubling in *Tess* comes from forces outside: it is Tess' fate and her fatality not to be singular.

While the forces of history, family, and class work against any easy notion of individualism in *Tess,* doubleness and duplicity shape the terms of erotic dialogue, just as they do in the two sensation novels discussed above. Moreover, in this novel haunted by class difficulties, doubling plays an important part in configuring the relation of class to sexuality.

Like Lady Audley and Isabel Vane, Tess is, from the beginning of the novel, many women at once; in *Tess,* however, these other selves within Tess appear as fragments of a personal, familial, and national history: each woman within Tess represents a stage of her development. As the novel opens and we see Tess in the first stages of sexual desirability, the narrator informs us that "(p)hases of her childhood lurked in her aspect still. As she walked along today, for all her bouncing handsome womanliness, you could sometimes see her twelfth year in her cheeks, or her ninth sparkling from her eyes; and even her fifth would flit over the curves of her mouth now and then."[12] The sense of individual history offered in this diachronic version of Tess is particularly intriguing in a novel interested in denying the heroine's personal agency. This description sets up the category of individual development only to undermine it by moving quickly into larger factors that determine the fate and even the contours of Tess' body.

The two competing determinants of Tess' corporeal fate are, of course, her paternal and maternal inheritances opposed, however problematically, in this novel as historical and "unhistorical." While Tess inherits her name and the D'Urberville history from her father, she inherits her beauty from her mother, from whose features, "faintly beamed . . . something of the freshness, and even the prettiness, of her youth; rendering it probable that the personal charms which Tess could boast of were in main part her mother's gift, and therefore unknightly, unhistorical." (Hardy, p. 25) Hardy is, of course, playing with the notion of history here; there are different types of history, and it becomes clear that Joan has one of her own when she warns Tess not to repeat the story of her sexual past to Angel. Joan's history, however, is unrecorded, and therefore, as we shall see later, illegible to Angel, even, and perhaps especially, when it gets rewritten upon the body of the daughter.

Like Lady Audley and Isabel, Tess carries within her, like a foreign but familiar body, the body and history of her mother. When Alec sees her for the first time he thinks that she is older than she is. As Hardy rather coyly puts it:

> She had an attribute which amounted to a disadvantage just now; and it was this that caused Alec D'Urberville's eyes to rivet themselves upon her. It was a luxuriance of aspect, a fulness of growth, which made her appear more of a woman than she really was. She had inherited the feature from her mother without the quality it denoted. (Hardy, p. 45)

Tess contains within her and projects outward to the world a body that is maternal not only in its literal resemblance to her own mother but in its fullness and maturity. Her body, poised at this point between childhood and maturity, forges a visible link between the past in the form of Joan D'Urbeyfield and the future, in the form of Tess' own shameful and public maternity. Like Isabel's cross, Tess' "fulness of aspect" acknowledges a legacy and foreshadows a future where that legacy will emerge replete with meaning. Unlike Isabel's, however, Tess' inheritance is written on her body; the broken cross might metaphorically represent a loss of chastity, but Tess' body bears a metonymic relation to its own destiny.

Tess is cursed with two male misreaders of her body and history. I discuss elsewhere the construction of Tess' autobiography and the refusal of Angel Clare to admit its existence or importance. (Michie, pp. 112–114) I would like now to reframe autobiography as doubleness; it is precisely Tess' multiplicity, the fact of the existence of many versions of Tess, that Angel is invested in denying.

Clearly, Angel's misreading of Tess centers on his fantasy of her purity; that purity, however, is itself inscribed in an economy of singularity reminiscent of Archibald Carlyle's. Not only is that singularity part of Angel's fantasy discourse of Tess' absolute monogamy, but it becomes mystified in the novel's ironic invocation of the Genesis story where all other men, all other histories, are mythically eliminated. Angel's repeated use of Edenic imagery is both seductive and dangerous. Passages like the following carefully set up its seductive qualities only to undermine them:

> Being so often—possibly not always by chance—the first two persons to get up at the dairy-house, they seemed to themselves the first two persons up of all the world. . . . The spectral, half-compounded, aqueous light which pervaded the open mead, impressed them with a feeling of isolation, as if they were Adam and Eve. At this dim inceptive stage of the day Tess seemed to Clare to exhibit a dignified largeness both of disposition and physique, an almost regnant power, possibly because he knew that at that preternatural time hardly any woman so well endowed in person as she was likely to be walking in the open air within the boundaries of his horizon; very few in all England. Fair women are usually asleep at midsummer dawns. She was close at hand, and the rest were nowhere. (Hardy, p. 134)

The mythic and indeed lexical inflation of this passage reflects Tess' own "largeness" in this magical world. As the passage progresses, however, Adam and Eve and their uniqueness and primacy disappear to be replaced by minuter, more realistic calculations. By the end of the passage Tess is only one of the prettiest women likely to be awake at a particular hour in a particular geographical area; her one merit is that she is "close." The deflation of Tess' mythical largeness works with a deflation from spiritual *to* physical largeness; by the middle of the passage we are reminded of Tess' "fulness of aspect," a largeness even Alec is capable of appreciating.

The irony of the passage depends to a certain extent on its identification as Angel's point of view; this identification is made two paragraphs later when the narrator, speaking explicitly for and through Angel, tells us: "It was then (in the morning), as has been said, that she impressed him most deeply. She was no longer the milkmaid, but a visionary essence of woman—a whole sex condensed into one typical form. He called her Artemis, Demeter, and other fanciful names half teasingly, which she did not like because she did not understand them." (Hardy, pp. 134–35) While feminist critics have commented on Angel's appropriation of Tess through his Adamic renaming of her, I want to focus here on the insistence of the "one typical form," in Angel's imagining of Tess; that oneness is, of course, itself a compound of different women, but it is precisely those differences that the "one typical form" masks and contains. Like his more obviously pathological parallel, Jocelyn Pierston in *The Well-Beloved,* who searches in three generations of women for one embodied form, Angel's version of eroticism disguises female multiplicity as sameness. In this, as in many other ways, Angel becomes only a more benign version of Alec, who tells Tess that "all women" say the same thing. While Tess can see through Alec's misogyny and can articulate her objections to it— "Did it ever strike your mind that what every woman says some women may feel?" (Hardy, p. 83)—she cannot resist totalizing rhetoric in its more benign form as it embeds itself in Angel's prelapsarian discourse: this form of unitary thinking is seductive to Tess and the reader alike.

Angel represents a gentle but coercive form of unitary thinking that links him directly to Archibald Carlyle. This connection becomes clearer in the infamous wedding-night scene, where issues of class and sexuality are finally given material form. Tess and Angel's "twin" confessions sever the night in two; even before their famous declarations to each other, class and sexuality become uneasily embodied in Tess as Angel encourages her to try on the diamonds his godmother has sent as a wedding present. In putting on the diamonds Tess becomes a specter of her own familial past, recorded and repeated in the D'Urberville portraits built into the wall of the house. Angel has already nervously noted the fact that "her fine features were unquestionably traceable in (the) exaggerated forms" of the portraits; now, despite, or perhaps because of that similarity, he turns Tess, on the night of their marriage, back into a D'Urberville:

> He suggested to her how to tuck in the upper edge of her bodice, so as to make it roughly approximate to the cut for evening wear. . . . He had never till now estimated the artistic excellence of Tess's limbs and features.
>
> "If only you were to appear in a ball-room!" he said. "But no—no, dearest, I think I love you best in the wing-bonnet and cotton-frock—yes, better than in this, well as you support these dignities." (Hardy, pp. 217–18)

This wedding night has done the work of many such nights in Victorian culture; it has transformed the bride into a member of another—higher—class. Ironically, however, in this case, Tess becomes a member not of her husband's class, but of one even higher—and in the terms of this novel—more dangerous. Tess is marked by the D'Urberville name, of course, in two ways; first, as a descendant of the D'Urberville family, and then, as Angel later insists, as the "wife" of Alec D'Urberville; both alternatives challenge the power of the husband to determine the identity of his wife, a power Angel complacently contemplates before the arrival of the diamonds:

> Looking at her silently for a long time; "She is a dear dear Tess," he thought to himself, as one deciding on the true construction of a difficult passage. "Do I realize solemnly enough how utterly and irretrievably this little womanly thing is the creature of my good and bad faith and fortune? I think not. I think I could not, unless I were a woman myself. What I am in worldly estate, she is. What I become, she must become." (Hardy, p. 215)

The simple and powerful equation with which Angel's meditation ends, is, of course, belied by what he learns about Tess' sexual past. Importantly, however, that past, that sexuality, is explicitly configured in class terms, and explicitly foreshadowed in the scene with the diamonds. Throughout the novel, class and sexuality have been, if not conflated, intertwined; when Tess first tries to tell Angel the secret of her past, by which she means her relationship with Alec, she loses her courage and substitutes another secret, her identity as a D'Urberville. Tess' instinctive replacement of one shameful revelation with the other is deeply true to the economy of the novel, and indeed to Angel's desires as they operate within that economy; as we learn from *East Lynne* among other Victorian texts, to be an aristocratic woman is to be sexually flawed, and to pair oneself as an aristocratic woman with a middle-class husband is to threaten the class and sexual assumptions of Victorian marriage. Tess, simultaneously a peasant girl and an aristocrat, challenges middle-class norms from both sides; as milkmaid and fine lady her doubleness exceeds the normative doubleness middle-class marriage is designed to contain.

One can read the wedding night as a struggle over the terms of that doubleness, as an effort on the part of Tess and Angel to find a way of managing female duplicity that seems safe and comprehensible to each. Tess initially experiences the wedding night as a time of merger between herself and Angel where she becomes part of him. When he asks her, early in the evening, as they wash their hands together " 'Which are my fingers and which are yours?' " she answers, "very prettily," " 'They are all yours.' " (Hardy, p. 215) Tess is, of course, thinking along approved legal lines; man and wife are to become one flesh and that flesh is the husband's. In one sense, Tess' remark is evidence of submission. In another, however, her point of view depends on a metaphor in which she inhabits her husband's body, becomes a presence inside him, acts, in fact, as a double within him contained and sanctioned by marriage. Her axis of symmetry is, as it were, heterosexual; marriage, in her idiom, involves a doubling between husband and wife.

This idiom finds its expression in the confession scene, where Tess listens with relief to Angel's story of his sexual experiences. Tess is "almost glad" about what Angel has to say because, as Angel confesses, he "seemed to be her double." (Hardy, p. 220) As she puts it, "now *you* can forgive me!" When Angel tells her that her confession can "hardly be more serious" than his own, she speaks from a sense of reciprocity and similarity: " 'It cannot—O no, it cannot!' She jumped joyfully at the hope. "No it cannot be more serious, certainly . . . because 'tis just the same!' " (Hardy, pp. 221–22) The tragedy of the novel is that according to Angel, her sexual past is not "the same"; in what is misleadingly called the double standard, doubling between husband and wife is disallowed, impossible, unthinkable. Angel cannot articulate what makes the cases different, but he feels irrevocably that they are so.

The very doubleness upon which Tess rests her hope becomes displaced at the moment of her confession as Angel sees Tess not as his own double, but as somehow double in herself, "a guilty woman in the guise of an innocent one." (Hardy, p. 227) Angel must, in Kleinian terms, actually split Tess into two; as soon as he can articulate his feelings he tells Tess that "the woman I have been loving is not you," but "another woman in your shape." (Hardy, p. 226) The axis of symmetry moves from between husband and wife to a place deep within Tess, as, through her confessed act of sexual fall and reproduction, she reproduces herself, although without the sense of purpose and agency involved in the self-replications of Lady Audley or even Isabel Vane. Tess is closer to Isabel in the inevitability of her doubleness; even less than Isabel does she seem in control of the multiple selves produced by and within her body.

It is not surprising that Angel's sense of sexual duplicity should be quickly followed by images of class doubleness, themselves multiple and contradictory. When Tess appeals to her mother's stories of similar problems with other couples, Angel throws Tess' peasant origins in her face: "don't argue. Different societies, different manners. You almost make me say you are an unapprehending peasant woman." (Hardy, p. 229) At the same time, Angel blames the aristocratic D'Urbervilles for Tess' sexual fall: "Decrepit families imply decrepit wills, decrepit conduct. Heaven, why did you give me a handle for despising you more by informing me of your descent!" (Hardy, pp. 229–30) In his anger following her confession, Angel splits his middle-class wife into the peasant and the aristocrat as he reveals the power of sexuality to undermine middle-class norms.

Tess' and Angel's competing discourses of similarity find conflicting expression as Tess' position, paraphrasable as "I am the same as you," gets rewritten by Angel's more culturally powerful "you are not the same person any more." Sexual experience in women is once again born of an inherent duplicity, and once again produces doubles, other women, from the body of the first. It is easy to read this reproduction of the other woman as a displacement or perversion of reproduction as it is normally understood; certainly in both *Tess* and *Lady Audley's Secret* the actual children are quickly disposed of as the plot focuses on this other kind of female production in some ways opposed to and in others causally related to the first.

Tess differs from the first two sensation novels in its ability to critique Angel's form of the "double standard" and its interest in showing how female doubling can be viewed as productive. From the time Angel leaves Tess— interestingly he stops on the way to Brazil to dally with an "other woman" in the conventional sense by inviting Tess' friend Izz Huett along—to the time he reappears in England asking for Tess under the wrong name, he is painfully coming to terms with, learning to accept, female doubleness. The ending of the novel, which I discuss as a sororophobic gesture in Chapter 1, becomes readable in terms of the text's consistent concern with female doubling. Liza-Lu emerges as a solution to the problem of doubling; at once Tess' double and a separate character, she can allow Angel access to female doubleness without duplicity. Even at the moment where Tess virtually hands Liza-Lu over to Angel, however, the specter of class difference haunts the text. At the time Hardy wrote *Tess*, the Deceased Wife's Sister Act was still in effect; marriage between Angel and Liza-Lu would, as Angel suggests, be illegal. Tess' response points back to her peasant origins: "That's nothing, dearest. People marry sister-laws (sic) continually about Marlott." (Hardy, p. 380) This act of replication, like the others we have seen, is class specific; the fact that Angel says nothing and that he ends the novel hand in hand with his sister-in-law might or might not suggest his acquiescence to a class tradition not his own. Whether he marries Liza-Lu or not, however, he has accepted another woman in Tess' shape and, perhaps, by extension the issues of class and sex which produced that dangerous other woman within Tess earlier in the novel.

Hardy's fascination with the erotics of class in relations between women occurs many times in his work, perhaps most vividly in two neglected pieces, *The Hand of Ethelberta* and his short story "On the Western Circuit." The first tells the story of a female storyteller who disguises her lower-class origins and becomes a celebrated beauty; the second is a complex tale about the relationship between an illiterate servant girl, her middle-class lover, and the lady who agrees to write love letters in the servant's name. Critics and biographers have suggested that we can read in Hardy's class fables his own anxieties about his birth; we can read him in the character of Ethelberta and in Hardy's family name, "Hand," in the title of the novel. However compelling this identification of Hardy with his working-class heroines, it is also important to take into account his preoccupation with class difference specifically between women, from the notorious homoerotic encounter between Miss Aldclyffe and her maid

Cytherea in *Desperate Remedies* to the rivalry between servant and mistress in "On the Western Circuit."

The erotics of class difference in *Tess* are contained—although this is hardly the word—within a single subject, a single body. Anxieties about class trespass become literally embodied in the heroine, moving from the interpersonal to the intra-subjective without losing their erotic force. If in "On the Western Circuit" the erotics of class are worked out through the sexual rivalry between mistress and maid, and if in *Desperate Remedies* they surface in more explicit homoeroticism, in *Tess* eroticism and class come together within the body of the heroine, that fertile textual space, that "gossamer tissue" on which so many things are written and in which so many lives are lived out.

When otherness between women becomes otherness within a single woman, when "single women" become necessarily double or multiple, the self gets revealed as fiction, and cultural institutions designed to contain the self—marriage and class, for example—get revealed as fictions about fictions. This might be the source of Victorian, and perhaps even contemporary, anxieties about sensation fiction. When the *North British Review* complained that the hair color of Braddon's heroines changed from page to page, perhaps the reviewer was responding not so much to bad writing as to the mutability of female desires for which hair was so frequently a sign in Victorian culture. Perhaps Angel's anxieties were not so much about adultery as they were about a kind of parthenogenesis toward which adultery might show the way.

Inter-Chapter 2

"Mama He's Crazy": The Judds

Their first hit album is called "Why Not Me." On the front cover two almost identical faces poised on two perfectly white necks stare seductively, cheek to cheek, at some point in the middle distance. (Figure 3) Each face is surrounded by red curls, carefully cut, angled, and backlit so there is no variation of shade to distinguish one head of hair from the other. The hair extends to the top and sides of the album cover, forms a frame within which the two faces shine in identical shades of carefully produced porcelain flesh tones. If the hair brings the two faces together, it also suggests separation; it bifurcates the cover, comes between the two faces, between one shining cheek and the other. Separation, distinction, difference, however, remain only suggestions; the hair that comes between the two women could belong to either, belongs somehow to both of them; the undifferentiated mass of hair that divides the faces becomes an emblem of the interweaving of the two personalities for whom the hair has become a public synecdoche. On the back of their next album cover, "Heartland," the faces have entirely disappeared. We see instead only hair, two red heads of it, from the back, neatly aligned under the numbers "one" and "two" that indicate the sides of the album. (Figure 4)

The two women, the two redheads, the two heads of red hair are the Judds, Naomi and Wynonna, country music's only mother-daughter singing duo. "Why Not Me" and "Heartland" are, in the compressed chronology of popular music, early Judd albums where Naomi and Wynonna, mother and daughter respectively, are represented as being indistinguishable from each other. The success of the Judds, their almost mythic stature in contemporary country music, begins with this fantasy of the identity between, the non-individuation of, mother and daughter, a fantasy that recalls other cultural

Figure 3. Front cover, *Why Not Me. Courtesy of BMC Music.*

moments from the famous Ivory Liquid commercial of the early seventies ("Can you tell whose hands are whose?"), to Fox television's mother-daughter beauty pageant where mothers and daughters answer questions about their relationship in matching bathing suits, to certain strands of French and American matriarchal feminism.

The Judds burst on the country music scene in 1984 as a living embodiment of the psychic and cultural possibilities of maternal fusion: at once a rare phenomenon—no one in country music remembers another mother-daughter singing team—and somehow representative of all that country music wants to be about (family harmony judiciously mixed with glamor), they enjoy the powerfully and paradoxically linked appeal of uniqueness and universality.

But fusion is not—and cannot be—the only axis upon which the Judds pose, sing, make public appearances, or stage their shows. The very identity between mother and daughter suggests difference; they can only preserve their sameness in the face of the mother's triumph over time and over her daughter. If there is a difference between the Judds it is at first blush an unexpected one; the familiar response to the Judds is that the mother is younger looking, thinner, sexier.

Mother and daughter join, through the institution of the Judds, to celebrate the youth of the mother, the youth to which the daughter sacrifices her own. Wynonna's physical and musical precocity are synecdochally represented through the pounds that separate her from her mother's youthful slimness; those distinguishing pounds of flesh serve, ironically, as a guarantor of the myth of sameness that fuelled the Judd's original success. As a visible reminder of her mother's transcendence of time, the daughter comes to stand for time and for decay; time, heft, even maternal curves reside not in her mother's body, but, strangely in her own (identical) form. The mother, in looking like the daughter, looks better than her daughter, for the likeness between them is the triumph of the mother.

And indeed, it is on that likeness which is both difference and transcendence that "mama"—Naomi Judd—seems to depend. It is mama who, at first glance, preserves the likeness between them, calling herself and her daughter, for instance, in their TV documentary-cum-video, "Across the Heartland," "just

Figure 4. Back cover, *Heartland*. *Courtesy of BMC Music.*

a couple of boogie-woogie red-headed babes," and who suggests a double date. Their likeness seems, on TV and on stage as on their album covers, intimately entwined with their hair, which, in turn, seems to stand in an almost pre-Raphaelite relation to their sexuality. On stage at Wolf Trap Wynonna introduces a new song by her mother, "Cadillac Red," by claiming that her mother wrote it while cruising. "And Wynonna was right there beside me," answers Naomi to the cheers of the crowd.

A glance at their living and highly public autobiography in the form of performances, interviews, and TV and radio specials—the Judds are not reticent about the story of their life—identifies Naomi, the mother, as the choreographer behind the Judd phenomenon; it was she who insisted that the two of them perform as a duo, she who resisted the idea that her daughter, universally acknowledged as the superior musical talent, should go solo. While this can, of course, be read as pure egoism on the part of Naomi, the issues at stake are far more psychodynamically and culturally complex than Naomi's individual desire to perform. As the Judds' biography repeatedly reminds us, the Judds as mother-daughter duo is a concept that *works;* it is Naomi's brainchild, part of Naomi's fantasies that she lived out with prescience and ferocity since, sixteen and unmarried, she became pregnant with Wynonna.

The Judds' biography by country music journalist Bob Millard details Naomi's abrupt and incessant journeys across the country—usually between her native Kentucky and California—to fulfill a vague dream that was somehow to be the amalgamation of both cultures: the rural, rooted, and religious culture of the Appalachians and the sophistication and glamor of San Francisco and Los Angeles. Naomi choreographed a series of lifestyles for herself and her two daughters; for her official narrative of the birth of the Judds she focuses on the four years the family spent in the mountains of Berea, Kentucky, without phone service or television. Naomi glosses over the equal number of years the Judds spent in California, as she glosses over the element of choice in her return to a rural life and a Kentucky town at a judicious distance from her own mother. According to Naomi and Wynonna, it was during evenings without television and without other distractions that Wynonna turned to music and specifically to the music of the Kentucky hills. The official Judds narrative generally ends here without mention of the next three years in Marin county where Wynonna learned the California sounds of EmmyLou Harris, the Eagles, and Linda Ronstadt which were also to have such an effect on what Naomi now refers to as "Judd music."

The fantasy of familial isolation—of mother and daughter singing with and to each other across a kitchen table oblivious to the rest of the world—feeds directly into the Judds' music and their joint public persona(e). Naomi both created and rewrote a personal history of herself and her daughter to provide the narrative behind the public spectacle that is the Judds. Both narrative and persona(e) were created early on in the Judds' musical career, perhaps even before their career could be said to have started; when the Judds came to Nashville several producers and artists noted that the résumé Naomi so vigorously handed out to all comers was more like a press release or the draft of a production concept than it was a list of the Judds' accomplishments. And the first step in the realization of such a concept is the complex story of the Judds' search for names.

Naomi was born Diana Judd; during her brief marriage to the father of her two daughters she took her husband's name and became Diana Ciminella. Naomi and her husband named their two daughters Christina and Ashley. A few years after the divorce, Diana officially returned to her old surname; at the same time she took on the name Naomi which she claims came to her from the biblical story of Naomi and Ruth. A little later, Christina changed her name unofficially to Wynonna Judd, having been attracted to the name of the tiny town of Wynona, Oklahoma. Presumably in the spirit of familial assonance, Naomi tried to persuade Ashley to rename herself Ramona Judd; Ashley, who features in Naomi's public discourse as "the non-musical Judd," agreed to use Judd at school but reportedly broke into derisive laughter over Ramona.

With the name changes came a series of associations and affiliations, a matriarchal network strengthened and made fluid by the amniotic syllables of "Wynonna" and "Naomi." If "Naomi" and "Wynonna" point at and refer to each other, the name "Judd" looks past Mike Ciminella and past Naomi's marriage to her birth family. Significantly, this name too becomes part of a matriarchal idiom; in "Across the Heartland" Naomi introduces her own mother as "the original Judd." The association of Naomi with one of the two books in the Bible named for a woman, a book in which one woman travels to a new land in the company of another, moves the origin of Naomi's public and private self back even further into a matriarchal and along a specifically female chain of identification. To insist, as Naomi does, that these names were conceived before she had any thoughts of a stage career and that they are therefore in no sense "stage names" is beside the point. The familial fantasy that produced the Judds is identical to the one that linked a matriarchal biblical and personal past with a hazy future in the original transformation of Diana Ciminella into Naomi Judd.

The Judds' early album covers create and display a fantasy of mother-daughter harmony based exclusively on linked principles of similarity and non-individuation. At the same time, the Judd's highly public life and their equally public relation to each other was clearly not as harmonious as their music or as their official persona(e). Soon after their first successful audition—where Naomi and Wynonna significantly converted producer Joe Galante with their rendition of "A Mother's Smile"—the Judds clashed (as they frequently did) over issues of control and responsibility and Naomi threw her daughter out of the house. Wynonna went to live with their manager, Brent Maher, and mother and daughter met only in the relatively controlled atmosphere of the studio. The Judds were understandably quiet about their living arrangement, although they began, after a while, to use their differences to their advantage in interviews that would often include playful and not-so-playful banter about the other's inadequacies.

As the Judds grew more confident in public, their banter became part of their persona(e); carefully staged conflict became part of their live act, and difference became the visual idiom of later album covers. Their "Greatest Hits" album (1988) and their most recent "River of Time" offer us differences of color, texture, and shape. Their hair is almost the same color, but it is differently styled. On the "Greatest Hits" album Naomi wears a clinging red dress which billows out to show her legs; she sits perched on a windowsill. Below her, standing with her arm barely touching her mother's dress, is Wynonna, swathed in, indeed almost obliterated by green fabric. (Figure 5)

Figure 5. Front Cover, *The Judds' Greatest Hits. Courtesy of BMC Music.*

Figure 6. Front cover, *River Of Time. Courtesy of BMC Music.*

Wynonna's costume is reminiscent of the "fat girl" dresses Millard tells us
Naomi forced her daughter to wear as a child, dresses which, as he points out,
emphasize rather than hide extra weight. This cover hints at the difference
implicit in identical mother-daughter pairs, and can be read either as the sexual
triumph of the bare-legged mother over her daughter weighed down by her
clothes and by her own body, or as the beginning of a public declaration of
Wynonna's physicality. Both bodies are dressed in conflicting codes; both
come to us through layers of public coverage and exposure.

If the "Greatest Hits" album simultaneously hints at and covers up the
question of weight through the draping of fabric, "River of Time" boldly
announces Wynonna's largeness and reframes it as power. In this album cover,
both women are dressed primarily in white, the mother in a form-fitting white
suit, the daughter in diaphanous and flowing white material that emphasizes her
difference from her mother. (Figure 6) Like the "Greatest Hits" album, and
unlike the early albums that showed the Judds only from the neck or chest up,

the full body shots on the "River of Time" cover offer us the fullness of Wynonna's body. This cover, however, is unique in its visual alignment of Wynonna's size with her musical talent, that other, less visible difference between mother and daughter; here, the daughter stands slightly in front of the mother, firmly holding a white guitar across the middle of her body. Fabric and guitar come together to underline Wynonna's physical presence and to reinterpret it as power and as music. Physical and sexual difference become, in addition, musical difference, a difference Wynonna has begun to work to her advantage.

No matter how close the visual similarity, we come inevitably to the question of the Judds' voices and to the startling difference between them. Wynonna's voice is powerful, deep, and throaty; perhaps more important, it is instantly recognizable. It is her voice that marks the songs they sing as Judd music, her voice that penetrates the crackle of a turning radio dial to announce the identity of the band, a song, a way of singing—a way, if you listen to the Judds, of being in the world. Naomi sings a gentle and intermittent harmony lost on any but the best equipment; to drive through the night with the car radio tuned to a country station is to hear only the voice of the daughter.

Country and western fans are used to rumors that Wynonna will leave her mother to go solo, that she will complete, in effect, the differentiation already at work in their singing.* Fan magazines are full of stories about quarrels between mother and daughter, of separations (Wynonna now has her own apartment) and shouting matches (Naomi admits they "hoot and holler almost daily"). Wynonna, who is usually the one directly to address the issue of tension between them, suggests an almost canonical paradigm of separation and reunion; "People assume we are joined at the lips . . . we're two very different people that come together 'cuz (of) something that binds us." "Joined at the lips" is, of course, a resonant metaphor for where mother and daughter come publicly together; it also suggests divergence below the surface, beyond the boundaries of the first two album covers that show only the Judds' faces.

But like the Persephone myth, that canonical story of mother-daughter separation, the Judds are also a parable of return and reunion. Their songs are dialogues in which something we might call a mythic maternal voice is stronger than Naomi's actual harmonies; they are dialogues that have developed and changed with the passage of time. One of the Judds' first smash hits, "Mama He's Crazy," is typical of their early efforts; its direct, familiar, and familial address, similar to the equally popular "Grandpa (Tell Me 'Bout the Good Old

---

* Since I finished this piece on the Judds, that differentiation has taken place in a tragic manner. Naomi has retired from the stage for health reasons; she was diagnosed in 1990 with the debilitating and sometimes fatal disease, chronic hepatitis.

Days)'' sets up a triangulated relation between mother, daughter, and lover. The "Mama He's Crazy" video shows mother and daughter together in a porch swing; the daughter's boyfriend has just left and "mama" replaces him for a confidential chat. Sexuality, in this song and fantasy becomes not a disruption of the original nuclear family, but a cementing of all relations, a reaffirmation of rather than a journey away from the originary relation with the maternal body. The song, written specifically for them by their friend and guitarist Don Potter, was not only their first hit, but the first song to capture and to formulate the sound and the ideology that were to become the Judds'. It quickly became their hallmark song, the one they were to highlight in their auditions:

> Mama, I've found someone,
> Like you said would come along.
> He's a sight, and so unlike
> Any man I've known.
> I was afraid to let him in,
> I'm not the trusting kind,
> But now I'm convinced
> That he's heaven sent,
> And must be out of his mind.
>
> Mama, he's crazy,
> Crazy over me,
> And in my life is where he says,
> He always wants to be.
> I've never been so loved,
> He beats all I've ever seen,
> Mama, he's crazy
> He's crazy over me.

In "Grandpa" the fantasy of reunion with the birth family takes on a specifically historical dimension as it works through the emotionally and culturally charged lexicon of nostalgia:

> Grandpa, tell me 'bout the good old days,
> Sometimes it feels like this world's gone crazy.
> Grandpa, take me back to yesterday,
> When the line between right and wrong
> Didn't seem so hazy.
>
> Did lovers really fall in love to stay,
> Stand beside each other come what may,
> Was a promise really something people kept,
> Not just something they would say?
> (Did) families really bow their heads to pray,
> Daddies really never go away?

It is easy to read this song biographically for the missing "Mr. Judd" in the person either of Mike Ciminella or Naomi's emotionally distant father, Glenn Judd, but what interests me is the repeated and resonant fantasy of familial union that can be read nationally as a lost American dream, historically as a longing for the period before the "sexual revolution," and psychoanalytically as pre-Oedipal desire.

Few of the Judds' most recent songs are as direct about the place of the birth family in the joint public fantasy they embody and represent. Their new songs—several of them significantly written by Naomi herself—tend to be more concerned with linked notions of psychic safety and sexual expression. If their songs grow increasingly sexual, they also grow increasingly insistent on monogamy. The relatively early "Love Is Alive"—"Love is alive and at our breakfast table/Every day of the week/Love is alive and it grows every day and night even in our sleep/ . . . Love is a man and he's mine"—becomes "I'm a One Man Woman":

> Well, I'm a one man woman
> I want a one woman man,
> I've got two arms to hold him
> To love him all I can.
> Now, it's a free world we live in,
> This I understand,
> But I'm a one man woman
> I want a one woman man.

The will to monogamy can underwrite that will to maternal fusion that is one of the many forces in operation in Judd music. The later desires—those that are explicitly sexual—come in the form of demands; there are no more questions of Grandpa, no more frame narratives of the relation between mother and daughter. The "mama," who is literally present—if silent—in "Mama He's Crazy," is now part of the Judd myth, present and listening in every song, answering, perhaps, in the voice of Naomi Judd as songwriter, or in her stage patter. We can even hear it—if we listen carefully—in her harmonies. The Judds are no longer voices on the radio, the stereo, the compact disc player, cameos on video stations, faces on album covers, confessions and non-confessions on documentaries; they are all these things at once and none of them as they play, perhaps over their heads, with some of the most resonant and deeply buried psychodynamic material of our culture. To complicate the picture and to bring it together, they must be seen—as the idiom goes—live.

Wolf Trap Farm Park, Reston, Virginia, June 1, 1989
Families picnic on the lawn; there is no room for latecomers to put their baskets, their neat squares of checked cloth. Blankets overlap promiscuously; the night

air comes down, and with it the flies. At the refreshment stand there is champagne and young women tell each other that "Mama Judd" has just married. No one seems to know who, exactly, but they are happy for her. Wynonna, or is it Naomi, you know the fat one, must be a handful. They are glad she is getting some pleasure after all these years. These are the Naomi fans; they like her legs, her slimness. Back on the lawn, the Wynonna fans do not leave their blankets. Many of them are large women with beautiful hair. Some wear cowboy hats like the one Wynonna wore in "Across the Heartland." The audience continues to eat as T. Graham Browne sings. Night falls suddenly, completely, but this far south the air seems to get warmer with the waiting bodies.

Naomi and Wynonna are due to rise at nine. At nine-fifteen the crowd grows restless, pushes closer together, close to the front of the lawn. They want to see. And they are right. The first thing to see are squares of light: two of them, waiting to be filled. Naomi appears in one, Wynonna in the other. Wynonna wears black pants, an oversize, diaphanous black top. She sports a guitar, a hat. Naomi wears lime green chiffon: a short, leggy dress, ruffled, draped, and ballooned at the thighs, the kind of dress you would die if your mother wore to a party when you were in high school. The kind of dress designed for the very young that the young rarely have enough money or courage to wear. Wynonna sings "I know where I'm going." Naomi—well, it is hard to say what it is she does. Occasionally she sings a line, occasionally she plays with the microphone as if it were a lasso. But Naomi does something her daughter rarely does. She moves. "Moves" doesn't describe it either. She circles her daughter like an electron. She runs up to her as if about to ask her for something, then runs back to the other side of the stage. The light moves off her, or she ducks out of the spotlight and she disappears only to reemerge, like Puck or Ariel, where you thought it least likely she would be. She teases her daughter, shakes her ruffles at her, makes faces, stops suddenly, jerks the microphone up to her mouth and sings something.

Mama can move up and down as well as from side to side. The stage has three or four levels; she jumps from one to the other in her lime green pumps, lands a little clumsily, but never quite hurts herself. You remember that Wynonna calls her "the Lucille Ball of Country Music." She does look a little like Lucy in one of those innumerable episodes where she schemes her way on stage into the middle of an act she's never seen before. But this is Naomi's act—Naomi's and Wynonna's. The song is over. Wynonna has sung it beautifully; her voice reaches the back of the lawn, filters out of the sold-out arena and onto the grass outside where people sit for free. She belts it out, she growls; her voice is full of sex. She smiles with triumph and suddenly you realize that she looks, sounds, and leers like Elvis. Mama slithers downstage, all elbows and shoulders; she looks like an appealingly clumsy teenage girl in her mother's dress. For a moment, Wynonna is the one with the sex; the song is hers, her voice is deep with experience. Mama flutters as the music stops.

The time between songs belongs to Mama. She is a riot of sexual innuendo; she calls the audience "girls." "You know what we want, girls," she growls, and the growl reminds us of Wynonna when she sings. This identity between the two women depends not so much on likeness now, but on reversal; one takes a position and gives it up, they take turns as mother and daughter, one sexy and one innocent. Sex passes between them like a flame or a gift to be lightly tossed back when the music stops or starts again. They sing "One True Love," turning toward each other with the word "one"; at the word "love" Naomi has melted into the darkness of the stage. Many of their songs feature the word "one"; the Kentucky drawl, or perhaps the growl, or even the acoustics of Wolf Trap make it rhyme with "love."

Toward the end of the second set Wynonna—it seems almost reluctantly—begins to talk between songs. She sounds more like Elvis than ever. "I love to watch Mama dancing her little life away," she says, in a voice that is all texture and no affect. Naomi bows as if in acknowledgment of a tribute. "Usually we don't like to sing about bad things—we've been so lucky," says Naomi, "But I wrote a song about how it feels when bad things happen." They move into "River of Time." Naomi's songs are less professional, less musically polished than many of the others the Judds sing, but there is more room for harmony in them. As the song progresses both voices get louder, as if competing for room in the warm air; Wynonna wins easily, and the speakers near the stage whine with the increased volume. Naomi has written another song they do often but will not do tonight, another song about bad things, "Mr. Pain."

The Judds swing into a rousing encore of "Have Mercy," a song about adultery with one of my favorite lines in the country-realist tradition:

> "Lipstick on your collar gives your game away
> It's strawberry red, and mine's pink rosé."

They have not sung one song that is not already part of an album, no old hymns, no rounds, no songs from future albums. The Judds play it surprisingly safe, surprisingly close to the chest for two women whose hearts are so often and so flamboyantly public property. Their stage show is not so much a live performance as it is, precisely a *staging* of their music, a way of showing their fans what is already there behind the scenes, below the chest, beyond the frame of the album covers, and finally, within the frame of the almost palpably vexed relation between mother and daughter.

Chapter 3

Writing Lesbian Difference

In 1977, when Bantam Books decided to reprint Rita Mae Brown's *Rubyfruit Jungle,* originally issued by the small feminist press Daughters Publishing Company, the novel became the first bestseller with an explicitly lesbian theme and the first lesbian novel[1] to make the crossover into the mainstream market. Most of *Rubyfruit Jungle*'s readers from a variety of reading communities— lesbian and nonlesbian, feminist and nonfeminist—encountered the novel in its Bantam edition which remained unchanged until 1988 when all of Brown's novels were reissued together. It is a small, white paperback with a discreetly abstract design on the cover that might or might not allude to the central image of a "rubyfruit jungle"—the name the novel's heroine, Molly Bolt, gives to the female genitals. The ambiguity of the image is played out in the apparently conflicting messages that adorn the two covers: the front cover titillates the reader with the specter of difference: "A novel about being different and loving it"; the back cover reassures, reintegrates: "Being different isn't really so different."

The design of the novel itself reflects the design of its covers; in the first half of the novel, Molly is repeatedly identified by herself and others as "different." Early on she finds out she is illegitimate, other to the family in which she is growing up; as the novel progresses we find that she is smarter, more athletic, less sterotypically feminine than other girls her age. Her other differences prepare our way, provide the structure for her sexual difference, for her lesbianism. Molly soon finds that the economy of difference defines her as inferior. When her adoptive mother taunts her with the news of her illegitimacy, Molly boldly tries to minimize its importance:

> "I don't care. It makes no difference where I came from. I'm here, ain't I?"
> "It makes all the difference in the world. Them that's born in wedlock are blessed by the Lord. Them that's born out of wedlock are cursed as bastards."[2]

Molly does, in fact, embody, at this point in the novel, "all the difference in the world"; like Jane Eyre, she proceeds through a journey to identity by comparing herself to other women, by making a space for herself as other that becomes the ground for her sense of self. While other girls dream of becoming nurses, Molly wants either to be a doctor or president. Her cousin Leroy warns her of the dangers of this position:

> I don't know, Molly, you're headin' for a hard life. You say you're gonna be a doctor or something great. Then you say you ain't gettin' married. You have to do some of the things everybody does or people don't like you.   (Brown, p. 36)

Again like Jane Eyre's, Molly's sense of self-as-other is powerful enough, her voice strong enough, to reiterate her separation from others as a sense of personal integrity. Molly's narrative "I," even more insistent than Jane's, resolutely refers back to itself:

> I don't care whether they like me or not. Everybody's stupid, that's what I think. I care if I like me, that's what I truly care about.   (Brown, p. 36)

As Molly grows older and discards the idea of being president for being a film maker, her otherness becomes implicated in the novel's consistent exploration of the economics and erotics of the gaze. In an important and very funny scene early in the novel, Molly watches a movie with her friend Connie. Connie is transfixed by Paul Newman, Molly by the unnamed leading lady:

> Connie kept nudging me, "What a bod. What a bod."
> I answered, "Yeah, so long and slender and smooth."
> "What are you talking about?"
> "Huh?"
> "Paul Newman's body is not long and slender and smooth, fool."
> "Oh." (Brown, p. 76)

This confusion of objects of desire, this disruption of and alienation from hegemonic erotic culture, is recast as comedy by the novel's investment in the picaresque "I" and its ability to absorb and transcend experience. Nonetheless, Molly's relation to looking and filming is always problematic and sometimes very painful. When she does go to film school, male students bond together to prevent her from checking out the film equipment; they are also not interested in the kind of work she does:

> Pornoviolence was in this year and all the men were busy shooting bizarre fuck scenes with cuts of pigs beating up people at the Chicago convention spliced between the sexual encounters. (Brown, pp. 222–23)

As Molly finishes high school and begins college, her otherness becomes more explicitly an issue of sexual preference. She learns to dress as if she had money and joins the appropriate sororities and school activities. Difference becomes circumscribed into small textual and sexual spaces: the airplane in the playground where she first makes love to the high school cheerleader Carolyn, the dorm room where she and her college roommate and lover Faye shut themselves up for weeks on end. Molly is eventually expelled from college for "moral reasons"; she walks down the hall for the last time, her hall-mates' "doors closing like clockwork," resolving to make it on her own. (Brown, p. 131) The image of the door is particularly important because, before Molly gets safely out of the dorm and into the second half of the novel, it reappears with a twist. Molly announces that she no longer believes in human nature, that she has "closed the door forever on idealism." (Brown, p. 131) The shift from having dormitory doors closed on her to closing figurative doors herself signals the transformation in the economy of otherness that is about to take place; Molly's difference from social norms will be rewritten as Molly moves from cultural periphery to center and becomes the normative figure in the second half of the novel.

The novel's change of location to the streets, bars, salons, and universities of New York also marks a shift in the location of both norm and other. Molly's "deviance" is nothing compared to the deviance of the people she meets in the city. The novel becomes even more picaresque as Molly meets one "character" after another: a black homosexual hustler, a man whose erotic life consists of having grapefruits thrown at him, a "diesel dyke," a kept woman, a university professor who studies Babylonian undergarments and likes to fantasize that she is in a men's bathroom at a urinal. Molly's encounters—sexual or not—with each of these people build on the reader's sense of her essential normalcy; as Molly breaks completely with each of the characters she meets in the second half of the novel, we can only feel that she is right. Molly has always been the moral center of the novel, brazenly taking over that ground by the sheer confidence of her "I"; in the second part of *Rubyfruit Jungle* she becomes the center in another sense, creating in the space of her narrative "I" a happy medium between the crippling conformities of homophobic culture and the perhaps equally crippling attempts to resist its hegemony.

The ending of the novel, as Molly goes back to the house in which she has grown up to make a documentary of her mother's life, tries to come to terms with issues of sameness and difference in the problematically integrative gesture of Molly's return to her foster-mother. The novel is saved from complete utopianism by the fact that Carrie is not Molly's biological mother and by her refusal to accept completely Molly's ambitions or her sexuality. Carrie represents a painful sameness-in-difference in the context of which

Molly returns home to capture Carrie in her own filmic and feminist idiom. It is an appropriate (and appropriative) ending to this novel that operates so often on the level of fantasy—Molly, slender and five foot two, can throw a football as far as her quarterback boyfriend Clark; no woman meets Molly without wanting to sleep with her—that the final fantasy should be of the daughter capturing her mother on film and editing the story of both of their lives. If all first-person narrative foregrounds the problem of editing, Molly's film of her mother makes the issue even more explicit; Molly learns, through the telling of her story, to write her own fantastical script.

It is nonetheless important that the integrative fantasy with which *Rubyfruit Jungle* ends is maternal rather than explicitly sexual; Brown does not posit a lesbian relationship free from or even in control of the issues of sameness and difference that haunt the novel. While psychoanalytically it could be argued that Molly has to come to terms with her mother before she can establish viable relationships with other women, it is also significant that the novel offers no such explicit promise, and that it ends with Molly thinking not about sexual relationships but about the always connected but by no means identical issue of her career as a film maker: "Damn, I wished the world would let me be myself. But I knew better on all counts. I wish I could make my films. That wish I can work for. One way or another I'll make those movies." (Brown, p. 246) *Rubyfruit Jungle* cannot resolve the problems of sexual difference that it consistently poses; the comic structure of the novel allows us to see the ending as Molly's triumph, but the outlook for sexual relations of any kind is bleak. That bleakness, I would argue, comes partially from the novel's inability to resolve the contradiction between its covers, its two halves, its double agenda. I would further suggest that this confusion has much to do with the historical moment in which it was written and with the particular valence attached to sameness and difference within lesbian communities in the United States at the moment of its reception as the first bestselling lesbian novel.

I will argue in this chapter that the history of homosexuality in general, and of lesbianism in particular, has been marked by an uneasy and fluctuating relationship to the concept of difference. That relationship shifts emphasis and valence according to the historical moment of its articulation: at different times lesbian feminists on the one hand, and homophobic interpreters of lesbianism on the other, have situated themselves variously with respect to difference. At times these oppositional accounts—homophobic and liberationist—have, for all their political differences, shared a position with respect *to* difference. At other times their accounts of the place of homosexuality within the idiom of difference have radically diverged. Historically, however, the construction of "homosexuality," "lesbianism," of "the homosexual," and of "the lesbian" has relied on a complex lexicon of the same and the different.

One could construct an account of the history of homosexuality that takes sameness and difference as its lexical and political poles. Homophobic culture has traditionally located difference in a specific and historically stable place: between gay men and lesbians on the one hand and "normal" people on the other. We have become accustomed, through the homophobic lens which our culture provides, to see homosexuality *as* difference. While this has been the way gay and lesbian sexuality has been constructed in the West for many hundreds of years, this certainly was not always the case. As John Boswell amply documents in his intricately argued book about male homosexuality, *Christianity, Social Tolerance, and Homosexuality,* ancient Greek and Roman cultures made very little distinction between sexual acts based on the gender of the erotic object choice:

> Neither the Roman religion nor Roman law recognized homosexual eroticism as distinct from—much less inferior to—heterosexual eroticism. Prejudices affecting sexual behavior, roles, or decorum generally affected all persons uniformly. Roman society almost unanimously assumed that adult males would be capable of, if not interested in, sexual relations with both sexes. It is extremely difficult to convey to modern audiences the absolute indifference of most Latin authors to the question of gender.[3]

Even early medieval penitential texts, according to Boswell (such as those condemning anal intercourse), in stressing the act and not the gender of the individual performing it, suggested an implicit continuity between homosexual and heterosexual behavior. Boswell explains that in the canons of Regino of Prum

> His approach to sexuality and sexual sins—like that of most of his contemporaries—was largely gender blind. To Regino it was the act, not the parties involved, which constituted the sin: the penalty for anal intercourse (three years) was exactly the same for two males as for a married couple, and no more severe than that for simple heterosexual fornication. (Boswell, p. 183)

Homosexuality was not until relatively recently seen as a discrete set of behaviors, and only since the end of the nineteenth century as a primary *identity* that separated the person engaging in certain forms of sexual behavior from the norm.[4] Gino Miller reminds us that "homosexuality" and the "homosexual" are constructions that imply difference; the nineteenth-century medicalization of erotic life produced taxonomies of sexual behavior that are dependent, by and through definition, on difference.

If Boswell's model for the continuity between male "heterosexuality" and "homosexuality" is rooted in history, that same continuity applied to relations among women is central to at least one contemporary feminist account of erotic possibilities: Adrienne Rich's influential lesbian-feminist notion of a "lesbian continuum":

> I mean the term *lesbian continuum* to include a range—through each woman's life and throughout history—of woman-identified experience; not simply the fact that a woman has had or has consciously desired genital sexual experience with another woman. If we expand it to embrace many more forms of primary intensity between and among women, including the sharing of a rich inner life, the bonding against male tyranny, the giving and receiving of practical and political support . . . we begin to grasp breadths of female history and psychology that have lain out of reach as a consequence of limited, mostly clinical, definitions of "lesbianism."[5]

If the continuum's almost palpable "embrace" includes a spectrum of resistant gestures by women, it also includes and conjoins moments common to much female experience:

> If we consider the possibility that all women—from the infant suckling her mother's breast, to the grown woman experiencing orgasmic sensations when suckling her own child, perhaps recalling her mother's milk-smell in her own; to two women, like Virginia Woolf's Chloe and Olivia, who share a laboratory; to the woman dying at ninety, touched and handled by women—exist on a lesbian continuum, we can see ourselves as moving in and out of this continuum, whether we identify ourselves as lesbian or not. ("Compulsory Heterosexuality," p. 194)

The strategies at work in constructing such a continuum are clear; if all women can be placed somewhere along its capacious spectrum, then "lesbian" loses its deviant status and becomes a name for moments and relations in all women's lives. Those who object to Rich's notion argue, of course, that the term also becomes diffuse and loses its power and meaning. The continuum allows Rich's "we" at the end of the passage to blur the distinctions between Rich as publicly identified lesbian and all daughters, mothers, colleagues, and friends. The woman reader becomes a lesbian, comes out as a lesbian, by reading the passage and by merging herself unconsciously with the all-embracing "we" with which it ends.[6]

Both Roman culture as Boswell understands it and the culture of Rich's lesbian-feminism announce, in their very different ways, the possibility of rewriting as similarity the perceived difference between heterosexuality and homosexuality. This rewriting has both costs and benefits for the dismantling of homophobic culture; lesbians and gay men can be accepted into mainstream culture because their differences from heterosexuals are minimized and collapsed; the price they might have to pay is a loss of identity *as* lesbians and gay men. Whatever the decision of individuals or of communities about this issue, the idiom of sameness ensures a radical rewriting of contemporary culture.

Difference from hegemonic culture is only one axis along which lesbian and gay sameness and difference have been charted. Perhaps even more vexed and deeply political is the question of difference as it is deployed *within* lesbian and gay communities. Like all political movements that depend on tropes of unity, the lesbian and gay liberation movement has historically been wary of exposing differences within its ranks to public scrutiny. One has only to look at how the women's movement in the early nineteen seventies denied the existence of lesbians within its ranks or at the stir Michelle Wallace's exposé of black sexism, *Black Macho and the Myth of the Superwoman,* created in black communities across the country to find analogies for the uneasiness with which lesbian and gay activist communities have often regarded those lesbians and gay men who practice sadomasochism, role playing, pederasty, or other forms of sexual behavior on the "fringe" even of lesbian and gay communities.

I am particularly interested here in how the lesbian-feminist movement has coped with difference within itself, and how, at different points in what I am loosely calling its twenty-year history, it has worked with the concepts of sameness and difference between and among lesbians to produce social change. The major challenges to lesbian-feminism from within have predictably articulated themselves within the idiom of difference, focusing on distinctions within lesbian communities from race to sexual behavior, from political style to personal appearance.

This chapter focuses on two recent and spectacular controversies within lesbian-feminism—the challenges to lesbian-feminism offered by the issues of role playing and lesbian sadomasochism—in an attempt to look at the stakes, costs, and strategics of difference deployed by those who have found the version of lesbian-feminism inherited from the nineteen seventies to be prescriptive, de-eroticizing, and ultimately homogenizing. The sometimes linked issues of role playing and sadomasochism are implicitly bound up in a political narrative that posits a hegemonic lesbian-feminist culture which in turn prescribes sameness and political correctness, and a challenge from the margin that posits an eroticized difference, a difference simultaneously construed as difference *from* mainstream lesbian-feminist culture and a difference between and among lesbians in the form of dichotomies such as "butch" and "fem,"[7] "sadists" and "masochists," "tops" and "bottoms."

In using role playing and sadomasochism as entries into the question of differences within lesbian communities and relationships, I am to some extent complicitous with a trend toward the eroticization of difference I will be discussing in some detail below. I am also reproducing what some lesbian-feminists, like Audre Lorde, consider to be an unfair emphasis on the part of the mainstream and feminist media on questions of sexual behavior at the expense of other issues of concern to the lesbian community. This emphasis, this appropriation of all differences into the lexicon of the erotic, is precisely my subject; in looking at role playing and sadomasochism we are looking at cultural synecdoches for difference within lesbian communities. It is that deeply eroticized synecdochal relation that interests me here and elsewhere; the debates within lesbian-feminism over role playing and sadomasochism represent moments in the construction of sexual difference—this time within lesbian communities.

It is no coincidence that the issue of difference within lesbian-feminism has been most spectacularly constituted as sexual difference, and that the most painful and public conflicts between lesbian-feminists have been over sexual issues, at conferences and in journals devoted to the analysis of female sexuality. While there are many individual writers, thinkers, and activists who see difference within the lesbian-feminist community in terms of class or race, sexual issues have, I think it is fair to say, occupied a much more visible place in mainstream and lesbian-feminist journals, newspapers, pamphlets, and other publications. While this probably (as I will discuss at greater length in Chapter 4) has much to do with the repression of racial and class issues by their immediate translation into sexual terms, I would also argue that all differences between women, from the competition between Victorian sisters, to debates between contemporary feminist theorists, to more overtly "sexual" conflicts between, say, cultural feminists and lesbian sadomasochists, partake in the eroticized idiom of sexual difference between women.

Conflicts over lesbian sexuality in the name of difference locate the source of the problem in the homogenizing notion of "political correctness," which, according to Esther Newton and Shirley Walton, in "The Misunderstanding: Toward a More Precise Sexual Vocabulary," impinges upon erotic life in the form of sexual prescription:

> Within the women's movement, the "politically correct" have had to believe in and practice "egalitarian sexuality," which we define as sexual partnering involving the functional (if not literal) interchangeability of partners and acts. Logically, there could only be one look and one role for all, which partly explains why lesbianism is assumed to be intrinsically more egalitarian than heterosexuality, and why lesbian feminists tend to look alike.[8]

For Newton, a lesbian, and Walton, who defines herself as primarily heterosexual, the confusion between egalitarianism and sameness is at the heart of the crippling ideology of the "politically correct." Their article, which ranges from personal experience to an overview of lesbian-feminist assumptions, attempts, as its title suggests, to find more and better words for the varieties of female sexuality, more and better ways to describe sexual differences among women. They claim that the "presumed psychological/social sameness'' of lesbian partners has simultaneously led to the privileging within lesbian feminism of lesbianism over heterosexuality and of certain limited forms of lesbian eroticism over others. Their article attempts to disrupt the symmetry of lesbian-feminist assumptions about sexuality by offering a term that intervenes in the category of sexual preference: "sexual role." According to Newton and Walton, sexual roles involve one's sexual persona in relation to one's partner: they borrow from the lexicon of sadomasochism to come up with "top" and "bottom," terms that, according to them, cut across sexual preference and gender.

Sadomasochism, then, provides among other things a vocabulary—however limited or limiting—for describing sexual difference between and among lesbians. In several anti-homogenist feminist texts it is paired with lesbian role playing as a way of marking difference. Amber Hollibaugh and Cherríe Moraga gauge the political effects of sadomasochism and role playing, as well as other sexual issues and cultures, in terms of their production and accommodation of difference:

> The point is that when you deny that roles, sadomasochism, fantasy, or any sexual differences exist in the first place, you can only come up with neutered sexuality, where everybody's got to be basically the same because anything different puts the element of power and deviation in there and threatens the whole picture. [9]

Both "The Misunderstanding" and Hollibaugh and Moraga's article, "What We're Rollin Around in Bed With: Sexual Silences in Feminism," struggle with the linked notions of difference and sexuality to produce a language that identifies and elaborates those connections. Significantly, both articles, each written by two women, are presented as explorations of sexual differences between the authors, either explicitly in the form of a shared sexual past or in a discussion of cultural differences that structure and are in turn structured by sexuality.

Both articles assume that eroticism depends on difference, and that sameness produces, in the words of Hollibaugh and Moraga, a "neutered sexuality." The term "neuter" returns us to the question of gender itself, sexual difference between women becoming interestingly associated with the production of different "genders" within the gender "female." Newton and Walton make explicit the presence of gender in their economy of difference. They speculate that "the dyke erotic identity is a modified butch look . . . because femininity is the mark of difference and inferiority which must be eliminated." (Newton and Walton, p. 249) The feminine then becomes a sign of difference, not only as Kristeva and others have posited, within a heterosexual economy, but within lesbian communities as well. According to Newton and Walton, lesbian sexual style excises and marginalizes the feminine in an attempt to assure the hegemony of the same.

The issue of femininity as difference resurfaces in the debate over lesbian role playing. In ''The Fem Question,'' an autobiographical exploration of the repression of butch/fem role playing by lesbian feminist communities, Joan Nestle argues that self-identified ''fems'' have consistently been perceived by other lesbian-feminists as ''the Uncle Toms of the movement'':

> A fem is often seen as a lesbian acting like a straight woman who is not a feminist—a terrible misreading of self-presentation which turns a language of liberated desire into the silence of collaboration. An erotic conversation between two women is completely unheard . . . by other women, many in the name of lesbian-feminism.[10]

The ''erotic conversation'' between butch and fem depends both on an historical context and an elaborate choreography of difference where each partner takes up an identity through her difference with the other. Nestle points out that fems, frequently accused of wanting to ''pass'' in mainstream culture, actually foregrounded the fact of their lesbianism through contrast with butch lovers. She points out that the more feminine a fem looks, the more obvious her lesbianism as she walks down the street with a butch lover. The ''erotic conversation'' of role playing becomes a conversation *about* difference and difference as sexuality; it is a conversation that can only be understood by ''reading'' the bodies of both women in relation to each other, by reading their differences from each other. Predictably, the reaction to butches and fems has not been symmetrical in most lesbian-feminist communities; the ''modified butch look'' that Newton and Walton see as central to the public presentation of ''politically correct'' lesbian feminism allows more room for a style that is— however complexly—marked ''masculine.'' Fems, like femininity, seem, in themselves, to embody difference in a prescriptive economy of the same.

If ''butch'' and ''fem'' provide problematic but accessible and historically resonant terms for the identification of lesbian difference, ''top'' and ''bottom,'' ''master'' and ''slave'' provide, within the context of lesbian sado-masochism, even more charged and difficult markers for the production and representation of that difference. Pat Califia, one of the most eloquent and prolific spokeswomen for lesbian sadomasochism and a founding member of SAMOIS, one of the first explicitly lesbian sadomasochist groups in the country, sees in lesbian-feminist unease with sadomasochism a potentially crippling pressure toward conformity. *Coming to Power,* a 1981 anthology of writings on lesbian sadomasochism edited by members of SAMOIS, was designed to challenge lesbian-feminist assumptions about power and sexuality. The pieces that constitute *Coming to Power* include personal narratives and fantasies from lesbians who have become involved in sadomasochism; how-to articles that take on issues of equipment, technique, and safety; poems and short stories celebrating sadomasochistic relationships or lifestyles; and "graphics": posed pictures of women in various costumes from the wardrobe of sadomasochism.

Coming to Power is also an implicit challenge to underlying notions of unity. Framed by two pieces—an introduction called "What We Fear We Try To Keep Contained" by Katherine Davis, and an epilogue by Califia on her view of the struggle between SAMOIS and other feminist groups—the book describes and explores various aspects of lesbian sadomasochism in the context of an ongoing debate within feminism over its political and moral legitimacy. Even the publication history of *Coming to Power* is colored by bitter debates within lesbian feminism; when rumors that SAMOIS was putting together *Coming to Power* circulated within the lesbian community, other self-identified radical feminists rushed to put together their own anthology called, succinctly, *Against Sadomasochism*, a formally similar compendium of interviews, essays, and fiction. The two anthologies came out in print at almost the same time, competing for space on bookstore shelves and for the attention of lesbian-feminist communities across the country.

Califia's personal narrative that ends *Coming to Power* explicitly frames the debate between anti-sadomasochist and sadomasochist feminists as a debate over difference. Califia claims that *Against Sadomasochism*

> . . . promotes a climate of suspicion and fear, a false conformity (where all lesbians pretend to be the same for fear of being condemned and excommunicated) and divisiveness in a community that needs all the unity it can get to face the Christian New Right and Reagan's repressive regime.[11]

Here unity is configured *as* the acceptance of difference; divisiveness gets paired with conformity in Califia's choreography of the different and the same.

Califia's critique of the "false conformity" of what she calls "vanilla lesbian" culture suggests that lesbian sadomasochists serve as scapegoats for the lesbian-feminist community's anxiety about difference. Some lesbian-feminists who position themselves as anti-sadomasochists, however, see the "difference" invoked and displayed by lesbian sadomasochists as a displacement or repression of more serious differences among lesbians, notably those accruing around race and class. Audre Lorde addresses this displacement implicitly when she asks, in an interview published in *Against Sadomasochism:* "When sadomasochism gets presented on center stage as a conflict in the feminist movement . . . what conflicts are *not* being presented?"[12] In another interview in the same collection black lesbians Karen Sims and Rose Mason see lesbian sadomasochism as an expression of privilege that inherently denies or trivializes the political resonances for black women of "master" and "slave." For both Sims and Mason sadomasochism involves a deeply problematic and ultimately racist reading of power. Sims explains:

> What I'm concerned about is one part of sadomasochism, the master and slave relationship. I have a lot of feelings about it. Some of the things that I have seen and heard about succumbing to the power of someone else are devastating for me as a Black woman, having grown up in Black culture and being subjected to someone else's power, and having to live with that all my life. . . . I wouldn't compare experimenting with power relationships on the same line with someone struggling to survive in this country. I have a question to the people that are into sadomasochism and talking about dealing with their own struggles. How do they align themselves with the day-to-day struggles of Third World people?[13]

For both Sims and Mason, sadomasochism is a lifestyle dependent on the privilege to "experiment"; both repeatedly use the term "luxury" to describe the culture of sadomasochism. Their arguments and others like them have been compared to arguments made in earlier decades against the articulation of lesbianism within the feminist community: like sadomasochism in Sims' and Mason's formulations, lesbianism was once thought by many people to be merely a "lifestyle issue" that would distract the movement from other, more important goals.

Defenders of sadomasochism have at times tried to protect themselves from charges of racism by pointing out that there are women of color in SAMOIS, and, perhaps more centrally, by invoking the analogy between cultural oppression of sadomasochists and racism. The term "vanilla lesbian," so frequently used in the discourse of sadomasochism for those who oppose sadomasochism on principle, has, I think, a racial valence; spokeswomen for sadomasochism not only use the analogy with racism but the idiom of color to suggest a continuity between their perceived oppression and the oppression of racial minorities.

Lorde, Sims, and Mason all suggest that it is not the practice of sadomasochism that is particularly pernicious, but rather its public presentation as a feminist issue. Although analogies can once again be drawn to strategic arguments in the early nineteen seventies when some feminists claimed that media attention to lesbians within the women's movement was disproportionate and therefore damaging to feminism, there is no doubt that the issue of sadomasochism in particular and of sexuality in general have been more public, more spectacular, and more accessible to the general public and to mainstream feminism than debates within lesbian cultures about race or class.

The debates over sadomasochism and sexuality are so painful, so fraught, and so divisive that it is impossible merely to chart or celebrate difference or to use these conflicts only as examples of the larger issue of sameness and difference. The conflicts within feminist and lesbian communities over sexuality have the status of meta-conflicts; they are as much about the deployment of difference as they are about local disagreements. Nonetheless these powerful debates about power threaten always to break the frame of the discourse with which they are engaged. This is why, to my mind, the sexualization of difference can be either useful or dangerous or both: useful if it is thematized and deployed to address cultural investment in the erotics of female difference, dangerous if sexuality is assumed to be the only or the privileged site of difference.

Lesbian Poetry and the Poetics of Sameness

The conflict over lesbian sameness and difference has its historical as well as its moral and political dimension: all the women discussed above are implicitly engaged in writing not only lesbian theory, but a history of lesbianism in the United States. The historical narrative that repeatedly underlies the texts of proponents of sexual difference depends on identifying the nineteen seventies and early eighties as a period characterized by sameness and unity and the present period which begins, say, around 1982 as one marked by difference and internal struggle. Implicit in this lesbian history is a relatively common notion of political movements as a series of stages in which the first depends on identification and similarity among group members and the second a questioning of the assumptions that formed the group in the first place. The historiography implied by the theory of progressive stages in turn privileges change and difference, identifying the present as a complication and a problematization of an overly simple and schematic past.

While any historical narrative that depends on such a self-serving assessment of the present—that is, almost any historical narrative at all—is always suspect, the narrative offered by proponents of sexual difference among lesbians is, to a certain extent, compelling. The remainder of this chapter turns to what over the last two decades has been called with increasing confidence "lesbian poetry," in order simultaneously to produce a tentative historical narrative of the interplay between lesbian sameness and difference, and to complicate that narrative with readings of the nuances of individual poems. The complications I offer come from the questioning of two major assumptions: first, that individual poems from either historical moment—the period before or after 1982—have an unvexed relation to their central identification with sameness or difference; second, that "difference" is purely an erotic category that transcends notions of race, class, or culture.

I begin with the work of a series of self-identified lesbian poets of the earlier period, to set up a taxonomy of sexual difference and of the poetic figures that exhibit and contain that difference. I then turn to the most canonized of contemporary lesbian poets, Adrienne Rich, and to her first explicitly lesbian-feminist collection of poems, the enormously influential *Dream of a Common Language,* to trace how her work has engaged with issues of sameness and difference within a lesbian poetics. While the history, or what Rich might call cartography of lesbian difference I offer is always provisional and can always be challenged by turning to other voices, I believe that I am describing with some accuracy a vexed and painful set of issues that haunts not only lesbian-feminism but all political movements struggling to define themselves in the double context of outside and inside, oppressor and oppressed.

The poems I choose to look at in detail here cluster around three issues and articulate these issues through three central images. The first issue, coming out as a lesbian, and by extension as a lesbian poet, most often works itself out in these poems as an exploration of the maternal body and of specular movements of identification with and separation from the maternal. The second issue, the poetic representation of a specifically lesbian erotics, also begins with the image of the mother but moves outward into a wider idiom of sisterhood. The third issue, the construction of a specifically black lesbian voice, also becomes manifest through the image of the sister which is used, often ironically, to identify both conflict and community within the category "lesbian." We can read these kinds of poems—coming-out poems, love poems, poems about race—as subgenres; we can also read them, less discretely, as positions along a metonymic familial chain in which mother becomes sister, and sister becomes lover, comrade, and/or outsider. The movement away from the maternal body and toward the unfamiliar is deliberate here; I set the poems up as a series of defamiliarizations which, nonetheless, are rooted in and sustained by a familial idiom. The currents of matrophobia and sororophobia, as we shall see, run frequently counter to the evolutionary, progressive, and euphoric movements also locatable in these poems and associated with a growing personal and political awareness. While lesbian poetry has often been dismissed as being in its infancy, and early lesbian poetry in particular as simple propaganda, the poems I discuss below (as well as countless lesbian-feminist poems which there is no room to discuss here) are complex, ambitious, and conflicted pieces of work that struggle—as does much of the lesbian-feminist movement—with the painful articulation of sameness and difference, identity and separation.

The beginning of the lesbian-feminist movement in the United States, which I locate for the purposes of this chapter in the early nineteen seventies, took as both idiom and methodology the process of lesbian "coming out"; the "coming-out story," like the stories of dissatisfaction, discrimination, and frustration of the consciousness-raising groups of the early feminist movement, became both organizing tool and the constituent of group identity. It is no wonder that early poems by lesbians are frequently concerned with the process of coming out, and that the first anthology of lesbian poetry initially published under the name *Amazon Poetry* in 1975 and expanded and reissued as *Lesbian Poetry: An Anthology* in 1981, should devote most of its introduction to the issue of what it means to identify and to come out as a lesbian *poet*. [14]

The process of coming out is, of course, deeply embedded in the linked notions of identity and identification. If the issue of lesbian sexual difference is worked out in contemporary political debates over sadomasochism and role playing, lesbian poetry from the nineteen seventies and early eighties explored the erotics of difference by exploring the maternal body. Adrienne Rich, in her extended essay on motherhood, *Of Woman Born,* charts some of the connections between the mother/daughter relationship and the relationship between female lovers by quoting the poet Susan Silvermarie:

> I find now, instead of a contradiction between lesbian and mother, there is an overlapping. . . . In loving another woman I discovered the deep urge to both be a mother and to find a mother in my lover. At first I feared the discovery. Everything around me told me it was evil. Popular Freudianism cursed it as a fixation, a sign of immaturity. . . . Now I treasure and trust the drama between two loving women, in which each can become mother and each become child. [15]

Motherhood and the process of lesbian self-identification come together in Jacqueline Lapidus' poem, "Coming Out" (1975), which puns on the act of being born, of leaving the maternal body, and on coming out in a more traditionally sexual sense. It chronicles and mourns the speaker's separation from "the first person I loved":

> the first person I loved
> was a woman   my passion
> for her lasted thirty years
> and was not returned
> she never let me suck her nipples
> she kept secrets between her legs
> she told me men would love me
> for myself   she couldn't tell me
> ways to love myself
> she didn't know   (*Lesbian Poetry,* p. 99, lines 1–10)

Elaine Showalter has suggested that the mid nineteen seventies were years when feminists in general were turning from the father to reclaim the figure of the mother so carefully repressed by matrophobia. This turning, according to

Showalter, was marked by the publication of *Of Woman Born* (1976), Nancy Friday's *My Mother/My Self* (1977), and Dorothy Dinnerstein's *The Mermaid and the Minotaur* (1976). While these were indeed years for feminists to bring their mothers—and their matrophobia—out of the closet, Showalter is, I think, underestimating the force of a specifically lesbian feminism and a specifically lesbian idiom in helping to produce this shift. Motherhood became a way for all feminists, but, I think, particularly for lesbians, to explore the fraught questions of resemblance and identity, to reexamine the paternal law that reads and writes attachment to the mother as immaturity and threatens women with the specters of incest and non-individuation.

There is no explicit reclamation of the mother in "Coming Out," no moment of reunion. The incest taboo works to keep the mother's secrets, her body and her love, from her daughter:

> Mother, I would like to help you
> swim back against the foaming river
> to the source of our
> incestuous fears
>
> but you're so tired
> out beyond the breakers
> and I am upstream among my sisters
> spawning.   (*Lesbian Poetry,* p. 99, lines 11–18)

The "breakers" that tear mother and daughter apart, that have broken the bond between them, are too powerful to allow for any easy reunion; the speaker turns from mother to sisters, accepts that the mother is too far away, too tired, to make the journey back to the "source" which the poet necessarily undertakes in writing this poem. Coming out, in the context of this poem, first involves a going back in, an exploration that will ultimately allow for a rebirth. If the speaker cannot rejoin her mother after thirty years of secrets and separation, she can invoke her, speak to her, in and through a poem.

The connection between mother and daughter is specifically erotic: that is, it is about eroticism, about sexual sameness and difference and their cultural deployment. The poem—and the connection it mourns and invokes—makes explicit the analogy between the mother and the female sexual self. "Coming Out" makes a familiar feminist argument: in order to know how to love oneself or to love other women, one must love and be loved by the mother. The maternal body is both metonymy and metaphor in a relationship that depends on closeness and similarity.

"Coming Out" is in many senses a poem about reproduction, a counterintuitive, although perhaps by now familiar, connection for a homophobic culture that labels lesbians as barren, childless, singular. The final line of the poem which gives us the one word "spawning" intervenes in an ideology that equates lesbianism and nonproductivity. The speaker is spawning many things: poems, other women who by her erotic intervention can also come to love themselves and each other, a vision of motherhood that does not depend on secrets and that reproduces the female body without shame. "Spawning" inserts itself as the principle of difference between mother and daughter, a difference that depends on the mother's denial of sameness.

In this poem, as in many of the period, difference between mother and daughter, between and among women in general, is seen as an effect of patriarchy, as a denial of a dangerous and always assumed sameness. If the speaker turns from her mother here it is because her mother has turned from her; it is too late to make up the difference: only one of them can return to come out again. The maternal body offers the promise of sameness and analogy to be turned, in the idiom of patriarchy, into a "secret," a denial of the body and of eroticism.

If "Coming Out" mourns the cultural necessity of the separation from the maternal body, Ruthe D. Canter's "The Resemblance" (1974) offers an ultimately less negative although equally problematic meditation on the physical similarities between mother and daughter. The poem begins with a promise of symmetry:

> My mother and I
> bear resemblance. (*Lesbian Poetry*, p. 215)

The use of the word "bear" takes us back, of course, to the act of carrying and giving birth to a child; mother and daughter carry resemblance between them. "Bear," of course, has another, more negative, connotation: women's bodies must be borne as well as born in this culture; the similarity between mother and daughter is a palpable weight which gives, like the unborn child, both pleasure and pain to the bearer. The pain both mother and daughter feel in this poem is, however, still bearable, if only because the two of them share it, carrying it between them. The "secret" of resemblance, of reproduction, moves from between the mother's legs to the place between mother and daughter, a place that announces and marks both their difference and their similarity.

The poem moves curiously and perhaps sinisterly to detail the sameness between mother and daughter:

> One eye at a time,
> one eye and we
> are one. Our breasts
> are silences that
> meet each other in
> a grace. (*Lesbian Poetry*, p. 215, lines 1–6)

The poem begins an assault on the female body, a fragmentation that is somehow a metaphor for unity; "one eye and we/are one" puns, of course, on "I" and "eye," suggesting that the "I" and the "we" are one, but only at the expense of a kind of dismemberment. Mother and daughter come together, perhaps, not despite their fragmentation but because thay have "one" eye, because their breasts are "silences." The unity so precariously described here is not the coming together of two whole women.

The relation between fragmentation, pain, and unity becomes clearer if more difficult in the last stanza, where the speaker asserts her right—perhaps her duty—to speak for her mother:

> I am sad, I am singing,
> my breasts become like
> yours, my hands with
> the same lines, I am
> singing for the mother
> whose sorrows I am.

The issue of advocacy, of one woman speaking for another, is a central political and poetic problem for feminism. The speaker takes for herself this right, the right to rewrite silences, through the power of resemblance, through the linked powers of being "like" and loving. Perhaps more important, the speaker feels compelled and empowered to speak because she is her mother's disturbingly plural "sorrows," sorrows that return us inexorably to resemblance and fragmentation.

Coming out, in the context of these and other poems about the mother, is both rebirth and separation, a return to and a departure from an origin based on morphological and psychological similarity. Both poems construct and contain difference between the mother and daughter; becoming a lesbian, a lesbian poet, is simultaneously an act of identification and differentiation.

Poetry about the maternal body cannot in any simple way be opposed to lesbian love poetry in the more canonical sense. Love too is often, predictably, represented as rebirth. Olga Broumas' "Sometimes, as a child" turns the language of rebirth into an adult erotics by interrupting an extended metaphor of reentry and devolution with the word "lover":

> in the arrested heat of the afternoon
> without thought, effortless
> as a mantra turning
> you'd turn
> in the paused wake of your dive, enter
> the suck of the parted waters, you'd emerge

clean caesarean, flinging
live rivulets from your hair, your own
breath arrested. Something immaculate, a chance

crucial junction: time, light, water
had occurred, you could feel your bones
glisten
transluscent as spinal fins.
                    In rain-

green Oregon now, approaching thirty, sometimes
the same
rare concert of light and spine
resonates in my bones, as glistening
starfish, lover, your fingers
beach up. (*Lesbian Poetry*, pp. 208–9, lines 10–28)

The "you" of the poem dives back into the sea where waters part to meet her and the birthing process is undone to prepare for a new kind of birth. The process of return is not painless; it makes its mark even on the amniotic fluid of the ocean: the almost oxymoronic "clean caesarean" reminds us that to go back is simultaneously to be purified and to be scarred. The movement toward a maternal sea is repeated phylogenetically in a movement backward along an evolutionary chain. The beloved's body inhabits the ocean like a fish, loses rigidity: years later, in "rain-green Oregon" the speaker's body responds in memory, curls and gives itself up into a shape Broumas elsewhere calls "curviform."

The poem ends with the twin vulvar images of the cupped hands and the starfish; between them the word "lover" eroticizes and gives meaning to the puzzling "beach up" of the last line. The three trochees that inhabit the two final lines ("starfish," "lover," "beach up") suggest an erotics that embraces and defines all three. "Starfish" and "beach up" take their meaning and power from "lover" and become, as Broumas promises in another love poem, "Artemis," "tongue-like forms/that curve round a throat/an arm-pit . . . like a curviform alphabet" (*Lesbian Poetry*, p. 208, lines 15–19). This new alphabet, the new words which, according to Broumas, "like amnesiacs/in a ward on fire, we must/find . . . or burn," opens up the possibility of a lesbian poetics once again based on return to the maternal, the amniotic, what Kristeva might call the semiotic.

To return to the maternal for and through the erotic is also to return to foremothers. M. F. Hershman's comic quasi-sonnet "Making Love to Alice" imagines Gertrude Stein and Alice B. Toklas in bed together:

> I imagine Gertrude making love to Alice
> her generous and wise mouth upon her
> breast her arms around hers the two
> bodies fitting together, strangely
> they are different and wonderfully they are
> together. Gertrude being warm and full and
> with Alice and Alice being warm and full with
> Gertrude who is with her and the way
> she is with her. Laughing. I imagine
> they must know each other, the two, the one.
>
> It is as with you and I. It is
> with us as them. She then she and you than I
> imagine. And in the act of imagining
> make love to love to love to love   (*Lesbian Poetry*, p. 235)

The poem is a tangle of bodies and parallels, the shifting pronouns marking, or perhaps refusing to mark, boundaries between female bodies. Gertrude and Alice make love chiasmatically: "Gertrude being warm and full and/ with Alice and Alice being warm and full with Gertrude." The two present-day lovers who appear in the final four lines make love by analogy: "It is as with you and I. It is/ with us as them." Names, positions, and bodies become entwined, it would seem, undifferentiated.

Things are, however, not so simple. Lines 6–7, however parallel, offer a remainder, a supplement, a word that sticks out of the first line and is missing in the second; the word, significantly is "and"; it is the hinge upon which these couples couple, the premise of their coming together. Gertrude is "*and* with Alice," Alice merely "with Gertrude." The "and" should remind us of two other words lost in the tangle: "strangely" (line 4) and "different" (line 5). Gertrude and Alice are by virtue of being Gertrude and Alice, respectively, different; their strange difference is joined, also by an "and," to their wonderful sameness: this difference is again sexual difference, buried in a sonnet that is itself not quite the same—metrically—as other sonnets.

The difference between Gertrude and Alice is more explicitly rendered in the final quatrain in the difference between the "you" and the "I"; while the several "hers" of the first few lines could belong to either Gertrude or Alice (but not both), the "you" and the "I" are distinct positions, however analogous to the "hers." The blank space between the first ten lines and the last four suggests a distance insufficiently expressed by the unconventional, unsonnetlike turn in line 10 to the "you" and "I." Gertrude and Alice can be used as inspiration, can become sexual, political, and/or literary fantasies, but the identity between the two of them and between the present-day couple *and* the two of them is necessarily incomplete. The poem sets itself up as a fantasy of identification, but breaks down in the process of constructing its own comparisons. The comic difference is also sexual difference; the laughter in line 9 is the laughter of one who knows that making love does not have the power to make two into one.

But whose is that laughter, which, like the arms and breasts of the opening lines seems to hang suspended between lovers? It is easy to read "laughing" as belonging to, emanating from, both Gertrude and Alice. The fantasy of simultaneous laughter, like that of the simultaneous orgasm, is attractive precisely because it occludes boundaries and dispels, however temporarily, the specter of difference from the act of making love. But "making" is precisely the issue. The "laughing" of line 9 is grammatically analogous to the "making" of the title, a making that belongs to Gertrude who is making love *to* Alice. This is not, after all, a poem entitled "Gertrude and Alice Make Love." The laughing, like the making, suggests Gertrude's control, Gertrude's agency in this sexual and comic act. The poem's last lines align the speaker firmly with Gertrude as they imitate Stein's characteristic verbal repetitions; the speaker, in aligning herself with Gertrude and not Alice, aligns herself predictably with making: the making of poetry and love. Sexual difference then becomes not only a moment in but the occasion of the poem; it is the difference between the "you" and the "I" that allows the poem—and the act of making love—to take place. The "I," as poet and agent, becomes the inheritor of Gertrude's poetic and sexual legacy, the poem a way of encoding and producing sexual difference within the act of lesbian making.

Difference in all four of the poems discussed above is explicitly contained as sexual difference, and more specifically as difference within a maternal idiom. The maternal body protects the daughter as it allows her to raise questions. Even more troubling than the question of sexual difference is the question of race; more troubling than the maternal is the sororal idiom used by several black lesbian-feminist poets to explore racial differences.

Julie Blackwomon's 1976 poem, "Revolutionary Blues" rings changes on the word "sister":

> and when I say to my sisters
> my lesbian feminist sisters
> my angry white sisters whose chains still mesh with mine
> when I say sisters help me
> the noose tightens on my neck
> I cannot breathe
>   it is because I am black
> my sisters say
>   yes,
> but what has that to do
>   with our revolution? (*Lesbian Poetry,* p. 132, lines 1–11)

Like "Making Love to Alice," this poem problematizes easy addition, easy notions of unity. The poem begins with an ironic gesture to the sign of the additive with the uncapitalized "and." The "and" pulls the reader into the middle of an ongoing debate, makes for an immediacy that is only more sharply rendered by additional additive ironies in the form of adjectival chains in lines 1–3 where "sisters" become "lesbian feminist sisters," and then "angry white sisters." The word "black" is never added to this oppressive litany of oppressions; it stands outside this ironized sisterhood in a line orthographically distant from the rest and bifurcated by a singular pronoun: "it is because I am black."

The poem moves symmetrically to accuse black men of analogous ignorance and oppression of lesbians:

> I am encircled by fire
> the flames grow nearer
>   it is because I love women
> my brothers say
>   yes,
> but what has that to do with our revolution?
> (*Lesbian Poetry,* lines 16–21)

Alone and segregated again, the "I" once more takes up a marginal position. The poem's painful symmetry underscores the repeated exile of the "I."

But this symmetry, like the apparent symmetry in "Making Love to Alice," will be, must be interrupted. The final lines move away from tensions with black men to focus asymmetrically on the issue of sisterhood:

> and when the revolution comes
> and it is time for choosing sides
> when militant black nationalists
> are fighting our oppression by whites
> I expect to be shot in the back
> by someone who calls me sister.

The word "sister" ends the poem and the debate, continuing within itself the escalating anger of the poem. A word that dominated the first half of the poem, it has significantly disappeared from the text until its sinister resurrection in this, the terminal position of "Revolutionary Blues." The ending of this poem is reminiscent of the last few lines of Barbara Smith's "Theft," dedicated to Angelina Weld Grimke:

> we must often play invisible,
> the Masquerade,
> must save our best and
> darkest selves for us. (*Lesbian Poetry,* p. 180, lines 46–49)

These lines explicitly take "Theft" out of the idiom of an integrated sisterhood and into a place of racial difference. Both poems work with a series of their own integrative gestures—the careful parallels of "Revolutionary Blues," the dedication to and invocation of Grimke in "Theft"—but both ultimately decide against a simple, benign, or simply benign sisterhood. Both poems explicitly refuse the homologizing discourse of sex in favor of the discourse of race: sexual difference becomes, finally and terminally, subordinated to racial difference. Both poems resist the erotization of difference between and among women; for "Revolutionary Blues" in particular, the body in question is the body in danger, and the act that signals difference an act of hate and not love. These poems situate themselves differently with respect to difference, refusing the erotics of difference that poems like "Coming Out" or "Making Love to Alice" construct for the reader.

Adrienne Rich and the Nightmare of Difference

Adrienne Rich's *The Dream of a Common Language* (1978) was and still is a landmark text in the shaping of lesbian identity and community. The collection served as Rich's coming out as a specifically lesbian poet; it is, on one level, a tribute to connections between and among women, working against the grain of hegemonic culture to construct a language to describe women's relationships with and to each other. The construction of connections between women is the collection's project and central anxiety. The collection and individual poems within it forge connections between women through dedications, impersonations, and recollections. Many of the poems, like "Phantasia for Elvira Shatayev" or "Transcendental Etude" (for Michelle Cliff), are explicitly presented as being *for* another woman or women; others, like "Power," about the life and death of Marie Curie, or "Paula Becker to Clara Westhoff," in the voice of one woman artist to another, make imaginative connections with particular historical figures; still others, like "Splittings" or "Sibling Mysteries," are more overtly autobiographical re-memberings of past relations with women relatives, friends, and lovers.

If the poems themselves speak the language of commonality between women, the history of its reading and reception by women is a case study in the formation of women's communities. I have three copies of the book; two are inscribed to me from women friends; one, which I must have forgotten to return, is dedicated from one woman friend to another. Women in the late nineteen seventies were giving, lending, reading, and forgetting to return the book, forging connections with the book's female presences and with each other.

The word "Dream" in the title reminds us, however, that this is not, cannot simply be a book about community or about coming together. The poems are filled with spaces: orthographic—Rich often leaves extra room on the page between words—and psychological—many of the poems, like "Splittings" and even the lyrical "24 Love Poems," are about breaking up or the impossibility of coming together in the first place. Spaces creep into lines, disrupting the connections between mother and daughter, between sisters, lovers, and friends. "A Woman Dead in her Forties," a poem about the re-membering of a friendship between women torn apart by death and denial, begins with a triple-edged image of separation: "Your breasts/sliced-off."[16] The slash and the spaces that follow it memorialize the act of cutting off, the fragmentation of the female body in the hands of medical culture. At the same time the poem explores and reproduces other scars—those caused by the refusal of the two friends to touch each other:

> I want to touch my fingers
> to where your breasts had been
> but we never did such things   (lines 14–16)

The poem that memorializes this separation, this cleavage of one woman from and to another, is itself simultaneously a connection and a scar, a sign both of the love between the two women and the slicing off made necessary by their lives as respectable women:

> we did each other's homework
> wrote letters   kept in touch, untouching
>
> lied about our lives: I wearing
> the face of the proper marriage
>
> you the face of the independent woman
> We cleaved to each other across that space   (lines 53–58)

"A Woman Dead in her Forties" inserts itself between the contradictory double meaning of the word "cleavage": simultaneously a clinging together and a cutting off, the space between a woman's breasts and the breasts themselves, cleavage and cleaving become apt metaphors for the double act of connection and separation that initiates the writing of this poem.

If Rich's poems in *Dream* embody the difficulty of connections between women, they also struggle with the inevitable and familiar distance between signifier and signified, relentlessly exploring the places where language fails women by failing to connect to their experiences. Rich charts a textured and difficult path through the difficulties and impossibilities of connection: in "Sibling Mysteries" she, like Lapidus, explores the contradictions of the maternal body; in "Twenty-One Love Poems" she records with, as she puts it elsewhere, "an unreturning stylus," the problematics of lesbian desire, and in "Cartographies of Silence" she thematizes connection and disconnection as a tentative female poetics.

"Sibling Mysteries" is Rich's attempt to re-member the maternal body through memories shared with the sister to whom the poem is dedicated. The poem, whose first section is framed and punctuated by the demand "remind me," is an exploration of a common past, a common body from which both sisters emerged and, in their own way, separated. The separation is described in almost perfectly Lacanian terms as the intervention of the paternal law between the bodies of mother and child:

> Remind me
> how her touch melted childgrief
>
> how she floated great and tender in our dark
> or stood guard over us
> against our willing
>
> and how we thought she loved
> the strange male body first
> that took, that took, whose taking seemed a law
> (*The Dream of a Common Language*, p. 48, lines 35–42)

The "remind me" which begins this passage announces a journey beyond paternal law to a pre-Oedipal relation between mother and daughter. Rich interrupts this familiar and utopian feminist journey, however, with the less-than-blissful line, "against our willing." Will and difference are already in place, it seems, *before* the intervention of paternal law: the many puns on "will" and "willing" compete for psychological resonance, as the two daughters are simultaneously "willing" to return to the mother and form their wills in opposition to hers.

However troubling the opening integrative fantasy, the poem ends with the replacement of the father by the mother:

> The daughters never were
> true brides of the father
>
> the daughters were to begin with
> brides of the mother

The marriage which so novelistically ends this poem recasts the story of return to the maternal body as a marriage plot whose resolution closes debate and brings an end to textuality. The fact that this is a marriage that has already happened only establishes more firmly its power to close and to resolve. Mother replaces father, and daughters return to mother through an act of poetic memorializing.

But "Sibling Mysteries" does not—quite—end here. The last five lines remind us that access to the fantasy of maternal return is in the hands and the bodies of the sisters who frame this poem with their mutual and mutually problematic presence. The marriage of mother to daughters is followed by a marriage of the two sisters:

> the daughters were to begin with
> brides of the mother
>
> then brides of each other
> under a different law
>
> Let me hold you and tell you

The word "different" in "different law" is hard to place. Does each sister live under a different law or simply under a law that is different from the mother's? The slipperiness of "difference" underscores its omnipresence, its ability to intervene in the spaces between women. The term enters the poem with the reentry of the sisters who become themselves principles of difference, contaminating the fantasy of maternal return.

The appearance of the sisters at the end of the poem forces us back to the problematics of sisterhood within the body of "Sibling Mysteries." If the sisters serve each other as gateways to the maternal body, they also come between the daughter and the fantasy of maternal sameness. The poem is split in two by a dated journal entry that begins "C. had a son on June 18 . . . I feel acutely that we are strangers." (Rich's ellipses) Like the maternal fantasy of return that opens the poem, the intervention of the journal material is simultaneously a gesture of integration and splitting. The poem opens up to include the journal entry about exclusion, and even the ellipses work two ways: as an effect-of-the-real announcing the inclusion of "real life," real autobiography, and as marks of secrets withheld from sister and reader alike. If the return to the mother is problematic, the relation between sisters pushes against the limits of poetry, intervening in poetic form. Before the journal entry the poem proceeds in tercets; after the entry, it becomes a series of couplets. It is as if the form of the poem itself turns from the relation among three women to the relation between two. Sisterhood comes to dominate the poem, as motherhood becomes, by comparison, unproblematic, relegated to a personal past that has achieved some kind of resolution.

Rich cannot, will not, resolve the problem of sisterhood, but the hope for these sisters, like the hope for so many other women in this collection, gets represented in linguistic terms. These sisters are "translations into different dialects/ of a text still being written/ in the original"; they come together—to the extent that they do—through a language that is itself deeply suspect, at times incomprehensible. Still, the act of reminding begins the poem, and the act of telling ends it. The physical embrace of the last line accompanies and in some sense allows for the telling of stories, the telling of different stories in different "dialects." This is the tentative promise of the "so-called common language" with which Rich ends her poem about language and about poetry, "Cartographies of Silence":

> what in fact I keep choosing
>
> are these words, these whispers, conversations
> from which time after time the truth breaks moist and green.

Both "Sibling Mysteries" and "Cartographies of Silence" end with a linguistic choice that works against the pain of the poem to produce some sort of poetic vision; both endings work against what Rich refers to in "Cartographies of Silence" as "the ice-floe split," and in "Sibling Mysteries" as "boats of skin on the ice-floe." Both poems acknowledge a drift, an iciness, a splitting, and, in the face of that acknowledgment, they attempt a poetics of unity between women and between individual poems.

If "Sibling Mysteries," produces a memorializing poetics as it reproduces difference between sisters, Rich's sonnet sequence, "Twenty-One Love Poems," tries simultaneously to find a language for the representation of lesbian love and a place for difference within that representation. A sequence of twenty-two short poems (one, the "Floating Poem" is unnumbered), "Twenty-One Love Poems" details the coming together and the breaking up of two lovers. The sequence begins in the full security of sameness; the splitting, to use one of Rich's favorite words, of the couple, foregrounds the issue of their difference from each other and tentatively locates that difference first between the lovers and then between the lovers and the world around them.

By Poem V, difference is located in and readable through the body. Bodies and voices seduce reader and lovers with a vision of sameness and connection, but difference inhabits hands, words, and sounds, even at moments of intense and erotic connection. The poems anatomize difference at the very moment of positing a physical similarity between the two lovers:

> Your small hands, precisely equal to my own—
> only the thumb is larger, longer . . .   (VI, lines 1–2)

Sleep—or, more properly, sleeping together—holds the promise of connection: "a touch is enough to let us know/ we're not alone in the universe, even in sleep," (XII, 3–4), but cannot fulfill the fantasy of union that grounds the poem:

> But we have different voices, even in sleep,
> and our bodies, so alike, are yet so different
> and the past echoing through our bloodstreams
> is freighted with different language, different meanings—
> though in any chronicle of the world we share
> it could be written with new meaning
> we were two lovers of one gender,
> we were two women of one generation.   (XII, lines 10–17)

At this point in the poem the lovers are still, in whatever sense the poem and the world allow them to be, together; their difference is part of their connection and subsumed—albeit with difficulty—by it. The last two lines turn the two lovers into the utopic ''one'' that earlier lines challenge with the presence of difference. Sleep acts as a suspension of an inevitable and fundamental difference; Poem XII takes place in sleep, offers a dream of unity in its final couplet. The opening of Poem XIII is an awakening into the world and into the idiom of ''breaking'':

> The rules break like a thermometer,
> quicksilver spills across the charted systems,
> we're out in a country that has no language   (XIII, lines 1–3)

The spilling of quicksilver is the first of many images of accidents, car crashes, and poison that haunt this sequence of poems and provide a counter-narrative to its euphoric love plot. The sequence begins to alternate images of coming together with images of breaking apart, poems that attempt the writing of a new gynocentric erotics like the ''Floating Poem'' and poems about the impossibility of such an idiom.

The conflict between the euphoric and dysphoric ''plots'' in this sequence itself generates a single movement outward where difference, once privatized, even eroticized, becomes a systemic problem. Poem XVII makes explicit for the first time that the search for a lesbian erotics is embedded in a culture ''ranged against'' such a project. The speaker imagines leaving a linguistic legacy, a ''ghost'' caught on a tape-recorder that

> . . . could instruct those after us:
> this we were, this is how we tried to love,
> and these are the forces they had ranged against us,
> and these are the forces we had ranged within us,
> within us and against us, against us and within us.   (XVII, lines 12–16)

The poem ends poised between what I have called ''difference from'' and ''difference within''; both are forces acting with parallel power on the two lovers. The ''they'' and the ''we'' mark a difference from, are ''ranged'' against each other, but work in psychological and syntactical tandem. Rich's language here, dependent as it is on repetition and analogy, cannot finally make a distinction between the "they" and the "we": only the pronouns remain as a mark of their difference from each other.

As the sequence progresses, difference becomes increasingly projected onto an outside world. The "they" of this poem becomes the "civilization" of Poem XIX:

> If I could let you know—
> two women together is a work
> nothing in civilization has made simple,
> two people together is a work
> heroic in its ordinariness   (XIX, lines 11–15)

Difference within has become difference from, as the poem ends with a celebration of loneliness and isolation, framed, as Rich frames her endings to many poems including "Cartographies of Silence," as a choice:

> I choose to be a figure in that light,
> half-blotted by darkness, something moving
> across that space, the color of stone
> greeting the moon, yet more than stone:
> a woman. I choose to walk here. And to draw this circle.
> (XXI, lines 11–15)

The circle with which the poem ends, and the choice the speaker makes to draw it around her, attest simultaneously to the power and the isolation of the "I." The ending of the sequence with its privatized vision of self and of womanhood conflicts brutally with the opening of "Twenty-One Love Poems" which emphasizes the ugly necessity of connection with the world:

> Wherever in this city, screens flicker
> with pornography, with science-fiction vampires,
> victimized hirelings bending to the lash,
> we also have to walk . . . if simply as we walk
> through the rainsoaked garbage, the tabloid cruelties
> of our own neighborhoods.
> We need to grasp our lives inseparable
> from those rancid dreams, that blurt of metal, those
>   disgraces   (I, lines 1–8, ellipses Rich's)

The urban landscape of the sequence has disappeared to be replaced by a mythic topography of moon, woman, and stone. The sequence moves inward from Manhattan streets to the lovers' apartment to a world removed from them both. Language need no longer grapple with the other, need no longer experiment to produce an erotics somehow different from the pornography with which the sequence opens. Words and syntax are stripped down; difference is replaced by identity.

The private and privatized vision that "Twenty-One Love Poems" ends with posits a safe space for the self within the image of the circle; the very word "circle," however, reminds us, indeed compels us, to go back to the beginning of the poem, to read circularly. If we read linearly we can only choose an erotics of the same, where otherness is systematically exiled. If instead we read the poem as an invitation to reread, that exile is never permanent, and we are embroiled in an erotics of difference horrifyingly similar to and exhilaratingly different from the pornographics invoked by the opening poem.

Caught between a homophobic culture that privileges sexual difference and a lesbian-feminist culture that has so far privileged sameness, lesbian poetry and practice are suspended in a painful struggle to represent difference while celebrating identity and sameness. For Rich, as for many lesbian poets and activists working today, one can only make the simple, powerful, and highly painful gesture of a choice between the different and the same.

Inter-Chapter 3

Eliminating the Other Woman: The Excremental
Fatal Attraction

Fatal Attraction is all the things its detractors have claimed it to be: misogynist, gynophobic, a hysterical and monogomist reaction to AIDS. A part of what makes it such an easy watch—and therefore for feminists so difficult and so painful—is the obsessive opposition of the two central female characters: the mistress and the wife. To say that this opposition is central to patriarchy is simultaneously to understate the case and risk feminist cliché; to call this virgin/whore, mistress/wife opposition "splitting" is to psychologize and risk a political soporific. These "risks" themselves suggest that we are not risking enough by simply suggesting that this splitting is harmful to women. In discussing a film that is about risking everything not to take certain other kinds of risks, feminists are, I think, compelled to look further.

What fascinates me about the film is not its obligatory parade of oppositions (the nuclear family lit up as if from within in their warm and glowing country house, and the mistress, crouched on the floor of her loft apartment insanely twitching at the light switch of a single lamp as it blinks on and off; the cuddlesome family sexuality that allows mother, father, and daughter to romp through their private times together in identical men's white T-shirts, and the lethally dyadic sex behind the bars of the elevator in the apartment house of the mistress), but the equally compelling series of images that connect the two women: to the body, to anger, to digestion, defecation, and waste.

Fatal Attraction is as much about the process that makes women different as it is about the cultural fact of that difference: it is about the desperate attempt to distinguish, to split, to render opposite what is overwhelmingly diffuse, what is, in the visual idiom of this movie, refuse. Female difference, in this film, comes out of the fear that all women are the same and that that sameness inhabits their reproductive, digestive, and eliminatory systems. It is also, of course, about the fear of difference: that female difference might spill over the boundaries erected for it, that it might spill, stain, soil, scar, or maim.

In the process of processing difference, this film tries consistently to locate that difference in the female body, and, more precisely, in the body of the mistress. What is remarkable about this otherwise conventionally triangular rendering of safe and unsafe sex is precisely the question of that location: while sex can and does take place anywhere—this is the trespass of the mistress—sexuality gets confronted, worked out, fought over not in the bedroom but in the bathroom.

We might begin, as the film does, in the wife's bathroom; we might begin, in fact, in any one of the film's many white-tiled bathrooms which serve as hygienic containers and displayers of the female body. The first bathroom we see serves its function perfectly; it is a benign extension of familial space entered visually through long white corridors that characterize the apartment that holds the wife and child. Dressed in their white T-shirts—signs at this moment, it seems, of family unity and cleanliness—the mother prepares for the fatal party at which her husband is to meet Glenn Close (Alex). The daughter, in a time-honored trope of acculturation, watches her mother dress and prepares with her, smearing her mother's red lipstick inexpertly and endearingly over the smooth white palette of her face. The smeared lipstick is a sign of the bond between mother and daughter; as such we revel in its cuteness. It is a cuteness, however, that must be cleaned up, erased: it is sex, and, in the context of the white-tiled walls, it is excrement. The daughter must be cleaned up before the mother can go to the party. Her lipstick simultaneously acculturates her, marks her as feminine—throughout the first scene the child's gender is up for grabs—and suggests that she has exceeded the boundaries of her little girlhood. The tiled walls behind her reproach with their whiteness and promise easy cleaning; this bathroom is a safe space for experimentation, forgiving, if ultimately disapproving of, sexual experiment.

The white bathroom is visually coextensive not only with the other walls and spaces in the apartment, but with what seems to be the family uniform: those white men's T-shirts. White bathroom walls, white T-shirts, and the little girl's boyish haircut make of androgyny a clean slate. Home is a retreat from sexual difference which, in this film, gets figured as sex itself. More dangerously, it is also, inevitably, where sexual difference is constructed in preparation for leaving, for going to parties in which sexual difference assaults you with its inevitability, where, inevitably, you wear a black dress and meet—or almost meet—your husband's future lover, also dressed in black.

There is, however, a layer under androgyny, a body under the white T-shirt, a gendered body, a female body that both mistress and wife uneasily share. Although the bodies are similar, their desires, as they are constructed in the film, are not. One can still read difference, desperately, in terms of sexual desire. The mistress wants sex all the time; the wife, with charming reluctance, breaks the sexual mood to open the bedroom door to the child who is hungry, and the dog who must go out to shit. More frightening than the association of the female body with sexual desire in this film is its repeated association with functions themselves not culturally gendered: eating, defecation, elimination. In his first sexual encounter with the mistress, the husband pushes her up against the wife's sink full of dirty dishes; her buttocks spill over the edge of the sink, nearly touching the leftover food on the plates. The mistress reaches behind her back to run the water, splashing it in the husband's face as they teeter together on the edge of the sink. This scene might at first be read specifically in terms of the mistress; she is defecating on the wife; she is dirty; it is she who must be eliminated. We must then, however, remember that the wife too is always in the bathroom; cleaning instead of defecating, it is true, cleaning up after sexuality, cleaning up after dinner, but nonetheless there, imprisoned in the sparkling site of elimination.

Both wife and mistress feed the husband; both cook spaghetti. Because of this, the husband can truthfully say he ate spaghetti the weekend his wife is away looking at a country house for the family, during the weekend he spends with the mistress. The spaghetti irony is one of the movie's small but resonant clevernesses, and one of the husband's. He has gotten away with the spaghetti story because women are predictable in their cookery; the two spaghetti dinners are redundant, and one must go to waste. The husband must go home and throw out his wife's spaghetti, or, more accurately, feed it to his dog, so she will not find it in the fridge when she gets home. As he spoons the pasta into the dog's dish it looks strangely like a regurgitation; the spaghetti has come up again, reminding us by its shape and color of the body in which it—or rather that other spaghetti—has begun to be digested. If the spaghetti is ironic because it is the same, it is also ironic because it is different. The two spaghetti dinners function oppositely in what we might call the opposed culinary lexicon of marriage and adultery. The wife's spaghetti is comforting, predictable, it lives in the fridge waiting the husband's convenience. It is spaghetti for dinner again. The mistress' spaghetti, although it looks the same, although it is regurgitated as the wife's spaghetti, is exotic: it is associated with sophisticated modern living, with opera, in particular with *Madame Butterfly* which both the mistress and the husband adore, and with the network of suicidal and erotic images the opera cooks up for both of them.

If the first bathroom scene involves the hygienic deployment of sexuality and elimination, the second takes us dangerously close to the body which desires, excretes, and bleeds. Nonetheless, it is a site of attempted control over bodily excess. Alex has just slit her wrists in an effort to get Dan to stay with her; in one of her quick changes from anger to victimage, she hangs over the edge of her bathtub as Dan bandages her wrists. The bandages figure ambiguously in this scene as manacles; they transform Alex from a murderous creature to a little girl, but are linked visually to her first appearance in the film where she sports a bracelet as a sign of her sexual power. The bandages absorb her anger as they absorb her blood; once bandaged Alex is exceptionally docile, falling asleep like a child with her wrists held pathetically outside the covers. Once again the bathroom functions as a black—or white—box where some mysterious and unnamed process cleanses, transforms, and domesticates female anger and sexuality.

The third bathroom is the famous one, the one that most dramatically challenges the ability of familial spaces and arrangements to contain bodily desire. Significantly, this bathroom is located in the country house, that place of retreat into privacy which is revealed to be fragile through Alex's many and violent intrusions. As the camera enters this final white-tiled space it lingers on its purity: Beth, the wife, scarred by her car accident and draped in a large unisex white bathrobe, is using the bathroom as a place of healing and relaxation: she is about to forget her troubles in a warm bath while her husband, domesticated at last, makes tea downstairs. The film is not subtle at this point about its project of defamiliarization: the steam from the soothing bath slowly builds into a fog through which the audience and Beth anxiously peer, Beth to look at her bruised face and the audience to see what or who lurks within the vapor. The film's most startling moment is, of course, a moment of identity between the mistress and the wife; as Beth looks through the steam into the mirror Alex's face appears horrifically close to hers within the frame of the mirror as she enters the room behind Beth's back. Mistress and wife occupy, for the first time, the same frame, the same space; for the first time they compete visually in the arena of the bathroom.

The entrance from behind is, of course, another trope of the film, another way the film foregrounds the problem of elimination. Alex's sexuality involves repeated reachings behind her back: the scene with the kitchen faucet is structurally repeated in the elevator of her building when, in the midst of sex, she fumbles behind her for the elevator buttons to stop it between floors. These moments are obviously in some sense about anal intercourse, and thus about the film's anxiety about AIDS; they also, however, become part of the film's accretion of waste images.

The final battle, the final bathroom, is of course a bloody one. Bodily fluids cannot be contained by bandages or motherly injunctions to clean up; both mistress and wife bleed all over the bathtub, the floors, and the walls. Their blood mingles, staining their clothing, turning the white tiles and the water red. The bloodiness of the bath water links this scene to Alex's previous act of literal trespass when she leaves the child's pet rabbit boiling in its own juices on the stove. The water of this final confrontation, like that of Lady Macbeth's speech, does not have the power to clean.

Caught up in this wash of bodily fluids are images of overflow; during the greater part of this life-and-death struggle in the upstairs bathroom, Dan sits calmly downstairs in the kitchen waiting for the kettle to boil for tea. The whistle of the kettle as the water boils over drowns out the sounds of struggle overhead. For Dan, the first sign that something is wrong is the dripping of the water from the bathtub through to the kitchen ceiling; female anger overflows, boils over, in this violent economy of fluids worthy of Irigaray: blood turns to water, water to blood; both overflow their bounds and threaten to destroy the very structure of the house.

The film's insistent transformation of the sexual into the excremental simultaneously betrays a fundamental anxiety about sexuality and allows sex to be represented in supposedly gender-neutral terms. It also consistently allows the film to locate representations of sexuality in the visually neutral or neutered space of the bathroom. White tiles, white T-shirts, and white bandages give the film an almost clinical look which holds out a place for and the promise of healing.

The third bathroom scene frames that healing as a choice between the two women, a choice, of course, that has already been made: by Dan, by the film, by the viewer. This affair which was only supposed to last one night is expendable, excretable from the white body of marriage. The struggle in the bathroom, with its visual insistence on the likeness between the two women, makes the act of finding a good woman quite literally a process of elimination; one gets rid of one woman and turns immediately to the one left standing. The final scene of the film, following closely on the horrifying bathroom scene, is one of completely restored calm. Dan and the police chief shake hands as Dan and Beth return to their home seemingly unscarred either by the death of a woman in their bathtub or by the specter of the complicated legal and psychological consequences that might follow. Little Ellen, repeatedly traumatized, first by the death of her rabbit, then by, in quick succession, her kidnapping by Alex, the car accident to her mother, the separation of her parents, and this final killing, does not reappear on the screen except as one of three smiling faces in the family portrait that serves as the film's final image. The binary structure of family—we are family and you are not—has worked to purge the film of any doubt or desire.

The process of elimination—in the idiom of this film, the elimination of elimination—is the cleaning up of bodily messes of all kinds. It is interesting, of course, that these messes get located in and on the female body; Dan's body remains intact throughout while both women, even when they try physically to injure him end up getting cut, battered, and bruised. Perhaps even more strange and more sinister is the fact that Dan is represented as having no agency; if he does not get bruised, he does not bruise or cut; even in the final scene it is the wife, not the husband, who kills the mistress. This lack of agency is more than an avoidance of responsibility, more than propaganda suggesting that women are the real perpetrators of family violence. The male body in this film is not a body at all; all bodily functions, whether traditionally sex-linked or not, are here gendered female. Finally, the film is interested only in difference because it fears, as we see through a series of parallel scenes, that women are somehow all the same. Splitting creates differences between women and sex creates difference between the sexes; these visual and political differences are repeatedly and horrifyingly undercut by the excremental images that raze difference. The film responds to the erasure of difference by attaching all mess, all excess, all excrement, to women and by carefully differentiating between mistress and wife. The work of difference is done over a body that does not differentiate between food and waste, sex and violence, love and hate.

Chapter 4

"And Now She Was Different": Sexuality and Differentiation Among Black Women In *Quicksand, Passing,* and *Sula*

The word "sister" in its political context, has, of course, its roots in the civil rights movement and in black culture.[1] The uneasiness of the translation of the term into white culture should remind white feminists of those roots, those debts, and the historical and cultural specificity of the term. To the extent that the word does evoke the civil rights movement and blackness for white feminists, I think it very often calls up a fantasy version of black sisterhood that serves white feminism in two ways. If we think of black women as somehow more intimately bonded to each other, less different from each other than "we" are, we can simultaneously simplify the position of black women in our culture and envy them a unity and direction that compensates for that dismissal. The notion of unity among black women allows us, as white feminists, to contain, for example, black women's writing, in one week—usually the last week—of feminist theory or women's studies syllabi; it allows us to allow one black woman—usually at the moment Alice Walker or Toni Morrison—to speak for all black women; perhaps most important it simplifies and contains guilt over racism by projecting onto black women a personal, political, and mythic power which suggests that we need not work with them to overcome racism.

There are many less ignominious reasons for white feminists not to concentrate on differences among black women, the most obvious of which is the problem of their authority to speak on the matter in the first place. Many black women, whether they call themselves feminists, womanists, or reject any public association with gender issues, have, after all, themselves refused to discuss differences, especially gender differences, within what is usually figured as the black "family" in front of a white public. Reaction to Michelle Wallace's *Black Macho and the Myth of the Superwoman,* perhaps the first bestselling book explicitly to critique sexism within the black community, was repeatedly criticized by some black women for its public airing of "dirty linen."[2] If black women are themselves hesitant to discuss differences, it seems at best presumptuous and at worst destructive for white women to try to talk about them.

I think, however, that to ignore issues of difference in black communities is to ignore the history of black people in the United States, and that to offer a uniform "black woman" is to offer only a cardboard figure all too easily assimilable to white fantasies. White feminists cannot step in to resolve debates between and among black women; they can, however, look at how such differences have been represented in those parts of black culture that have been made available to a white audience.

Differences between black people have taken different dominant forms at different historical moments: the field hand versus house slave (a difference in the process of being undermined by historians of slavery) and the free black versus the slave under slavery; the true Negro versus the assimilationist in the Harlem Renaissance, the mulatto versus the (always relatively) "pure" black in the literature of the nineteenth and early twentieth century, and, some would argue, the black man versus the black woman in the literature and culture of the last few years. All these differences, like differences in sexual preference discussed in the previous chapter, have been talked and written about from the point of view of the disenfranchised community itself as well as from the point of view of hegemonic culture. There are racist and liberationist versions of all these differences, as well as versions that cannot easily be categorized as one or the other.

This chapter focuses on two often linked differences within black communities as they are represented in literature—differences in skin color and sexuality. Differences in skin color among blacks evoke, of course, the figure of the mulatto and the tradition of literature embodied in that doubly marginal figure. Nella Larsen's novels, *Quicksand* and *Passing,* work with and against the tradition of the mulatto to produce a spectrum of colors, a lexicon of color that underwrites the notions of race in her fiction. As Deborah E. McDowell suggests in her influential essay which serves as an introduction to the Rutgers University Press edition of Larsen's two works, the racial issues that bifurcate the text of *Quicksand*—Helga Crane's double attachment to and distance from her two ancestries—are reflected in and amplified by the novel's sexual doubleness and Helga's attempts to locate herself with respect to sexuality as well as race. This chapter begins with *Quicksand* and *Passing* to open up the issue of color as sexual difference, and moves on to a reading of how these terms for and about difference are revised in Toni Morrison's *Sula*. My discussion of *Sula* takes this chapter into an almost exclusively black community and translates the problem of skin color into other physical markings, and the problem of racism into, additionally, one of community making and unmaking.

To read *Quicksand*, as Anne Hostetler notes,[3] is immediately to be absorbed in the idiom of color: people, objects, and places are identified first by their color. Color operates, however, not only thematically or imagistically: colors, their various shades and connotations, their relations to each other, generate the lexicon of verbal, racial, sexual, and political difference upon which this novel unfolds. The dichotomy between black and white, always present as a background to the novel, is continually interrupted by the articulation of different shades of skin. The students at Naxos, the school where Helga teaches as the book opens, have "ebony, bronze, and gold faces"; Helga's first patron, Mrs. Hayes-Rore, is "a plump lemon-colored woman"; a physician is "saffron colored"; Helga herself has "biscuit-colored feet" and "skin like yellow satin." Larsen mines the language of food, fabric, and precious metals for a language of colors that is both precise and various. Blackness explodes into shades of yellow, brown, and tan, themselves—sometimes lovingly, sometimes angrily, but always carefully—calibrated.

Color does not rest with or in skin tone; it flows outward from individual bodies to mark the landscape and infiltrates the foundational metaphors of the text. Many chapters open with a reference to color that serves as an index of location, a sign of place and placement that is one of the novel's central concerns. Chapter 5, the first after Helga leaves Naxos to travel north, begins with the words "Gray Chicago": "Gray Chicago seethed, surged, and scurried about her. Helga shivered a little, drawing her light coat closer. She had forgotten how cold March could be under the pale skies of the North."[4] The next chapter opens by repeating, breaking down, and amplifying the signal grayness of the first: "Helga woke to the sound of rain. The day was leaden gray, and misty black, and dullish white." (*QS*, p. 31) To live in a city even for the space of one day, one chapter, is to begin to complicate the vocabulary of color as grayness dissolves into its component parts and re-forms as a metaphor for many colored things: weather, psychology, race relations.

Color marks the language of individual characters and describes and distills institutional relations. Naxos, with its Southern proprieties, is twice described in the terms of "red tape" which produces and impedes her desire to leave it:

Suddenly she longed for immediate departure. How good, she thought, to go now, tonight!—and frowned to remember how impossible that would be. "The dignitaries," she said, "are not in their offices, and there will be yards and yards of red tape to unwind, gigantic, impressive spools of it." (*Quicksand*, pp. 5–6)

Helga repeats her fantasy of leaving several pages later. This time she pulls herself short with the single phrase, "red tape": "sharply she began to probe her decision. Reviewing the situation carefully, frankly, she felt no wish to change her resolution. Except—that it would be inconvenient. Much as she wanted to shake the dust of the place from her feet forever, she realized that there would be difficulties. Red tape. James Vayle. Money. Other work." (*QS*, p. 10) Red tape becomes shorthand for Naxos, concentrating its essence in a single image. It is as if Larsen's own language had cut through red tape in producing the phrase, in reproducing the color.

When members of the Naxos community are told of Helga's upcoming departure, they mobilize the lexicon of color against her. Helga's friend Margaret warns that Helga will be put on a "black list," while Dr. Anderson, the strangely compelling president of Naxos, mourns that Helga is giving up what he considers to be service to the community: "Service," he says, "is like clean white linen, even the tiniest speck shows." (*QS*, p. 20) Caught predictably between black and white, between threats and promises, and between allegiances, Helga moves North into a landscape that is simultaneously colorless and burgeoning with color.

If colors are multiple and various, they are also relational. The structure of the novel reminds us that Helga feels black when she is around her white relatives and—to a lesser extent—white when she is in Harlem. Larsen demonstrates the fluidity and the relationality of color by consistently producing images of foreground and background, displaying for the reader faces and bodies against contrasting backgrounds.[5] The novel begins with such a contrast as it opens upon Helga's intensely colorful room with its "reading lamp, dimmed by a great black and red shade," its "blue Chinese carpet" and its "many-colored nasturtiums":

An observer would have thought (Helga) well fitted to that framing of light and shade. A slight girl of twenty-two years, with narrow, sloping shoulders and delicate, but well-turned, arms and legs, she had, none the less (sic), an air of radiant, careless health. In vivid green and gold negligee and glistening brocaded mules, deep sunk in the big high-backed chair, against whose dark tapestry her sharply cut face, with skin like yellow satin, was distinctly outlined, she was—to use a hackneyed word—attractive. (*Quicksand*, p. 2)

Helga's skin articulates itself against her clothes, and her clothes stand out against the tapestry of her chair. Objects and people in *Quicksand* do not so much take their colors from their surroundings as much as they take on color in a complex and shifting relation to other things, other people. From the beginning of the novel, Larsen invents a language of colors, a lexicon vast, exact, and scrupulous that takes into account not only difference but change.

It is easy to see *Quicksand* as a novel in two parts demarcated by Helga's shifting sense of identification with black and white culture. The novel opens with Helga's decision to leave Naxos and the assimilationist culture it represents, follows her to Harlem, and through a series of identifications with and withdrawals from the community she finds there, moves on to represent Helga's extended visit to her white relatives in Sweden, and closes with a highly ambivalent depiction of Helga's life as a wife and mother in a tiny, rural Alabama town. Although Helga's travels take her to many places, the primary movement of the novel is binary; not only is her struggle to find a place structured by the ever-present conflict between black and white, but it is characterized by a series of local oscillations: approaches and withdrawals, attractions and repulsions.

Indeed, the bifurcations that structure the novel and Helga's divided self become thematized in the language of the novel. Chapter 4, which describes Helga's encounter with Dr. Anderson, ends with a series of images of a division so powerful that language itself breaks down. In retrospect, Helga blames herself for not being more honest:

> Why hadn't she grasped his meaning? Why, if she said so much, hadn't she said more about herself and her mother? He would, she was sure, have understood, even sympathized. Why had she lost her temper and given way to angry half-truth?—Angry half-truths—Angry half—. (*Quicksand*, p. 26)

The three "half's" of the final question point partially to its answer; in Helga's case there are only "half-truths"; from moment to moment, she can only tell half the story, even if this means that she will be misunderstood. The "angry half-truths," the divison and the anger persist into the rest of the novel, forcing Helga into a pattern of identification and withdrawal from a series of characters and communities.

Once again, this division is worked out in terms of color and clothing. At Naxos, Helga wears bright colors, standing out from the rest of the teachers and students who are warned, in what Deborah McDowell sees as an imitation of ninteenth-century white ideals of proper womanhood, that "bright colors are vulgar."[6] If such colors are inappropriate for all proper young women, they are especially so for the women of Naxos, who wear "Drab colors, mostly navy blue, black, brown." (*QS*, p. 17) As she gazes out of the window at the drably attired women outside her dormitory window, Helga hears the disembodied voice of Naxos' dean of women: "Black, gray, brown, and navy blue are the most becoming colors for colored people''—''Dark-complected people shouldn't wear yellow, or green or red.'' (*QS*, pp. 17–18) What is at stake in the Dean's proscriptions is, as the shifting meaning of ''color'' from clothing to body suggests, not merely the elimination of colored clothing, but of ''colored'' people, of their difference from mainstream culture. It is as if by dressing colorlessly, these women not only hide but undo or erase their own color.

If Helga's attempt to declare her color and her colorfulness structures the first half of the novel, her sense of discomfort about color structures the novel's closing half. Helga's relatives in Sweden dress her in bright colors and bright, expensive jewels, going so far as to suggest that she use rouge to add ''high color'' to her cheeks. (*QS*, p. 69) Helga's discomfort with her aunt and uncle's costuming can be related here to the Barthean figure of the clown or the exotic I mention in the Introduction; Helga here is deliberately staged as a ''savage,'' her difference, her color, heightened for a spectacle about which Helga feels typically ambivalent:

> Marie had indeed ''cut down'' the prized green velvet, until, as Helga put it, it was ''practically nothing but a skirt.'' She was thankful for the barbaric bracelets . . . for the beads about her neck. She was even thankful for the rouge on her burning cheeks and for the very powder on her back. No other woman in the stately pale-blue room was so greatly exposed. But she liked the small murmur of wonder and admiration which rose when Uncle Poul brought her in. (*Quicksand*, p. 70)

The two halves of the novel, if we see it this way, can be aligned with the two sides of the Barthean paradox: Helga at Naxos is the mirror, in Sweden, the clown, the exotic, the savage. At Naxos, the teachers explicitly imitate the white normative culture. ''Naxos,'' the name itself a mirror image of ''Saxon,'' promotes the absorption and erasure of difference. In Sweden, difference is staged, exaggerated, and commodified as Helga is produced and promoted for the marriage market. Circus and stage imagery pervade the depiction of Helga's visit to Sweden from the moment she is first displayed at her aunt and uncle's evening party to the moment of her identification with two black vaudeville clowns.

The binary structure of the novel, with its symmetry of color and form, is itself mirror-like, neat, predictable. The comparison of Naxos and Sweden, however, ignores the two most complex and in many ways painful parts of the novel: Helga's extended stay in Harlem and her final relocation to Alabama. Both these sections, which take place within very different black communities, foreground the question of sexuality, which, as McDowell suggests, is present in some form throughout the novel. The Harlem section, however, is the first in which Helga articulates sexual desire, the first in which difference becomes clearly a matter of both race and sex and in which racial difference gets rewritten as sexual difference. The final section in Alabama, with its insistent scrutiny of Helga's many and painful pregnancies, announces Helga's sexual and racial difference, ironically enough, at the very moment that she most perfectly reproduces the womanly roles of wife and mother.

It is also in Harlem that the novel most explicitly anatomizes otherness among women and constructs two "other women" through whom Helga explores the linked questions of race and sexuality. The first woman whose presence puts Helga in the position of sexual other is Audrey Denney, infamous for "going about" with white people. The disgust felt for Audrey by, among others, Helga's friend Anne, which casts her out of the community of good women, itself brings together issues of sex and race through the barely articulated specter of miscegenation. Anne can only hint at what she feels to be the real dangers of mixed race parties: " 'And the white men dance with the colored women. Now you know, Helga Crane, that can only mean one thing.' Anne's voice was trembling with cold hatred. As she ended, she made a little clicking noise with her tongue, indicating an abhorrence too great for words." (*QS*, p. 61) At stake here for Anne is the nature of black female sexuality, or, perhaps more properly, black female purity. Mixed race parties, and, by extension, Audrey Denney, serve as a visible reminder of questions about sex and race too painful to be confronted or put into words.

Helga's response to Anne reminds us of what Anne herself does not know: that Helga's mother was white. Helga changes the sexual configuration of Anne's nightmare to reenact her own racial history and the sexual history of her mother in hypothetical terms: "Don't the colored men dance with the white women, or do they sit about, impolitely, while the other men dance with their women?" (*QS*, p. 61) This revised scenario points us toward the text's original and silent "other woman," the mother whose sexuality Helga at times tries so hard to understand. At the beginning of the novel, Helga explicitly compares her own at best lukewarm feelings for James Vayle with what her mother must have felt for her father; literally nauseated by James' kisses, she finds herself unable to identify with a mother set apart by race and sex.

McDowell has discussed in some detail Helga's discomfort with her own desire for Robert Anderson; interestingly, in terms of the sexual and racial economy of the novel, it is through another woman—one whose skin, despite her race, is white as alabaster—that Helga comes for the first time to feel desire for a man. When Helga first sees Anderson at a party in Harlem, she "blush(es) furiously," and "averts" her eyes. (*QS*, p. 60) She cannot keep them turned away, however; her gaze returns "immediately," not to Anderson, but to "the girl beside him who sat indifferently sipping a colorless liquid from a high glass." (*QS*, p. 60) The term "colorless," here signals not a lack of desire or sexuality, but a connection between Audrey and her drink: the contraband gin of Prohibition. Audrey's pallor, carefully articulated in the next paragraph, both likens her to Helga and sets her apart; like Helga, she is a very light-skinned black woman, but, in this world of minutely calibrated color, she is a shade lighter, even more different than Helga herself.

The description of Audrey, through Helga's eyes, like the earlier narrative descriptions of Helga, depends for its vividness on the contrast between clothing and skin:

> She was pale, with a peculiar, almost deathlike pallor. The brilliantly red, softly curving mouth was somehow sorrowful. . . . The extreme *décolleté* of her simple apricot dress showed a skin of unusual color, a delicate, creamy hue, with golden tones. "Almost like an alabaster," thought Helga. (*Quicksand*, p. 60)

The exquisite balance of sameness and difference between Helga and Audrey sets up an identification that allows Helga, a little later on, to use Audrey as a way of identifying, of identifying with, her own sexuality; careful contrast serves as the idiom both for the description of Audrey and her position in relation to Helga herself.

In light of Anne's remarks about dancing, it is significant that Helga's revelation about her own desires should come while Audrey and Robert are dancing together. Perhaps more significant, however, is the fact that, in this instance, Audrey is not dancing with a white man, but with someone whom Anne regards as an eligible property: the man, indeed, whom Anne eventually marries. It is as if this dance between Audrey and Robert is in some sense already a mixed race event; Audrey's history of dancing with white men, inscribed perhaps in her own pallor, makes of the dance something titillatingly forbidden, especially for the gazing Helga who insets herself voyeuristically into the scene:

> At the first sound of music Dr. Anderson rose. Languidly the girl followed his movement, a faint smile parting her sorrowful lips at some remark he made. Her long, slender body swayed with an eager pulsing motion. She danced with grace and abandon, gravely, yet with obvious pleasure, her legs, her hips, her back, all swaying gently, swung by that wild music from the heart of the jungle. Helga turned her glance to Dr. Anderson. Her disinterested curiosity passed. While she still felt for the girl envious admiration, that feeling was now augmented by another, a more primitive emotion. She forgot the garish crowded room. She forgot her friends. She saw only two figures, closely clinging. She felt her heart throbbing. She felt the room receding. She went out the door. (*Quicksand*, p. 62)

This extended description is, of course, powerfully erotic; its erotics, however, emanate not so much from Helga's appreciation of Anderson, as from a shifting and often painful identification with Audrey. Robert's body is strangely absent during this scene; it is "the girl" who is the focus of Helga's sexual feelings. Helga's desire is mediated through her identification with Audrey, an identification that causes Helga, for many reasons, acute discomfort. It would be easy enough, of course, to see a simple displacement at work here; Helga focuses on Audrey because she cannot bear to look directly at Robert's unsettling gray eyes. This, however, is only part of the story in a novel that depends on repeatedly choreographed identifications with and withdrawals from other women, their race, and their sexuality.

Audrey's sorrowful lips remind us both of her sexuality and of the literary icon of the tragic mulatto: the figure, usually female, caught between two worlds, whose beauty is at once her power and her downfall. Helga, like Audrey, is a descendant of that figure, although Larsen deliberately endows Helga with an irony and subtlety that complicate her. Audrey represents a link to that tragic figure, while she is at the same time tragically updated in this scene which, as McDowell notes, is resonant with images of hell.

If Helga can escape the specter of Audrey by walking out the door, she cannot so easily walk out on her friend Anne, who, by marrying Anderson, replaces Audrey in the sororophobic economy of the text. In a text marked by Helga's exits, Anne is the one figure to whom Helga—however ambivalently returns. She is the only one about whom Helga feels guilty, the only person for whom she delays a departure. Although Helga's relationship with Anne remains largely unrepresented, Anne is the only character with whom Helga keeps up a sustained dialogue about race. Helga sees Anne as "obsessed" with "the race question," and notes the contradictions between Anne's "hatred" of white people and her attempts, as the narrator puts it, to "ape their clothes, their manners, and their gracious ways of living." (*QS*, p. 48) Helga's political differences with Anne are, of course, partly a function of the unspoken racial difference between them. Despite her accusations of obsession, Helga is as concerned with race as is Anne; her concern, however, derives from a different position within the highly differentiated structure of racial relations offered and explored by the novel. Indeed, as Helga debates her return to Harlem from Sweden, it becomes clear that her anger toward Anne is in many ways a sign of her own anxieties about race. Helga refuses to return to the United States for Anne's wedding for a reason Anne herself might recognize, although Anne would cast it in different terms:

> Go back to America, where they hated Negroes! To America, where Negroes were not people. To America, where Negroes were allowed to be beggars only, of life, of happiness, of security. To America, where everything had been taken from those dark ones, liberty, respect, even the labor of their hands. (*Quicksand*, p. 82)

Helga's own "obsession" with race takes a different form from Anne's, but race is nonetheless a dominant factor in her many attempts to find a home. Anne's positions on race are simpler than Helga's, if equally contradictory.

It would be easy to see Helga's refusal to attend Anne's wedding as "purely" a matter of sexual jealousy; in a novel in which purity of all sorts—sexual purity, purity of race or of motivation—is deliberately undermined, it is only possible to read racial explanations simultaneously with and against sexual ones. Certainly, there are moments in the text when sexuality, and, in particular, sexual jealousy between Anne and Helga, become dominant. Significantly, these moments are explicitly cast in terms of the sexual difference between two women. The most vivid moment occurs after Helga's return to America, when it becomes clear that Anne does not want Helga to share a house with her and her new husband:

> Anne had perceived that the decorous surface of her new husband's mind regarded Helga Crane with that intellectual and aesthetic appreciation which attractive and intelligent women would always draw from him, but that underneath that well-managed section, in a more lawless place she herself never hoped or desired to enter, was another, a vagrant primitive groping toward something shocking and frightening to the cold asceticism of his reason. Anne knew also that although she herself was lovely—more beautiful than Helga—and interesting, with her he had not to struggle against that nameless and to him shameful impulse, that sheer delight, which ran through his nerves at mere proximity to Helga. (*Quicksand*, pp. 94–95)

The "lawless place" Anne herself does not want to enter is, of course, one of the many places in this novel on whose fringes Helga is constantly hovering. This place, like white culture, like Sweden, is clearly out of bounds for Anne, and far less clearly so for Helga. This sexual doubleness both in itself and as a metaphor for racial doubleness produces the sororophobia so fundamental to this novel. Anne, who from the beginning of the novel is "too good to be true," can ultimately only act as a foil against which Helga's tenuous sense of self develops. Helga's friendship with Anne is worked out through a series of departures and absences: Helga carefully lays out Anne's silk pajamas as Anne returns from a trip; Helga leaves Anne to visit with her Swedish relatives; she returns to America, but, by mutual and unspoken consent, not to Anne's home. Helga's most important sexual encounter takes place in suspension between Anne's absence and presence; at a party, behind Anne's back, Anderson grabs Helga and kisses her. Both women come to an assessment of their own sexuality by contrast with the other; theirs is a rich and contradictory sororophobia, made up of political and moral differences transcribed onto the more palpable differences of sex and race.

Helga's final journey propels her away from Anne, away from Harlem, and into a world where there are no friendships, no individual relations among women. The other women in the small Alabama town to which Helga moves with her pastor husband act as a disapproving chorus, a community of other women onto which difference is painfully projected. As I mentioned above, that difference arises and increases at the very moment Helga's body is making a series of connections to experiences supposed to be common to all women: in Alabama, through her many pregnancies and childbirths, Helga is reduced to the level of an everywoman without the consolations of community support. This ending, traditionally read as Larsen's punishment of her heroine, is as cruel in how it works out its sororophobia as it is in its use of the heterosexual or marriage plot; if Helga's husband is philandering, judgmental, and neglectful, the women who surround her are of little help. Helga's otherness to women is complete, ironic, and totalizing.

If *Quicksand* links the exploration of race to sexuality through a series of sororophobic contrasts, *Passing* intensifies the relationship between racial and sexual identity by focusing the story more closely on a single pair of women. *Passing,* even more than *Quicksand,* explores the constructedness and the relationality of race and sexuality. Both are contingent terms; race and sexuality find their meaning only through a series of binary oppositions that get embodied as characterological and positional differences between the two main female characters, Irene Redfield and Clare Bellew. The relationality that characterizes the novel's sense of racial and sexual identity gets embodied as a complicated, ambivalent, and important relationship in which the two women act out, sometimes simultaneously, the positions of childhood friends, sexual rivals, potential lovers, and, finally—according to most readings of the novel—murderer and victim.

Passing begins with the construction of self through difference. In one of the novel's first scenes, where Irene and Clare meet again after many years, both are "passing" for white, but they are passing differently. Irene is passing, as she says later, "only for convenience," only publicly and only temporarily; she is taking advantage of her light skin to drink an iced tea at an exclusive restaurant. For Clare passing is a way of life: her husband, an unabashed racist, thinks she is white. The scene of their encounter in the rooftop restaurant of Chicago's Drayton Hotel is a marvelous encounter of loyalties, allegiances, and duplicities, in which Irene, from whose point of view the novel unfolds, struggles to come to terms with the degree and kind of Clare's otherness to herself.

The scene opens with an interchange of gazes as Irene watches Clare watching her. The clash of gazes is a battle both for control and identity, as Irene finally turns Clare's toward herself to wonder if Clare has seen through her attempt to pass. The visual economy set up by this exchange of looks complicates feminist notions of the heterosexual gaze, as the two women negotiate their differences and their power through looking and turning away. Irene begins with a casual appraisal of the other woman's face and clothing: "An attractive-looking woman, was Irene's opinion, with those dark, almost black, eyes and that wide mouth like a scarlet flower against the ivory of her skin. Nice clothes too, just right for the weather, thin and cool without being mussy, as summer things are so apt to be."[7] Irene's evaluative glance objectifies the other woman; "that mouth" and "those eyes" suggest a distance appropriate to this almost instinctive judgment of one woman by another. For a brief moment, the more general allusion to the propensity of summer clothes to be "mussy" marks an identification of Irene with the unknown woman, a sense of a common feminine problem, an inhabitation, however brief, of the body of the other woman. Irene's gaze, with its familiar attention to the contrast between skin and clothing, mimics that of Larsen's narrator in both *Quicksand* and *Passing;* again, it suggests a female self constructed out of difference and opposition that takes the form of a subtle dialogue between colors.

Irene's summary glance judges not only the other woman's beauty, but her sexuality as well. Irene takes in and tries to evaluate the smile Clare bestows on the waiter: "it was an odd sort of smile. Irene couldn't quite define it, but she was sure that she would have classed it, coming from another woman, as being just a shade too provocative for a waiter." (*P,* p. 149) Before Irene recognizes Clare, the smile is mysterious, hard to categorize: nonetheless Irene's categories, inescapably sexual, remain in place. The hypothetical "other woman" ironically foreshadows Clare's identity and the part she will play in Irene's life. After their mutual recognition, Clare smiles at the waiter again, and this time "Irene was sure that it was too provocative for a waiter." (*P,* p. 152) Irene's judgment depends on a careful calibration of race and class; she is able to "class" Clare's smile only when she knows the background of the other woman. The smile, "a shade too provocative for a waiter," must be calculated not only in terms of color, but in terms of the slight shades of color that make up the racial and psychological grammar of this novel. It is no accident that Irene's final judgment is articulated in sexual terms, for eroticism is the lexicon into which all differences are finally translated.

If Irene conventionally, almost automatically, "sizes up" the other woman, she also, out of convention, turns away. Clare's returning gaze cuts across the visual etiquette of the glance:

> The dress decided, (Irene's) thoughts had gone back to the snag of Ted's book, her unseeing eyes far away on the lake, when by some sixth sense she was acutely aware that someone was watching her. . . . Very slowly she looked around,

and into the dark eyes of the woman in the green frock at the next table. But she evidently failed to realized (sic) that such an intense interest as she was showing might be embarrassing, and continued to stare. Her demeanor was that of one who with utmost singleness of mind and purpose was determined to impress firmly and accurately each detail of Irene's features upon her memory for all time, nor (sic) showed the slightest trace of disconcertment at having been detected in her steady scrutiny. (*Passing*, p. 149)

Clare's power throughout the novel will lie in her ability to cut through convention, her ability not to turn other people's opinions, assumptions, glances, back upon herself. Her eyes are magnetic, seductive; Irene turns *into* them as if she is drawn not only to but inside Clare. Clare, on the other hand, cannot, will not internalize; she draws people in without allowing them to change her.

The battle of the gazes is over, not so much when Irene establishes Clare's reason for gazing, as when Irene turns her own gaze toward herself, first superficially—"had she, in her haste in the taxi put her hat on backwards? . . . Something wrong with her dress?"—and then more deeply: "Did that woman, could that woman, somehow know that here before her very eyes on the roof of the Drayton sat a Negro?" (*P,* pp. 149–50) The ironies here are manifold: that Clare, whose "passing" is so much more dangerous, so much more problematic than Irene's, should cause Irene to question her own safety; that Clare, who refuses, at least as the narrative itself presents it, any self-reflection, should produce such reflection, such reflexiveness, in another woman; that Irene should at this point calibrate her racial identity against Clare's supposed whiteness when later she will calibrate it against the always unquantifiable sense of her blackness.

The scene sets up the axes of difference between the women—whiteness and blackness, proper and improper sexuality—that will remain the constant structuring principles of the novel while the position of the two women on these axes will shift from situation to situation, from moment to moment. The movement of the novel is always in the direction of the complication and the eroticization of difference: as the novel progresses, the stakes of difference also get higher, its price more painful and its negotiation more violent and destructive.

McDowell sees *Passing* as a novel in code, where racial difference provides a cover for questions of sexuality, where racial "passing" becomes an oblique way of talking about the covert operation of lesbian desire between Irene and Clare:

In *Passing* (Larsen) uses a technique found commonly in narratives by Afro-American and woman novelists with a "dangerous" story to tell: "safe" themes, plots, and conventions are used as the protective cover underneath which lie more

dangerous subplots. Larsen envelops the subplot of Irene's developing if unnamed and unacknowledged desire for Clare in the safe and familiar plot of racial
passing. (McDowell, p. xxx)

While I have no trouble with a lesbian reading of the relationship between Irene
and Clare, I do think the hierarchization of the two plots is unnecessary and
untrue to the complex and contradictory gestures toward the presentation of
selfhood that this novel attempts. While on a narrative level racial paasing is a
relatively "safe" topic that cozily establishes Larsen in the literary tradition of
the tragic mulatto, passing—on the level of story—is fraught with danger.
Clare continually risks her husband's violence if she is ever found out; his
hatred of "niggers" and "black devils" is made abundantly clear in the
wonderfully complex tea party scene in which he openly avows his racism as he
is surrounded, unknown to him, by three black women who represent various
degrees of passing.

It is true that as the novel progresses, racial passing is continually eroticized,
both by Clare's presumed affair with Irene's husband and by Irene's conflicted
desire for Clare. In the end, of course, it is not John Bellow who pushes Clare
out the window, but Irene, the other woman, in whose murderous impulse
questions of race and sexuality come fatally together. Racial passing and
sexuality are inextricable; both are brought painfully to bear, for instance, on
Irene's decision not to betray Clare to her husband: Irene keeps quiet, as we
shall see, because of a curious mixture of racial loyalty and sexual self-
preservation. No matter how self-deluded or hypocritical we find Irene, the
truth is that she is herself torn between racial and sexual alliances; McDowell's
privileging of sexuality, her sense that race is merely a "cover," makes Irene
too scheming, too sure of herself in a novel in which, as in *Quicksand,* the
category of self is constantly under investigation. The privileging of one
category over the other also disrupts the almost obsessively neat balance of race
and sex in the novel—a balance and an obsessiveness that McDowell would
probably see as itself an indication of the novel's need to provide a tidy
framework for a disruptive "subplot." Nonetheless, Irene's relations to
everyone in the story are mediated equally by sexual and racial concerns; this is
clear with Clare, but also in her half-glimpsed relations with her children: Irene
has two arguments with her husband about Brian junior—one in which she asks
Brian not to encourage his son to talk about sex and one in which she tells him
not to tell Brian junior too much about the "race problem." Both problems are
unspeakable for Irene, both are spoken through her by the structure of the
novel.

Both race and sex get explored through female difference in this novel as in
Quicksand. Passing, however, complicates an already eroticized notion of

female difference by simultaneously making Clare and Irene rivals for Brian's affections and by making more explicit than in *Quicksand* their desire for each other. Again, this does not seem to me an "either or" situation; just as in the dance scene in *Quicksand* Helga feels desire for and through Audrey Denney, so Irene oscillates between—to the extent that they can be separated at all— desire for Clare and identification with her.

Both kinds of erotics work through sororophobic contrast, a contrast that simultaneously links *Passing* to *Quicksand* and suggests that *Passing* somehow moves beyond its predecessor. Clare acts in this novel as Helga does in *Quicksand*; it is as if *Passing* is an attempt to tell *Quicksand* from Anne's point of view; Irene even has a moment of introspection almost identical to Anne's when she acknowledges the ability of the other woman to feel more, and more deeply, than she can:

> Her voice was brittle. For into (Irene's) mind had come a thought, strange and irrelevant, a suspicion, that had surprised and shocked her and driven her to her feet. It was that in spite of her determined selfishness the woman before her was yet capable of heights and depths of feeling that she, Irene Redfield, had never known. Indeed, never cared to know. (*Passing,* p. 195)

Like many passages in *Passing,* this one takes advantage of pronominal confusion to make a point. The "she" here as elsewhere is constantly shifting, and we need the "Irene Redfield" of the penultimate sentence to make sense of the paragraph. The explanatory phrase simultaneously suggests the stability of a self we could call Irene Redfield, and works as a defensive gesture that exposes the relationality of self-making. The reassuring contrasts Irene is constantly invoking between herself and Clare are undermined both by their similarities and Irene's inexplicable, to her, desire *for* Clare.

Like Helga, who, in the dance scene in *Quicksand,* simultaneously identifies with and desires Audrey Denney, Irene feels at the same time a desire for and a desire to be Clare. Irene's senses of self and sexuality come tenuously together in Clare's presence, over Clare's body, in response to Clare's beauty; as we have seen, that sense of self is itself divided and shifting, but it shifts primarily in response to Clare.

At the end of the first half of the novel, Irene thinks, for the second time, that she has exorcised Clare from her life. After the humiliating scene at Clare's tea party in which she was forced to pass in front of John Bellew, she has no desire to see or to hear from Clare again. Clare reenters Irene's life and the narrative through the mail; her letter, on "foreign" paper, directed in purple ink, lies at the bottom of Irene's "little pile of mail," looking "out of place and alien." It is the only letter without a return address. (*P,* p. 143) This letter scene represents an attempt on Irene's part to construe Clare as "foreign," to persuade herself that she and Clare live in different worlds. The lack of return address suggests, besides secrecy, Clare's continual denigration of the universe she inhabits with her husband, her insistence that, despite her decision to pass, Harlem is somehow the pertinent address: that it is still, in fact, her home.

Canonically, mysterious letters suggest love affairs, and it is precisely as an affair that Clare's return to Harlem is structured. Not only must Clare hide her visits to Harlem from her husband as she would an extramarital relationship, but her rhetoric about Harlem and its inhabitants is explicitly erotic. When she complains that Irene has not returned her letter, Clare claims that she has taken to haunting the post office for a reply: "every day I went to that nasty little post-office place. I'm sure they were all beginning to think that I'd been carrying on an illicit love-affair." (*P*, p. 194) The suggestion of adultery points simultaneously at Clare's future relationship with Brian and at her feelings for Irene; it also suggests what might be called an erotics of passing; both Irene and Brian speak at times of the excitement and danger both passing and "going back" entail.

Irene's response to Clare's sudden appearance in her bedroom is—to her—completely unexpected. She is shocked out of her disapproval and composure by Clare's beauty: "Looking at the woman before her, Irene Redfield had a sudden inexplicable onrush of affectionate feeling. Reaching out, she grasped Clare's two hands with her own and cried with something like awe in her voice: 'Dear God! But aren't you lovely, Clare!' " (*P*, p. 194) This is only the first of several scenes in Irene's bedroom where Irene works out her complicated relationships with her husband and her friend: alone with Clare in her own bedroom, Irene seems capable of admiring Clare without resentment or envy; it is only when the two move downstairs and into the gaze first of Brian and then of the Harlem community, that Irene sees Clare's beauty as a threat to herself. When Irene first descends the stairs to meet Clare and take her to her first Harlem dance, she makes a "choked little exclamation of admiration at Clare's beauty." It is Brian's presence that constructs an opposition between Clare and Irene. Under Brian's gaze, Clare, "exquisite, golden, fragrant, flaunting, in a stately gown of shining black taffeta," makes "Irene, with her new rose-colored chiffon frock ending at the knees, and her cropped curls, (feel) dowdy and commonplace." (*P*, p. 203) Alone, the two women have their differences; in public, with Brian, these differences are frozen into canonical forms.

Clare's body takes on a different value, a difference valence, under Irene's private gaze and under a more public, heterosexual one. To Brian, they appear as conventional rivals; he even refers to Irene's assessment of Clare's intelligence as "feline"; to a casual observer, a conventional gaze, Irene is simply being "catty." And indeed, Brian is, in this novel, a stock figure, a sign of a conventionally rivalrous plot, a plot that in some sense, for all the pain it causes her, Irene seems desperate to enter. It is important to note that Irene has no real evidence that Brian and Clare have actually embarked on a sexual relationship; it is simply the easiest and most plausible solution of racial and sexual identity infinitely more painful than "infidelity" as it is usually construed.

Significantly, the scene where Irene "discovers" Brian's infidelity takes place in their bedroom as Irene makes up her face for one of her endless series of tea parties. Brian has invited Clare in spite of Irene's reluctance; it is this conflict that sets up the discovery. After Irene explains why she did not invite Clare, Brian is silent: "He continued to stand beside the bed, seeming to look at nothing in particular. Certainly not at her. True, his gaze was on her, but in it there was some quality that made her feel that at that moment she was no more to him than a pane of glass through which he stared." (*P*, p. 216) Once again, Irene is the subject of the gaze; this one unmakes her, renders her invisible. Unlike Clare's more overtly dangerous gaze on the roof of the Drayton, this does not take into account her face, her features, or her past. Irene both challenges and submits to the authority of this gaze by continuing, as Brian stares at and through her, to make up her face in the mirror, "complet(ing) the bright red arch of her full lips." Brian's gaze is a challenge to her self-making, her making up; despite the bright red mouth she creates, she is invisible.

It is in the mirror that Irene first sees what she reads as signs that her husband has been unfaithful:

> Brian's head came round with a jerk. His brows lifted in an odd surprise. Her voice, she realized, *had* gone queer. But she had an instinctive feeling that it hadn't been the whole cause of his attitude. And that little straightening motion of the shoulders. Hadn't it been like that of a man drawing himself up to receive a blow? Her fright was like a scarlet spear of terror leaping at her heart. Clare Kendry! So that was it! Impossible. It couldn't be. In the mirror before her she saw that he was still regarding her with that air of slight amazement. She dropped her eyes to the jars and bottles on the table and began to fumble among them with hands whose fingers shook slightly. "Of course," she said carefully. "I'm glad you did (invite Clare). And in spite of my recent remarks, Clare does add to any party. She's so easy on the eyes." (*Passing*, p. 217)

It is tempting to argue that the adulterer Irene sees in the mirror is not her husband but herself, that this is a scene in which she realizes her own desires and projects them onto a tired story of sexual betrayal. Whatever the explicitly erotic relationship between Irene and Clare, however, this is still a scene about self-making, the production of public and private self through sexuality and color. The red spear of anger mimics the red arch of Irene's lips as her public persona becomes internalized, private, and vulnerable. Irene's contention that Clare is "easy on the eyes" is both a joking pretense of alignment with a male desiring gaze and an appropriation of that gaze in self-assertion and self-defense. Clare is "easy on the eyes" both because she is beautiful and because she allows Irene access to a desiring and inquiring exchange of gazes which Brian does not. Again, in one sentence, Irene moves between identification and distancing as she articulates in the most deliberately offhand and hackneyed terms the convolutions of sororophobic looking.

Again, it is not because Clare takes her husband away from her—whether she wants to do this in the first place is completely unclear—that Clare is dangerous. It is because, in this exchange of gazes as in the one on the rooftop, she forces Irene to look at herself and the constructedness of her marriage, her sexuality, and her racial position. Clare challenges Irene through the idiom of displacement: from the beginning of the novel, Irene is desperate to defend her social, racial, and geographical position against all "foreign" challenges whether they be Brian's desire to move to Brazil or Clare's entry into her life. It is as a challenge to self-making that Clare menaces Irene; she can neither keep Clare in the place of difference nor in the place of sameness. Clare is other, but at the same time someone with whom Irene must at moments identify.

Clare's unmaking, her undoing of Irene, must ultimately be challenged by a final and instinctive displacement; Irene's murderous dislodging of Clare from her life, from Harlem, and from the windowsill on which she is leaning while she confronts the intrusion of her husband John Bellew into her "other" life in Harlem. The instinctive violence of Irene's gesture dramatizes in a single instant the intensity of the sexual and racial conflict between the two women. Irene takes her revenge on the body that has both tantalized and infuriated her; when she mourns, she mourns her friend's "glorious body mutilated." Even in death, Clare is not exorcised; neither, significantly, is the entanglement of Irene's body with Clare's. The novel's final paragraph describes Irene's swoon into unconsciousness as her body mimics—again with a difference—the trajectory of Clare's: "Her quaking knees gave way under her. She moaned and sank down, moaned again. Through the great heaviness that submerged and drowned her she was dimly conscious of strong arms lifting her up. Then everything was dark." (*P*, p. 242) Irene, unlike Clare, will rise again in life; the "strong arms"—perhaps John's—hold out that promise. She must first, however, travel through a darkness that is both her own and Clare's, a darkness whose completeness suggests a welcoming back into the world of Harlem, into a simpler and more comprehensive notion of race and community.

Sula is a novel that has broken free of the tragic mulatto; it is, however, as interested as either of Larsen's novels in the question of female difference within the black community. In *Sula,* Morrison offers a series of sororophobic and matrophobic relations: the novel focuses on the complex friendship between Nel Wright and Sula Peace as it explores each of their equivocal matrilineal legacies, and positions them within the larger black community and specifically within the female community of Medallion, Ohio. Difference between women is, as it is in *Quicksand* and *Passing,* indelibly written on the body; in this case the inscription of difference is located not so much in skin color as in other bodily markings: Sula's birthmark, Eva's missing leg, Hannah's physical beauty. These marks foreground their otherness from other women and from the community, which, through different strategies, they learn to negotiate.

Sula operates on one level as a searching investigation of the meaning of community. The novel opens not with Sula, Nel, or their families, but with a figure of even more profound and more difficult otherness: Shadrack, the damaged veteran, the hermit, the founder of Suicide Day in Medallion. Shadrack leaves Medallion to go to a war that psychologically cripples him; he returns after a year in a psychiatric hospital, attended by hallucinations that his hands are swelling to monstrous size and preoccupied with thoughts of death and violence. His invention of Suicide Day is an effort at controlling death by limiting violent impulses to one day and to a peaceful ritual of parading and ringing bells. Despite the villagers' initial terror, Shadrack and Suicide Day become institutions, incorporated into the language and customs of the community:

> As time went along, the people took less notice of these January thirds, rather they thought they did, thought they had no attitudes or feelings one way or another about Shadrack's annual solitary parade. In fact they had simply stopped remarking on the holiday because they had absorbed it into their thoughts, into their language, into their lives.
>
> Someone said to a friend, "You sure was a long time delivering that baby. How long was you in labor?" And the friend answered, "'Bout three days. The pains started on Suicide Day and kept up till the following Sunday. Was borned on Sunday. All my boys is Sunday boys."[8]

The absorption of Suicide Day into the everyday discourse of the community, its incorporation into the temporal and biological calendar of daily life, is a testament to the power of community to transform the different into the familiar. As Morrison's narrator tells us, "Once the people understood the boundaries and nature of (Shadrack's) madness, they could fit him, so to speak, into the scheme of things." (Morrison, p. 13)

This "scheme of things" has both its generous and its sinister side; Morrison's exploration of community dwells on both through a series of experiments in which outside becomes inside, the marginal hegemonic. Shadrack's story, like Eva's, like Sula's, is both a story of tolerance and colonization; the latter is hinted at in the novel's repeated invocation of the concept of privacy, first alluded to in Shadrack's stay in the hospital. Awakening out of a coma, Shadrack is addressed by a nurse as "Private": "'Private? We're not going to have any trouble today, are we? Are we, Private?'" Disoriented, Shadrack misinterprets the term: "He wanted desperately to see his own face and connect it with the word 'private'—the word the nurse (and the others who helped bind him) had called him. 'Private' he thought was something secret, and he wondered why they looked at him and called him a secret." (Morrison, p. 8)

Despite his title, privacy in the other sense is systematically denied to Shadrack: in the war, in the hospital, in jail, and even, eventually, in Medallion. In Medallion, his most private acts become cause for comment and therefore part of the public discourse; his very desire to be alone becomes a fact of community life. His Suicide Day rituals are public, in the sense that they take place in front of other people, from their inception; as time goes on, however, they become more and more institutionalized, to the extent that they become reference points for other people in the community.

Medallion, on the whole an accepting and flexible community, routinely sets boundaries on privacy as it challenges the notion of a private self. The people of Medallion routinely mark their acceptance of an outsider by changing his or her name; Helene Wright is, after several years, welcomed into the community at the price of her name: "She lost only one battle—the pronunciation of her name. The people in the Bottom refused to say Helene. They called her Helen Wright and left it at that." (Morrison, p. 16) More sinister, because it is more complete, is the incorporation of "the deweys" into the Bottom and into Eva's household. The deweys, when they first arrive upon the scene, are three young boys of different ages and different ethnic mixes; Eva changes all three of their names to "dewey" referring to them only collectively, as in "send one of them deweys out." (Morrison, p. 33) Eva's kindness in providing a home for the boys is undercut by her sense that there is no need to tell them apart; moreover, her denial of their difference has the shaping force of a command or a prediction: after a while no one in town can tell one dewey from the other. The obliteration of difference in the case of the deweys is intimately entangled with the obliteration of their sexuality; the deweys officially do not grow up, do not in any way enter the novel's sexual economy. While this, of course, does not mean they are not in some sense sexual, they are barred from the community's definitions of sexuality, from the public discourse about sex or even gender.

The deweys are only the most extreme example of the homogenizing forces at work in the world of the novel. Other characters, like Eva, Hannah, Nel, and Sula, struggle against and ultimately make different compromises with the community to come to some sort of sense of identity. In the cases of these four women, difference is explicitly sexual: Hannah's openly acknowledged sexual encounters in the pantry under shelves of provisions she has put up and Eva's flirtations with male visitors are part of community life. The women of the Bottom disapprove of these exhibitions of sexuality, particularly Hannah's, but the community accommodates even Hannah's affairs with newly married men just as Eva accommodates an ever-increasing household of boarders. When Hannah is burned to death in front of the eyes of several of her neighbors, the women, jealous of her in life for her beauty and attractiveness to men, take her body lovingly to themselves in a final ritual of community: "the women who washed the body and dressed it for death wept for her burned hair and wrinkled breasts as though they themselves had been her lovers." (Morrison, p. 67) One can, of course, read this passage too benignly; it is possible to suppose that the women can only express affection for Hannah after they are safely rid of her. Like all sororophobic gestures, the preparation of Hannah's body is both contradictory and erotic: an act of both love and resentment, identification with and repulsion from the wrinkled breasts.

It is no accident that Hannah's evocative burial and reintegration into the community should be in the hands of women. Communal norms in *Sula* are embodied in a chorus of usually nameless women who make judgments on the behavior of other women. Men, of course, judge as well; Nel and Sula are proud and excited to merit the term "pig meat" as they walk by the men idling in front of the pool hall. Male judgments do not seem, however, in the world of the novel, to be community-making; it is, by and large, the women who literally and figuratively decide whether to make room for other women.

The linked sense of judgment, hostility, and accommodation that marks female relations to the community of Medallion is also worked out through a series of parallel intergenerational female relationships: the relations between Nel, her mother Helene, and her mysterious grandmother Rochelle, and the relations between Sula, Hannah, and Eva. Each woman on each chain of relations takes up a position across the body of her mother, her daughter, or her grandmother.

We are first introduced to Nel when, as a young child, she leaves Medallion with her mother Helene to be at the deathbed of Helene's grandmother Cecile. For Helene, it is a journey back to and through a world she has, with the help of her grandmother, completely rejected; Helene's mother, Rochelle, from whom her grandmother "rescued" her, and with whom Helene wants nothing to do, is a prostitute still living in New Orleans, and the journey itself, in a segregated train, is filled with racial and sexual humiliation.

As Helene and Nel travel toward the source of their matrilineal inheritance, Nel begins for the first time to form her own sense of self in opposition to her mother. In one of the novel's most powerful and painful moments, Helene, caught by the conductor coming through the white cabin, humiliates herself and Nel and alienates the black men in the colored cabin by smiling flirtatiously at the conductor who calls her "gal":

Pulling Nel by the arm, she pressed herself and her daughter into the foot space in front of a wooden seat. Then, for no earthly reason, at least no reason that anybody could understand, certainly no reason that Nel understood then or later, she smiled. Like a street pup that wags its tail at the very doorjamb of the butcher shop he has been kicked away from only moments before, Helene smiled. Smiled dazzlingly and coquettishly at the salmon-colored face of the conductor. . . . Behind Nel was the bright and blazing light of her mother's smile; before her the midnight eyes of the (black) soldiers. She saw the muscles of their faces tighten, a movement under the skin from blood to marble. (Morrison, pp. 18–19)

Caught between her mother and the soldiers, her loyalty to her family and to her race, Nel realizes that she and her mother have come to a moment of choice. It is a moment charged with racial and sexual tension; Nel's shame at her mother's racial betrayal is also shame at her sexuality, or rather at the sexual form of the betrayal. Nel's anger takes on the canonical matrophobic form of repulsion for her mother's body:

In the silence that preceded the train's heave, she looked deeply at the folds of her mother's dress. There in the fall of the heavy brown wool she held her eyes. She could not risk letting them travel upward for fear of seeing that the hooks and eyes in the placket of the dress had come undone and exposed the custard-colored skin underneath. (Morrison, p. 19)

Nel's nightmare of maternal exposure is simultaneously based on an identification with her mother's shame and a deep sense of being ashamed of her mother. The custard-colored skin is both only equivocally black and a sign of Nel's diagnosis of her mother's cowardice. She is afraid that her mother has been stripped naked by the experience both because she, for the first time, sees her mother as vulnerable, and because she recoils from her mother's sexuality with its overtones of racial betrayal.

If the journey south begins the process of separation between Nel and her mother, it forces both Helene and Nel to position themselves in relation to Helene's mother, the infamous Rochelle. In New Orleans, Helene must simultaneously occupy and enact what recent feminist theorists have called the "daughter position" and the "mother position"; as daughter she repeats and reestablishes her rejection of Rochelle, while as mother she protects her own daughter from Rochelle's influence.

Helene's relation to her mother is physical and primal; she first discovers that Rochelle has been in her own dead mother's house by the perfume that marks her presence: "No one other than Mr. Martin seemed to be in the house, but a sweet odor as of gardenias told them that someone else had been." (Morrison, p. 21) Rochelle's perfume marks the house of the mother who rejected her as her own territory; Helene and Nel find her in Cecile's bedroom, presiding over her mother's dead body.

It is in this house, crowded with the warring presences of four generations of women, that Nel first begins to order, in her own mind, her own matrilineal legacy. Helene reluctantly introduces Rochelle as "your . . . grandmother" (Morrison's ellipses). Nel, confused, gestures toward the bedroom door and toward Cecile's body. Helene corrects her: "'No. That was your great-grandmother. This is your grandmother. My . . . mother'" (Morrison, p. 22) Helene defines herself against her mother's sexuality, against what she sees as her sexual trespass, just as Nel, on this journey, begins the process of defining herself against her mother.

The oppositional nature of self-definition for the women of this family produces a binary structure that allows or forces Nel, in the process of separating from her mother, to become attracted to Rochelle. As Helene is bathing her daughter, Nel wonders out loud about her grandmother "She smelled so nice. And her skin was so soft."; Helene answers tartly, "Much handled things are always soft." Nel is also fascinated by the Creole French that punctuates her grandmother's conversation. When Rochelle takes her leave with a "'Voir! 'Voir," Nel asks what "'vwah'" means; again Helene tries to distance herself and her daughter from her mother. "'I don't know,' (Helene) said. 'I don't talk Creole.' she gazed at her daughter's wet buttocks. "And neither do you.'" (Morrison, p. 23)

These exchanges between mother and daughter, as Helene carefully soaps Nel's body, are in a sense exchanges *about* both their bodies and the choices each will make about her own. In bathing Nel, Helene does what she can to purify her daughter, to wash away the gardenia smell and all it signifies. She tries, in this scene, to reestablish the dyadic intimacy of mother and infant daughter, so aping her "head to toe," lingering on the innocence of her daughter's body.

The person who breaks up this mother-daughter dyad, who provides Nel with another voice, another language, is not her father, so frequently absent on long sea voyages, but her grandmother. Like the father, who in the Lacanian oedipal scene is associated with language and with the symbolic, the grandmother in this scene initiates the daughter into a new language and a new world. Unlike the world of the Lacanian father, this one is not dominated by prohibition; unlike the Lacanian father, the grandmother teaches not only what is not but also what it is possible to be. Her "'voir," a condensation of "au revoir," is simultaneously a sign of parting and a promise of return. Nel will, somewhere, in some sense, see her grandmother again. "'Voir" is also, of course, a command to look, to look around, perhaps to look with desire: it hints at a world of gazing and being gazed at, the world Nel will enter with Sula two chapters later when the two girls deliberately engage the gaze of the men in front of the Medallion pool hall.

There is no doubt that the journey which was supposed to introduce Nel to her dying great-grandmother and instead brought her into the vibrant presence of her errant grandmother and began the process of recoil from her mother, is identity-making for Nel. When she gets home, Nel begins the frightening and empowering process of creating a "me":

> It had been an exhilarating trip but a fearful one. She had been frightened of the soldiers' eyes on the train, the black wreath on the door, the custard pudding she believed lurked under her mother's heavy dress, the feel of unknown streets and unknown people. But she had gone on a real trip, and now she was different. She got out of bed and lit the lamp to look in the mirror. There was her face, plain brown eyes, three braids and the nose her mother hated. She looked for a long time and suddenly a shiver ran through her. "I'm me," she whispered. "Me." Nel didn't know quite what she meant, but on the other hand she knew exactly what she meant. (Morrison, p. 24)

In a novel that consistently undoes any simple notion of identity, Nel's construction of a "me" is fraught and dangerous. Her sense of self, itself provisional, unspeakable, comes to life through her mother's hatred of her own mother and her own recoil from Helene. It takes its form across her mother's custard-yellow flesh, her grandmother's flamboyant canary-yellow dress, and her own nose which her mother hates so much and tries so hard to change. It is a self born of hate, love, fear, and difference; it is a self created in opposition to generations of sexual choices, sexual differences.

If the women of the Wright family come to terms with sexuality, race, and self in vexed relation to each other, the three generations of women who live in the ironically named Peace household—Eva, her daughter Hannah, and her granddaughter Sula—make their provisional peace with their own identities through far more violent interactions. Eva, who has literally sacrificed part of her body to construct a household that will hold both members of her biological family and a variety of people, sets fire to one of her children and tells her other child, Hannah, that she never really loved her, but throws herself from the window in an attempt to save her from burning; Sula watches fascinated as her mother burns, and, toward the end of the novel, has her grandmother put away in a home against Eva's objections and those of the entire community.

All three of these women enter a complex negotiation with their own sexuality and the sexual mores of the community. Eva's missing leg places her, in a certain sense, outside the sexual marketplace; at the same time, it allows her—with relative authority and safety—the luxury of prolonged and institutionalized flirtation with most of the men in the community: "Eva, old as she was, and with one leg, had a regular flock of gentleman callers, and although she did not participate in the act of love, there was a good deal of teasing and pecking and laughter.'' (Morrison, p. 36) The missing leg operates as a source of both weakness and power, a conscious appropriation and redirection of sexual energy. Eva controls and directs the male gaze by training it both toward and away from her missing leg:

> Whatever the fate of her lost leg, the remaining one was magnificent. It was stockinged and shod at all times and in all weather. Once in a while she got a felt slipper for Christmas or her birthday, but they soon disappeared for Eva always wore a black laced-up shoe that came well above her ankle. Nor did she wear overlong dresses to disguise the empty place on her left side. Her dresses were mid-calf so that her one glamorous leg was always in view as well as the long fall of space below her left thigh. (Morrison, p. 27)

Eva courts the male gaze and controls it; the missing leg, the presumed self-mutilation, is the price for that control, that compromise with male desire. The missing leg provided her with money for the ''house of many rooms'' she builds to fill with the people with whom she chooses to live.

Hannah's sexual compromises are different, but no less complex. She ''refuse(s) to live without the attentions of a man,'' after the death of her husband, and has ''a steady sequence of lovers, mostly the husbands of her friends and neighbors.'' (Morrison, p. 36) Her sex is frequent, simple, and casual, so fully integrated into her domestic routine that she frequently has sex in the pantry, ''stand(ing) up against the shelves she had filled with canned goods, or l(ying) on the flour sack just under the rows of tiny green peppers.'' (Morrison, p. 37)

Both Peace women are beloved by the men of the community for their ''manlove,'' their ability to stimulate or soothe men as part of their daily existence: ''While Eva tested and argued with her men, leaving them feeling as though they had been in combat with a worthy, if amiable, foe, Hannah rubbed no edges, made no demands, made the man feel as though he were complete and wonderful just as he was . . . and so he relaxed and swooned in the Hannah-light that shone on him just because he was.'' (Morrison, p. 37) This ''manlove'' itself has its limits; Eva and Hannah never marry again after their first experience, and continue to live in what is clearly a matriarchal household. It is as if not living with men as lovers allows them to love all men, allows them the luxury of loving them with safety and distance. However similar the basic structure of compromise, mother and daughter arrange, display, and live their sexuality in opposite ways; Hannah's ease and Eva's intensity are equally erotic, equally successful as strategies in the management of community, identity, and sexuality. Sula's sense of sexuality comes to her both from her mother, from whom she learns that "sex was pleasant and frequent, but otherwise unremarkable" (Morrison, pp. 37–38), and from "outside" where her mother is uneasily tolerated and where "children giggled about underwear." (Morrison, p. 38) We see Sula watching her mother, coming upon her on one of the rare occasions in which she has actually slept with a man and lies "curled spoon."

Although we see attitudes, gestures, and personality traits transmitted from mother to daughter, only rarely do we hear significant conversations between Eva and Hannah or Hannah and Sula. Hannah's one conversation with her mother about their relationship appears in the text, significantly enough, as a series of "strange things" that culminate in Hannah's death and are themselves presented "strangely"—that is, out of chronological order—by the narrator. The "second strange thing" is Hannah's asking Eva: "Mamma, did you ever love us?" (Morrison, p. 58) The question accompanies, as do all of Hannah's significant actions, the carrying out of a simple domestic chore; Hannah asks her momentous question in the middle of shelling green beans for supper. Eva's answer is self-contradictory; she begins with a simple, "No, I don't reckon I did," and, then, significantly revises with a "not the way you thinkin'." Her more elaborate answer to the question takes the form of a family parable; she tells the story Hannah has heard many times before about one particularly bad winter when she shoved her last pieces of food up Plum's rectum to save him from constipation. The story, all too familiar to Hannah, does not somehow "count"; Eva's lexicon of love, which depends on acts taken in the context of extreme poverty and privation, is not the relatively affluent Hannah's. The conflicting definitions of maternal love and nurture at work in the Peace household are embedded in familial and communal history; love and its language, are, like selfhood, relational, entangled in generational opposition.

Hannah's death must be understood in the context of her question to her mother, just as Eva's attempt to save her daughter must finally be understood as the answer to that question. Love for both women is intimately related to violence directed at self and other; it is articulated as a mute but flamboyant lexicon of the body, of scarring, of fire. The coming together of mother and daughter in the death of one and the near-death of the other is an expression of love through and over the body; it powerfully connects mother and daughter as it separates them for the final time.

The double "conversation" between Hannah and Eva—the literal discussion of Eva's love and the enactment of that love minutes later by a woman who has historically had no time for words—is, however unsatisfactory, still textually present. Sula and Hannah never discuss their feelings for each other; Sula does, however, overhear the one thing Hannah says in the novel about her daughter. In a discussion of "the problems of child rearing" with her friends

Patsy and Valentine, Hannah makes a crucial distinction between liking and loving one's children: "I love Sula. I just don't like her. That's the difference." When her friend answers "Likin' them is another thing," Hannah agrees, "Sure. They different people, you know." (Morrison, p. 49)

Hannah's differentiation of herself from her daughter, her acknowledgment that children "are different people," is an inversion of the train scene in which Nel begins to differentiate herself from her mother. Hannah's calibration of the "difference" between "love" and "liking" is also an attempt to calibrate the difference between herself and Sula. Like Isabel Vane whose distinction between liking and erotic love gets her into so much trouble, Hannah is struggling to make a linguistic and emotional distinction that language does not allow women. While an upper-class woman in the nineteenth century could have only one feeling toward her husband, a black mother in the mid-twentieth century was only supposed to have one feeling for her child. In a brief moment of union with other women from the community of the Bottom, Hannah explores the spectrum of her feelings in the context of a community toward which she is also ambivalent.

Sula's reaction to overhearing her mother's words is to summon up, as if in self-defense, the presence of Nel. Sula leaves her mother for her friend, and enters a different struggle with and for identity. In the fire scene, that moment of violent connection between Eva and Hannah, Sula quite literally stands apart, watching. Her connection to love and to a beloved other is equally vexed and painful, but it is a sororophobic rather than a matrophobic one. Sula's self is shaped by her relation to Nel: by their mutual love, their sexual difference(s), and by the violence between them. Several of the most influential readings of *Sula* focus on the relationship between Sula and Nel; theirs is a relationship that must be understood within the context of community and maternal inheritance—within, in other words, a context of other vexed and violent relations between and among women.

Much critical writing about the relationship between Sula and Nel has focused on naming that relationship. From those who focus on the "narcissism" or "self-indulgence" of one or both of the two characters, to those like Barbara Smith, who are interested in the homoerotic nature of female friendship, most critics of *Sula* engage in the problem of definition at the level of character and psychology.[9] It is, however, possible, as Deborah E. McDowell suggests, to see *Sula,* despite the presence in the book of an eponymous heroine, as undermining notions of individual and racial identity. Self is, according to McDowell, always in flux in *Sula:* the novel becomes, in her account, a story about the *process* of self-making, of self-configuration.[10]

If we keep this in mind, the relationship between Sula and Nel becomes one of a series of experiments in self-definition; even more than the relations between community and outsider, or between mother and daughter, this curious symbiotic relationship becomes a site for the staging of female difference. The relationship between Sula and Nel, however, offers something these others do not; embedded as it is in a bildungsroman structure, the relationship offers us not only difference, but differentiation, not only rationality, but the process by which it is lived and encoded. The textual presence of Nel and Sula as young girls takes us behind the scenes of a process already stabilized in *Quicksand* and *Passing;* it adds to the notion of relationality a temporal component present in the novel's concern for generational opposition, but figured most vividly in the sexual difference of "growing up." The differentiation of Sula and Nel, the process of individuation, is, as in *Passing,* both sexual and visual. Nel and Sula move from a visual economy where they share a single point of view, a single gaze, to a double and contradictory focus.

We first see Sula and Nel at the moment of their entry into a sexual and visual economy; despite the fact that it is "too cold for ice-cream," Sula and Nel walk to the ice-cream parlor, Edna Finch's Mellow House, as an excuse to pass the Time and a Half Pool Hall and meet the gaze of the men who stand outside it: "Nel and Sula walked through this valley of eyes chilled by the wind and heated by the embarrassment of appraising stares. The old men looked at their stalklike legs, dwelled on the cords in the backs of their knees and remembered old dance steps they had not done in twenty years." (Morrison, p. 43) The communal gaze of the men makes no distinctions; the "stalklike legs" belong to both or either of the girls who, at this point, are joined within the gaze like a four-legged creature both attractive and slightly monstrous.

If the two girls are joined in their receipt of the gaze, they are also joined in looking back: "Years later their own eyes would glaze as they cupped their chins in remembrance of the inchworm smiles, the squatting haunches, the track-rail legs straddling broken chairs. The cream-colored trousers marking with a mere seam the place where the mystery curled. Those smooth vanilla crotches invited them; those lemon-yellow gabardines beckoned them." (Morrison, p. 43) This passage replicates in miniature the process of differentiation at work in the novel as a whole; in a litany of luscious sameness and difference that could come straight out of "Goblin Market," this passage moves from the general ("the inchworm smiles", *"the* cream-colored trousers" [italics mine]), to an edible difference (*"the* smooth vanilla crotches" *"those* lemon-yellow gabardines." [italics mine]) As in "Goblin Market," but more explicitly, it is the phallus and the phallic economy that turn sameness into difference: crotches divide into the lemon and the vanilla, just as in "Goblin Market" goblin men move from purveyors of generic fruit to dealers in cherries, figs, and pineapples.

Even as Sula and Nel's erotic gaze begins the work of selection and differentiation, it remains one gaze: desire belongs equally and similarly to both at this point in the novel. In the next encounter between the two girls, the famous and famously erotic scene of their frenzied digging of two holes in the sand, their sense of sameness is momentarily and perhaps utopically enhanced. The relevant passage, with its meticulous interplay of sameness and difference, is so complex it is worth quoting at length:

> Sula lifted her head and joined Nel in the grass play. In concert, without ever meeting each other's eyes, they stroked the blades (of grass) up and down, up and down. Nel found a twig and, with her thumbnail, pulled away its bark until it was stripped to a smooth, creamy innocence. Sula looked about and found one too. When both twigs were undressed Nel moved easily to the next stage and began tearing up grass to make a bare spot of earth. When a generous clearing was made, Sula traced intricate patterns in it with her twig. At first Nel was content to do the same. But soon she grew impatient and poked her twig rhythmically and intensely into the earth making a small neat hole that grew deeper and wider. . . . Sula copied her, and soon each had a hole the size of a cup. . . . Together they worked until the two holes were one and the same. (Morrison, pp. 49–50)

This passage begs for a satisfying reading, and it has been read in many ways, most of them focusing on its resonances of sexual exploration. It has been read oppositely and convincingly as a moment of heterosexual initiation and lesbian eroticism; if it does nothing else, the scene maps out the problematic terrain of sexual desire in this novel.

I prefer to read this passage, as I read startlingly similar passages in "Goblin Market," not so much as a play between the "heterosexual" and the "lesbian" as between the concepts of "same" and "different." Nel and Sula copy each other in their sexual experimentation; each in turn takes the lead at introducing change. This part of the passage ends with a symbol of unity and sameness as the two holes collapse into one; it is a unity, however, quickly erased as they fill the hole(s) with dirt and move on into an adventure—the killing of Chicken Little—that will place them in different positions in the visual economy of the text.

The killing of Chicken Little is an especially mysterious moment in a text filled with mysteries and secrets. It begins, however, to establish a difference between Sula as actor and Nel as watcher, a difference that will come up again only to be questioned at the end of the novel. Up to this point it is Nel who has had the adventures, Nel who has left Medallion for the exoticism of New Orleans and maternal separation; in this scene Sula literally seems to leave Nel behind.

The division between the watcher and the watched is, at this point, tentative; in the structural and thematic mirror scene where Hannah burns to death, Sula takes on Nel's position as watcher. It is significant, however, that Nel is absent from the scene and that Sula replaces her rather than connecting with her. At this point, Sula and Nel watch separately. The metonymic relation of the scene at Chicken Little's funeral where their identity to and with each other is based on touch becomes a metaphoric relation based on replacement and absence.

The process of differentiation begun in violence continues and finds a public shape in marriage. Nel's marriage to Jude places her firmly inside the community; Sula's mysterious years of absence mark her, even and perhaps especially in her return, as exile. Sula's departure from Medallion during Nel's wedding inscribes the sexual difference between them in the act of marrying and in Nel's institutionalized heterosexuality. The closing paragraph of Part One of the novel sets up the juxtaposition of Nel's marriage with Sula's departure. Toward the end of the wedding, Jude looks at Nel and reads impatience and sexual desire in her eyes:

> As if reading her thoughts, Jude leaned down and whispered, "Me too." Nel smiled and rested her cheek on his shoulder. The veil she wore was too heavy to allow her to feel the core of the kiss he pressed on her head. When she raised her eyes to him for one more look of reassurance, she saw through the open door a slim figure in blue, gliding, with just a hint of a strut, down the path toward the road. One hand was pressed to the head to hold down the large hat against the warm June breeze. (Morrison, p. 73)

The chain of metaphoric replacement now includes Jude; Jude's entry into Nel's life is the occasion for Sula's exit. Less obvious, and perhaps more important in this feminocentric text, however, is the development in the relation between Sula and Nel; Nel's thick veil and Sula's hat become signs of their different positions within the economy of marriage and within the community of the Bottom. Jude's "Me too," that sign of empathy across gender and through heterosexual sexuality, is also an echo of Nel's "I'm me," a sign that Nel's sense of self is now embedded in a different system of sex and gender.

The blankness at the center of this novel, those unrepresented ten years in which Sula is absent from Medallion, is itself an echo of the blank space in Eva's biography. Eva, of course, returns to Medallion with a missing leg; Sula returns in a costume from another world, another class: "A black crepe dress splashed with pink and yellow zinnias, foxtails, a black felt hat with the veil of net lowered over one eye. In her right hand was a black purse with a beaded clasp and in her left a red leather traveling case, so small, so charming—no one had seen anything like it before, including the mayor's wife and the music teacher, both of whom had been to Rome." (Morrison, p. 78) Sula's departure and return have amplified and reified the difference between Sula and Nel, now the somewhat dowdy mother of several children. That difference resides not only in Sula's clothing, but in the mysterious mark over her eye which has become more noticeable than ever: "It was darker than Nel remembered." (Morrison, p. 83)

Sula's return to Medallion and her re-entry into Nel's life is, at first, only a pleasure for Nel. She thinks back to her childhood history for a way of thinking about their relationship: "talking to Sula had always been a conversation with herself. Was there anyone else before whom she could never be foolish? In whose view inadequacy was mere idiosyncracy, a character trait rather than a deficiency? . . . Sula never competed; she simply helped others define themselves." (Morrison, p. 82) This is, in part, the utopian language of nostalgia, a memory that reaches back behind the shadow of sexual differentiation, of self-construction in a heterosexual economy. It is this economy, of course, which intervenes, which announces in canonical and predictable terms the difference between Sula and Nel, between mistress and wife, between outsider and insider.

Sula's "affair" with Jude, Nel's discovery of them together, naked, on the floor, freezes the two women into position in relation to each other. Neither of them can understand the other: Sula is bewildered by what she feels to be Nel's possessiveness, while Nel cannot comprehend what she feels as a betrayal by her best friend. The institution of marriage has changed the tone, indeed precluded, the "conversation with herself." This is not to suggest, of course, that outside of patriarchy, outside of compulsory heterosexuality, Sula and Nel would not be "different," would not disagree, but only that that difference might take other less predictable and less institutionally powerful forms.

Nel's compromising discovery of Jude and Sula reiterates not only the positional difference between mistress and wife, but also between actor and watcher. Nel's gaze and Sula's, no longer identical, break apart in this moment of sexual opposition:

> But they had been down on all fours naked, not touching except their lips right down there on the floor where the tie is pointing to, on all fours like (uh huh, go on, say it) like dogs. Nibbling at each other, not even touching, not even looking at each other, just their lips, and when I opened the door they didn't even look for a minute and I thought the reason they are not looking up is because they are not doing that. So it's all right. . . . They are not doing that. I am just standing here and seeing it, but they are not really doing it. But then they did look up. Or you did. You did, Jude. (Morrison, p. 90)

Nel's traditional position as the watcher is challenged here by the consequences of looking; Jude and Sula's position challenges, in its unexpectedness, the dichotomy between looker and actor upon which Nel's relations to Sula have hitherto been based. Nel still looks, Sula refuses to look, but Nel's gaze quickly translates itself into reality and into action. Her position vis-à-vis Sula and Jude forces both of them out of her life.

Soon after this perhaps more than primal scene, it becomes clear that the act of looking has in some sense replaced the act of sex for Nel, and that the look has become—sexually speaking—everything. After Jude leaves, Nel realizes it is looking that is really the problem:

> Now her thighs were really empty. And it was then that what those women said about never looking at another man made some sense to her, for the real point, the heart of the matter, was the word *looked*. Not to promise never to make love to another man, not to refuse to marry another man, but to promise and know that she could never afford to look again. . . . (Morrison, p. 95)

Nel becomes frozen within the sexual economy of the gaze into a parody of her own position. The act of adultery, however, parodies not only Nel, but Sula as well; through the rupture of communal norms Sula becomes as isolated, as one-dimensional as Nel.

Sula does not propose an unequivocal solution to the problem of difference between women; it does suggest, however, that the place of even a partial answer is in the gaze. Nel's return to Sula's sick-bed is explicitly framed as a painful decision to look, and to look specifically at what is different about Sula. As Nel contemplates seeing Sula again, Nel realizes that "for the first time in three years she would be looking at the stemmed rose that hung over the eye of her enemy." (Morrison, p. 119) That "rose," which takes on different meanings with different onlookers, is both a mark of Sula's difference and the relationality of that difference: it embodies difference in motion while challenging any simple binary distinction between the different and the same.

It is tempting to see the last few pages of the novel as an attempt to collapse the distinction between Sula and Nel; Nel's conversation with Eva in which she is forced by the older woman to realize her own complicity as watcher in the murder of Chicken Little, and her final acknowledgment that it is Sula and not Jude whom she has been missing for the last few years, make it relatively easy to see the ending of the novel as an acknowledgment of Nel's complete identity with Sula. Certainly, this novel comes closer than any of the others in this book to seeing difference between women as a function of hegemonic culture. *Sula* is, however, too savvy about the homogenizing pressures of community life to end with an image of complete absorption. Like *Passing, Sula* ends with one woman dead, with a reunion that is both earthshaking and impossible. Nel's difference from Sula, Sula's difference from Nel, cannot be disentangled from the sexual, racial, and visual economy in which their lives unfold and are represented. The bildungsroman structure tempts us with a prelapsarian fantasy of unity, while the cracks, lapses, and interstices of that structure remind us that identity is always constructed through difference and that development and differentiation are neither simple nor linear.

Inter-Chapter 4

Between Two Carmens: Olympic Ice-Skating and the Choreography of Otherness

The Olympics, 1988. The dance of the Other Woman takes shape, etched on ice before what American announcers describe as a "hugely partisan" crowd. Debi Thomas: American, pre-medical student, athlete, amateur. Katarina Witt: East German, performer, beauty, consummate flirt. Both women, by some remarkable coincidence, are to skate to music from "Carmen." Katarina's choreography demands that she end her program dramatically prone on the ice as she mimics Carmen's death. Debi will not, must not die, will remain unfallen, triumphant; as both skater and doctor she enacts what might be a peculiarly American fantasy of healing.

In this ballet of East and West, American and East German take on counterintuitive roles. Katarina is a seductress from a country whose women are usually portrayed as grim, unerotic, and masculine, a kind of third sex that might at any moment be exposed through a post-game chromosome test as not really women at all. Katarina occupies no such ambiguous gender territory; her femininity is not a matter of science but of spectacle, her body an open secret that announces the project of its own femininity. Katarina's costumes—their beads, feathers, gaps, and spangles—reveal, amplify, parody the femininity of her body. In the media the costumes become an occasion to pronounce upon her body, synecdoches for the body they display. Western coaches express their uneasiness with her performance through strictures on her clothing: "We're here to skate in a dress, not in a G-string," says Canadian coach Peter Dunfield. Sometimes the body bursts through the costume; the media lingers on costume failure:

> [In Paris] carrying this stressing-what's-attractive concept to the extreme, Witt popped out of the front of her costume during a camel spin, an accident that was

captured on film by the West German magazine *Sports International* and made its February issue a hotter trading item in Calgary than even a Jamaican bobsleigh pin.[1]

Unable to say "breast," *Sports Illustrated*—itself, in its annual swimsuit issue, deeply invested in the convergence of sexuality, sport, and costume— substitutes "Witt." It is "Witt" herself who "pops out" of her costume. She becomes, through the substitution of her proper name for the unnameable and the improper, a sexual force, restrained by a few inches of gossamer net, cloaked unconvincingly by a few blue feathers added at the last moment by her coach to diffuse the controversy over her costume.

The lexicon of costume has, of course, its athletic register, and it is in that register that Debi Thomas does, and sometimes fails to do, her triple-jump combinations. In the short program, while Katarina wore her controversial blue-feathered costume, Debi wore a black unitard:

> Thomas and Witt gave the judges a clear contrast. Skating in her familiar black unitard to a Euro-synthesized disco tune, *Something in My House,* by the rock group Dead Or Alive, Thomas wasted little time in getting the Saddledome crowd clapping to the beat. But the judges were less easily impressed. "It was very dangerous music," said one judge after the competition. "It's hard to look pretty [skating] to that." (*Sports Illustrated,* 40)

The terms of this "clear contrast," like Thomas' unitard, are familiar. The unitard highlights muscular development, athleticism; a unitard is almost, in this scenario, unisex, or perhaps more accurately, unsexed. It is also, of course, "familiar," reassuring; there are no surprises, no fear of "popping out" here. Thomas wears this suit over and over again, nonchalantly, as if she does not care how she looks. A unitard is full costume and no costume at all; it covers all parts of the body, refuses the play of covering and uncovering that makes Katarina's feathers so unconvincing as signs of modesty.

In staging this contrast between the erotic East German and the simple American pre-medical student, the American media inverts another opposition that has been used to critique America's highly sexualized consumer culture. In this instance, Katarina is the consumer—she has her own car in a country where many people who have worked for decades do not—while Debi, daughter of a middle-class black nurse, is a true amateur, struggling to be a doctor. The economic, like the erotic, "facts" are hard to ascertain, harder still to compare across cultures; the issue is how they are deployed in the media. It is as if Katarina's consumptive Carmen becomes a symbol for all kinds of consumption; we as Americans resist being consumed with and by Katarina Witt, retain our distance as she "melts the ice."

Before the opening chords of Katarina's long program—she will be one of the first to skate among the medal contenders and Debi will be last—the opposition between them is firmly in place. Like so many scenes of difference between women, this one has publicly and spectacularly been produced as a clash between the fallen and the unfallen. If Katarina draws the audience down with her into that last dramatic collapse, Debi invites us to take joy in her athleticism, her astonishing ability to leap upward into space and land upright on the thin blade of her skate.

From the moment the competition begins—and it cannot be said to have begun until Katarina steps out on the ice—the fantasy of opposition begins to unravel. Katarina's program is "lackluster," mechanical, unadventurous. Her final fall is not, as I at least had imagined it, a death spiral, slow, then faster and faster, into an inevitable, delicious collapse. Instead, the music ends, and after a moment of visible hesitation, Katarina, the queen of grace, of "artistic merit," plops awkwardly on the ice. Prone on the rink, in her black and red costume that looks like something off the set of a saloon scene in a bad Western, Katarina looks like an inert parody of herself. Crumpled like a puppet on the ice, she literally shows us her strings: the camera angle allows us to see the loops at the end of her sleeves that all figure skaters wear to keep their sleeves from moving during their program.

If the drama of the competition is over, if we will not see as we saw in the men's figure skating, two champions skating their finest programs, at least we—America—will have the excitement of the upset victory. Katarina's marks are mediocre; the judges are clearly "leaving room" for Debi Thomas. This was the moment for Debi's worth to shine through. As the *Washington Post* put it the next day, "All Thomas had to do was be her dazzling self. She wasn't."[2] In this drama of the fallen and the falling, it was Debi who actually fell—two-and-a-half times. The first slip came on her very first jump, her hallmark triple-toe-loop combination, the very move that had served as a sign of her athleticism, her difference from the cautious stylist, Witt. After the first failure, the other falls seemed as inevitable as Carmen's death, seemed, sinisterly, like signs of the mortality Debi's program had been designed to repress. Debi, it seems, fell victim to an ethos of consumption that had little to do with Carmen, with herself, or with Katarina Witt.

Debi's failure was so spectacular, Katarina's performance so unspectacular, that the very framework of the competition seemed to come unglued. No Olympic sport is more predictable in its outcome, less prone to upsets than figure skating; indeed, for several days before the women's finals, figure skating judges had been publicly criticized for being too inflexible and for marking in accordance with a pre-ordained ranking of the contestants.

Cutting across skating tradition, the teleology of world-class figure skating, the binary opposition between the two Carmens, however, was a third figure, who insinuated herself in the rankings between Katarina and Debi, leaping, twisting, and turning almost unnoticed for second place and the silver medal.

This third woman was Elizabeth Manley, a Canadian skater known for her talent and for her instability on and off the ice. She was rumored to have had one or more nervous breakdowns, to be unable to reach her potential in clutch situations. In this dance of women, this test of true womanhood, she figured, even and perhaps especially in victory, as a child: "Manley . . . was marvelous, bounding around the ice like a charismatic child on a playground." (*SI*, p. 40) It might seem strange that this woman of bitter experience should be remade as an innocent; perhaps this "interloper," as the *Post* called her, in the primal scene of figure skating could only be so cast. If, in the end, Manley's burden of emotional and athletic crises was easier to bear than the burden of womanhood imposed upon the two Carmens, it is no wonder that Manley seemed, despite her personal history, carefree and spontaneous.

Manley's intervention in the monogamous drama of this figure skating event had, of course, its geopolitical as well as its psychodynamic resonances. She served as a reminder that, among other things, Canada is not the United States, not perfectly and indistinguishably aligned with this country on the East/West axis. Manley's victory made clear that the majority of the fans in Calgary's Dome had, perhaps, another agenda, another fantasy than the one embodied in Debi's healing of Carmen. Manley, who had somehow acquired a cowboy hat for her medal laps, reminded the audience that this was Calgary, that we were north of a border over which, among other things, acid pollutants pass from the United States into Canada.

If borders were blurred and binarisms collapsed that night in the Saddledome, it was not long before the American media found a substitute for Debi Thomas to occupy the position of sexual purity. By the time *Sports Illustrated* had come out at the end of the week, it had consolidated the sexual anxiety of the figure-skating championships into another figure of pure athleticism, this time the only American double medal winner, "little" Bonnie Blair:

> There are no sequins in women's speed skating. No death-drop necklines or feathered hats. Nobody gets points for lipstick or for meaningful eye contact. . . . There are only fast women waiting for a gun. They are tough, and they dress not to flirt but to fly. One such woman is Bonnie Blair of Champaign, Ill. . . . (*Sports Illustrated*, p. 50)

America had tried to find its essence in Debi Thomas and had failed, not perhaps because Thomas was not good enough, but because the sport of figure skating itself is somehow tainted; if Debi could not, would not compete for "meaningful eye contact" with the judges, America would turn for its heroine to a sport where the only judge was the time-clock, where feminine curves were obliterated by more than skintight speed-skating suits.

No one was more perfect as an antidote to Katarina than Bonnie Blair, that tiny and powerful woman who combined Manley's insouciance and childlike glee with the strength and competitive drive of a "tough chick." Moreover, Bonnie's victory was family drama, a victory for the American family:

> Not until much later . . . did she get to run into the arms of her family and friends. They formed a giant scrum outside the oval, where they chanted "Gold! Gold! Gold!" and took turns biting the medal to see if it was real. Talk about genuine. Does there breathe a family more real than this one? (*Sports Illustrated*, p. 52)

The answer, in case we are in doubt, is "no"; both the family and the gold were in fact genuine, solid, things you could sink your teeth into. Bonnie Blair with her numerous speed-skating brothers and sisters, backed financially by the Champaign Police Department, was in the end a better heroine than Debi Thomas could have been for a country that depends on images of the heartland.

The opposition between Blair and Thomas highlights yet another which the discourse of nationalism obscures: Blair, in replacing Witt, places Debi Thomas unequivocally in the position America typically assigns to the black woman. The fact of Thomas' race can be read back upon the story of her carefully contained sexuality. The decorum of Debi's costume, of her public presentation, refers not only to the opposition of East and West, but to the muted opposition between black and white brought into play by the spectacle of any black woman entering a primarily white sport in a primarily white culture. Thomas' race, once an issue in articles about her as the first important black figure skater, is simultaneously referred to, contained, and obliterated by the omnipresent black leotard. Its blackness covers hers; its conspicuous anti-eroticism turns the black woman whom it covers from an icon of lawless sexuality into something, as far as the American commentators were concerned, sexless. Debi's race blurs in a conspiracy of silence and opposition: it is her Americanness the audience back home wants to see. It is, not surprisingly, an Americanness that depends on the desexualizing of black womanhood. In a year in which Doug Williams, one of three black quarterbacks in the National Football League, became the first black quarterback to guide his team to the Superbowl, in a year where race reentered the idiom of sports journalism, if only to be repeatedly and unconvincingly dismissed, it cannot be an accident that the official story of Debi Thomas had no access to the lexicon of race. In a year in which a black man's blackness filled the January sports pages, a black woman's blackness was covered up so the story of the two Carmens could be more easily, more dramatically told. The silence surrounding Thomas' race became the final and most spectacular proof of America's liberalism: unlike Doug Williams', Thomas' body came to stand—and to fall—for an entire nation.

If we need Blair to foreground Thomas' race, and in doing so, to restore some of her sexuality—it is "figure skating" in general that is the subject of *Sports Illustrated*'s rebuke—we need Blair, Witt, Thomas, and Manley to give us the fuller story of Carmen. It is a story endlessly retold with different and equally complicated racial, sexual, and national configurations, by the two fastest sisters-in-law in the world, Jackie Joyner-Kersee and Florence Griffith-Joyner, in the Summer Olympics, by the "ice queen" Chris Evert and the officially "bisexual" Martina Navratilova on the tennis courts, and by countless swimmers, gymnasts, and divers of years to come.

Chapter 5

The Colleague and the Washerwoman:
The Other Woman in Feminist Theory

I have suggested in the Introduction that contemporary feminism is still embedded in the familial idiom that has given us, at different moments and for different purposes, the "patriarchy," of early second-wave feminism, the "sisterhood" invoked as its enemy, and the "m/other" of feminist psychoanalytic theory. All these terms and the master trope of family in which they are embedded are still part of the language of feminism and continue to have profound and at times deeply productive political and psychological resonance.

Contemporary feminism has also, however, taken upon itself, again in different ways at different historical junctures, the work of looking beyond the family, of imagining economic, political, and psychological arrangements that would radically contest the hegemony of familial structures. This work should also, I think, take us, as far as it is possible to do so, outside what Gallop has called "the pitfall of familial thinking," outside the familial lexicon, and, in the project most central to this book, toward the figure of the woman who is not part of the family: the woman who is "other" in some way, the "other woman."

Mainstream—that is, white middle-class—feminism's interest in, anxiety over, and guilt about, otherness in the form of race, class, and sexual preference has embodied itself in the figure of the other woman whose textual presence lurks at the edges of some of the most powerful pieces of feminist writing. The other woman—other usually because of her race, class, or sexuality—is a visible and often acknowledged presence in texts of feminist theory written in the last two decades. Her presence, however, is more para-textual than textual; even in texts that announce their concerns about otherness, she appears in footnotes, parentheses, orthographic gaps, and other contested or marginal textual sites. This chapter is an exploration of rhetorical gestures toward the other woman; it begins with a brief discussion of two profoundly different texts whose titles include the phrase "other woman," and moves on to discuss in some detail five texts of feminist theory that in some sense confront the problem of otherness between women by constructing, naming, and containing a particular "other woman," a specific figure who embodies the anxieties of otherness. These texts—Catharine Stimpson's "Feminism and Feminist Criticism," Jane Gallop's "The Monster in the Mirror: The Feminist Critic's Psycho-analysis," and "Annie Leclerc Writing a Letter, with Vermeer," Julia Kristeva's *About Chinese Women,* and Gayatri Spivak's "French Feminism in an International Frame"—are all products of French and U.S. feminism of the nineteen seventies and eighties. They represent, to me, a crucial moment or series of moments in Western feminism when mainstream academic feminist theory was just beginning to complicate its discursive position from one of simple victimage and marginalization to one that took into account feminism's—or one version of feminism's—increasing academic cachet and institutional power. All five are anxious pieces of work; all five project that anxiety onto the figure of the "other woman" and create a complex rhetorical relation to her otherness that is simultaneously dismissive and desiring.

The "other woman" as a phrase, a name, a non-name, finds a place in a veritable litany of popular and academic book titles. To name a few: the best-selling novel, *Other Women* by Lisa Alther, about the relationship between a female psychologist and a lesbian patient; *The Other Woman: Stories of Two Women and a Man,* an anthology of short stories edited by Susan Koppleman; *The New Other Woman,* by Laurel Richardson, a sociological study of single women who have affairs with married men, and, of course, Luce Irigaray's critique of the phallogocentrism of Western metaphysics, *Speculum of the Other Woman.* The very similarity of the titles hints at a problem central to feminist perceptions of otherness; these titles, hardly other to each other, at once name the other woman and insert her into familiar sexual tropes.

Feminist unease with otherness lurks behind issues of title and entitlement; all four of these texts, in their different ways, can be read as strategies to control otherness, either by displacing or removing it from the speaking subject—the female structuring "I"—or by incorporating the other into the family, into sameness. An example of the first rhetorical strategy, *The New Other Woman* opens, remarkably, with a statement about the author's motives in writing the book that is at once personal and disjunctive. The very first sentence invokes the familiar, improbable fiction of the "friend" who makes possible so many confessional moments: "A friend had been an Other Woman for almost two decades. . . . Her experience was the initial impetus to do the research leading to this book."[1] Literally true or not, the explanation of the book's inception as a response to the situation of a "friend" has the rhetorical effect of projecting otherness onto the life and the body of the other, of establishing a boundary between self and other that is rigorously maintained by socio-sexual law, by, in other words, the law that produces and maintains the family. The other woman, exiled from the family, provides a convenient and articulable space for the exile of otherness. All that is troubling, adulterous, troublingly adulterous within the family and within the wife, can be impersonated by the other woman. The idea that one can be an "Other Woman" for "two decades" suggests the permeability of the boundary between "Other Women" and those who are not, in whatever sense, "other." The rhetorical distancing of "friend" resurrects these boundaries even in the face of an admission that one's status as other or not other can change.

Speculum of the Other Woman employs an opposite strategy by naming otherness between women only to reproduce it in its more familiar context of heterosexual difference. The "Other" of the title, in both French and English, would seem to modify "Woman" and to hint at the presence of at least two women, other in some sense to each other. In Irigaray's only discussion of otherness as a category, however—which significantly and tantalizingly takes place in the course of her critique of Freud on female homosexuality—women's sexual identity becomes a matter of identity between women, lesbianism becomes a form of autoeroticism, and women's relations with each other, in the absence of men, become, quite explicitly, the relation of like to like, same to same. Irigaray begins her critique by problematizing the words "like" and "same" by setting them off in quotation marks: "That a woman might desire a woman 'like' herself, someone of the 'same' sex, that she might also have auto- and homosexual appetites, is simply incomprehensible to Freud, and indeed inadmissible." Yet the quotation marks, those marks of difference, disappear as "same" and "like" get absorbed into the text and into the undifferentiating and capacious trope of sisterhood: "Yet what exhilarating pleasure it is to be partnered with someone like oneself. With a sister, in everyday terms."[2] Sisterhood as "everyday" term, as the infinitely iterated rhetorical move, surfaces here to erase difference between women and close down its possible orthographic location between ironic quotation marks. Irigaray mirrors Richardson in her need to delimit otherness; like all mirrors, perhaps more vividly like all specula, *Speculum* both reproduces and inverts what it reflects.

If these mirror strategies for the containment of female otherness surface at critical moments in Richardson and Irigaray, they serve as structures for the five important texts of feminist criticism that make up the body of this chapter. In examining how these texts simultaneously are and are not about the other woman, how they make textual space for her entrance onto the scene of feminist criticism, and close it off, I necessarily become both absorbed by and into the texts of other women as I absorb them into my paradigms. I hope throughout the process of these close readings of texts of my feminist sisters/mothers to disrupt the very familial metaphor that Harold Bloom suggests is the basis of all re(mis)reading. To begin to acknowledge the possibility of the other woman one must work through the texts of other women; to move outside the family is to chart the places made accessible by its idiom. I begin with Catharine Stimpson, who in her role as creator and first editor of *Signs* clearly occupies a maternal position in American feminist critical discourse, and with Jane Gallop, who repeatedly and disingenuously figures herself as daughter, sister, and rival in the field of psychoanalytic and feminist criticism.

Catharine Stimpson's essay is, on first reading, a triumph of the family of feminism, of a marriage not only as its title suggests between feminism and feminist criticism, but between and among a polyphony of feminist voices and enterprises. It summarizes for an indulgent but perhaps uninformed public, the multiple projects of feminism. As a review essay it promises synthesis and integration. In describing feminism as a "mosaic" of women's voices, it comfortably subsumes differences among feminisms and feminists into a structuring metaphor that sees pattern and beauty in difference. More problematically, perhaps unconsciously, the essay seems at the same time to be a deconstruction of the mosaic, and an exploration of the otherness(es) within feminism. The specter of the other in what at first reading seems to be a manifesto of pluralist coherence makes its entrances into her text through a series of linguistic slips and shifts. From her invocation of *Jean* Foucault, to whom she refers as "the other Foucault," to her concluding account of the rape of a colleague, another woman at her university, the other is simultaneously invoked and kept at bay.

On the surface, the essay's function is to integrate otherness, to make it other than other through a systematic dialectical pluralism that sympathetically includes and mediates among a number of disparate voices. It is also meticulously integrative on a rhetorical level, moving with ease from the personal to the academic to the political and refusing to see any rupture between them. Some of the most successful integrative moments in this essay are its numerous lists, which move lyrically among categories of feminist experience. In describing what she calls the contemporary feminist aesthetic, she deliberately mixes genres and styles:

> The new woman's culture self-consciously produces a feminist aesthetic that reconciles the flavorful gratuitousness of style with the imperatives of ideology. It appears in posters; clothing, such as T-shirts; demonstrations (those in Italy have a special elegance, verve, and theatricality); fine arts; films, and texts that experiment with a voice both personal and collective, that alludes to ricotta and Adrienne Rich, wool and Virginia Woolf, the domestic and the public.[3]

Separated only by semicolons, the objects that make up these lists flow naturally into each other; they are litanies of inclusion, testaments to the graceful ease of feminist bridge-building. They promise a continuum, a seamless fabric: the mosaic naturalized and made fluid. This survey of feminist topography knows and inhabits all spaces, moving with equal freedom from the public world of demonstrations to the private world of wool, from England to (parenthetically) Italy.

The alliteration of the final list-within-a-list, "Rich . . . ricotta," "wool . . . Woolf," adds to the incantatory quality of prose based on the most liquid of metonymies and free-associative techniques. The movement from Rich to ricotta undermines the potential grammatical impasse of the proper name, while the transmutation of wool into Woolf makes even the canon a matter of feminist weaving. Stimpson's parentheses absorb and contain difference, the foreign, in an expansive and expanding political syntax.

The larger structure of the essay repeats and amplifies the structure of the lists; there is an exhilarating sense of motion throughout as Stimpson moves with ease from topic to topic, from allusion to allusion. The authority of logic, of phallogocentrism, has been replaced with the enabling authority of experience. The essay's assured experiential voice moves with ease from paragraphs about Emily Dickinson to a Yale University computer program named Boris, to the New Testament, to Gertrude Stein. The structure of the essay, like that of the lists, proclaims that within feminism there is no other, or rather that otherness can be enveloped in feminism's fertile and nurturant embrace.

It would seem that the fluidity that marks the structure of the essay extends to its pronomial shifts. Apparently untroubled by the pain Monique Wittig and other feminist theorists have reproduced in the engendering of their female narrative "I's" and "she's," Stimpson begins with a historically situated "she": "In 1861, Emily Dickinson cut one of her shard-like poems about language," and moves immediately in the second paragraph to the academically forbidden narrative "I." Indeed, the "she" and the "I" come together in this act of producing the mosaic that structures this essay:

> I place Emily Dickinson as the first inlay in the mosaic of my argument to the power of women writers . . . I do not want to subordinate criticism to feminism, complexities of analysis to the severities of ideology. Neither do I wish to subordinate feminism to criticism. Rather, I seek a "dialectical mediation between them." (Stimpson, p. 272)

In demonstrating her power to "place," Stimpson has *created* a place for the "I" and the "she," the contemporary feminist and the nineteenth-century female poet, to create together. The "I," however, subsumes the "she" in creating both metaphor and mosaic. Like Derrida's "choreographies" of gender, Stimpson's mosaic both disguises and foregrounds the agent and her/his agency; a mosaic, like a dance, is an arrangement of seemingly spontaneous gestures and pieces.

It is not only women who have a place in Stimpson's mosaic. The embedded quotation in the passage just cited—"dialectical mediation between them"—represents the voice of a male Marxist critic. Stimpson need not have depended on a footnote here; the term "dialectic" is common enough. The quotation marks, like the parentheses around Stimpson's earlier sentence about Italian demonstrations, serve precisely as marks of incorporation. Something foreign, something outside the nuclear family of Anglo-American feminism has been swallowed but left undigested as a testament to the power of feminist inclusion.

If the essay opens with a choreography of positions, of voices, to borrow from Stimpson's remarks about Emily Dickinson, "at once monolithic and polyphonic," it closes with an attempt to simplify and personalize these voices. In the last paragraph of the essay, the "I" reappears for the first time; the paragraph is worth quoting in full:

> I began with a quotation. I wish to end with a difficult anecdote. I was thinking about feminist criticism one night as I was driving home from my university work. On either side of the highway's twelve lanes were oil refineries, with great curved pipes and round towers. I smelled industrial fumes. I saw no green, except for paint and neon signs. Earlier that day, after a meeting, a woman colleague had told me about an experience. She had been raped, at knife-point, in her car, with her son watching. She was in her late twenties, her son only six. She was no Leda, the rapist no swan. To remember that story, to keep it as a fire within consciousness and political will, is the feminism in feminist criticism. Such a memory is a base of our use of language, no matter how skeptical we might be of language's referential power, as feminist criticism annuls powerful cultural arrangements, anneals again the materials of history, and reclaims language's push of joy. (Stimpson, p. 274)

By self-consciously calling attention to the narrative framing of her essay, Stimpson prepares us for both symmetry and teleology. The line "I wish to end with a difficult anecdote" simultaneously reminds us of the quotation that begins the piece, and promises us a change of direction, a movement inward that runs counter to symmetry, perhaps even to coherence. The "I" in "I wish to end" prepares us for its vulnerability; for the first time something is "difficult."

Significantly the "I" is one that both does and does not appear; it announces a violent opening up (in the sense of both rape and discourse) that does and does not happen. The essay has set itself up for the rape of the author, for the personal to overwhelm the critical, for the "I" that has "placed" Dickinson to lose all control and distance. At the beginning of the paragraph we are made aware for the first time of the narrator's body. "I was thinking . . . I smelled . . . I saw" is both familiar in its integrative movement from thinking to smelling, from the intellectual to the sensual, and radically defamiliarizing in its announcement of the presence of the body. Catharine Stimpson's body is the last piece of the mosaic to fall into place. We are prepared to move inward, to violate it, to share its violation, to be moved by it, to move below the surface of the mosaic. At this moment, tentatively embodied by the difficult, the vulnerable narrative "I," we are presented suddenly with a "she." She is the other woman.

The words "a woman colleague" appear uneasily to us as the narrative "I," reassuring even in its vulnerability—we do, after all, know that the "I" survived, wrote, and is writing—disappears. "She had . . . she was . . . she was" becomes the sinister mirror-burden of a song that began "I was thinking . . . I smelled . . . I saw." The other woman appears only briefly; she is raped and vanishes. We only know that she is other, that "she was no Leda." We do not know who she is except that she is not Catharine Stimpson, not Leda. The answer to the question, "Who is this other woman?" does not of course lie in her name or in any facts about her life before or after the rape. What interests me here is who she is not, and how who she is not allows her painful entrance into Stimpson's lyrical text.

The power of Stimpson's feminism depends on the somewhat problematic power of the tropes of analogy and metonymy at work within this final, moving paragraph. The author remembers the story of the rape of her colleague when she, like her colleague at the time of the rape, is in a car. Stimpson's body positions itself in an act of remembrance and recreation, at the wheel of her car. The author's body, in not being raped as she drives, simultaneously alludes to the body of the woman colleague and allows her the safety to speak for her; the text becomes a witnessing by someone whose speech is made possible because she was not a witness in the usual sense. The "real" witness, the colleague's little boy, cannot speak here of this nightmarish amplification and deformation of the primal scene; Stimpson substitutes for the little boy as she substitutes for his mother. The family idiom of feminism allows her to speak what for the family is unspeakable.

On one level, of course, this "difficult" personal/impersonal anecdote acts as a displacement, a way of mediating terror, an attempt to incorporate even the ultimate otherness of rape into feminist discourse. The other woman and her body become a test case for the integrative "I," for the warmly integrative yet respectful phrase "woman colleague." The strangely inappropriate phrase "push of joy" that ends this paragraph and this essay brings us back to the beginning where Stimpson quotes the same line from Dickinson. It is too much to say that the rape, through the triumphantly rhetorical ending, has become "a push of joy," that feminist language has been produced by the rape in the act of reproducing it. It is not too much to say that otherness appears briefly, violently, only to be "reclaimed" by feminism and its language.

It might at this point be useful to recall the beginning of Stimpson's essay, the opening invocation of Dickinson, whose name was the first to be placed in the mosaic. Running counter to the dominant metaphors of connection and coherence is a more troubling set of images that have to do with cutting, pain, and violence. "In 1861 Emily Dickinson cut one of her shard-like poems about language." Dickinson's voice, then, is not easily or unambiguously placed; her poems are "shards"—perhaps bits of mosaic broken into sharpness. Dickinson's voice severs connections even in the act of making them. In this context, Dickinson, the heroine in the romance of literary foremothers who constitute the feminist narrative of literary history, becomes herself other, not only to the series of editors who tried to remove her shard-like dashes, not only to the patriarchy that kept her imprisoned in her father's house, but to the women who read her, identify her, identify *with* her, write about her, and try to "place" her.

Dickinson joins the colleague whose rape disrupts but is accommodated by the end of this essay to construct a frame that belies the body of Stimpson's argument; both colleague and literary foremother hint at the presence of otherness within the family, be it biological, academic, or literary. If the shard-like frame of Stimpson's essay implicity undercuts its pronouncements of unity in diversity, the ending of Gallop's "The Monster in the Mirror" explicitly forces us to reread them with a view toward the crevices, cracks, and dislocations that signal the presence of the other woman. Making familiar a rhetorical closing move out of the family, Gallop repeats in "Monster" the structural strategics of *The Daughter's Seduction*. In *Daughter*, Gallop moves chapter by chapter through the family as she discusses the daughter's struggles with and against her father, her mother, and her sister/rival. The final chapter disturbs the symmetry and intimacy of family relations by invoking otherness within the home in the person of the governess. "Monster" also turns toward the other woman, offering her the last word. The other woman of "Monster" is the woman of color, the Third World woman. In a paragraph orthographically separated from the body of her essay, Gallop concludes with a brief appreciation of Gayatri Spivak's "French Feminism in an International Frame":

> I see a connection between the problem I am pursuing and Spivak's critique of Western feminist theory. She argues that Western elite feminism can only project onto Third World women. As an antidote to such narcissistic projection, she advocates a new question for feminism to ask. That antidotal question seems equally appropriate to the dilemma I have traced here . . . so I will close with Spivak's words: "However unfeasible and inefficient it may sound, I see no way

to avoid insisting that there is a simultaneous other focus: not merely who am I? but who is the other woman?''[4]

By quoting the ''other woman'' on otherness, Gallop would seem, in so far as this is possible, to be resisting the domestication of otherness. She has not only given Spivak the last word; she has given her the last question—and it is one Gallop will not try to answer. By placing a blank space between the body of the essay and the paragraph in which Spivak's words appear, Gallop refuses the temptation to deny or absorb otherness; she is, in effect, acknowledging the blank spaces between the pieces in Stimpson's mosaic. This gesture that closes but does not end the debate on otherness is a gesture toward other answers, the answers of other women.

Something happens, however, in the move from ''Monster'' to ''Annie Leclerc''; the quotation from Spivak appears in identical form, but this time within the body of the essay. The appearance of the same other woman in identical guise familiarizes her, makes her part of the family, makes her a Gallop. In quoting something she has already used, Gallop is now, in effect, quoting herself.

In ''Annie Leclerc'' Gallop structures a critique of the two covers of the *Critical Inquiry* special issue, *Writing and Sexual Difference,* much as I have structured my critique of Stimpson's two framing paragraphs. She looks first at the apparent sexual symmetry between the paintings reproduced on the two covers:

> Together they compose a particularly well-articulated illustration of ''writing and sexual difference.'' The woman is writing a letter, the man a book. Women write letters—personal, intimate, in relation; men write books—universal, public, in general circulation. The man in the picture is in fact Erasmus, father of our humanist tradition; the woman without a name. In the man's background: books. The woman sits against floral wallpaper.[5]

In and between these covers, then, oppositeness, otherness, will be defined as sexual difference. *Writing and Sexual Difference* will find its place within that difference, between the two covers that represent Man and Woman. The space between these covers is also, however, the space between marital, familial covers; it is a space defined, like heterosexual marriage, as the space between a man and a woman, a place of and constituted by their difference. There is certainly conflict in *Writing and Sexual Difference,* just as there are ''differences'' in the best regulated marriage, but the paintings on the covers stand like sentinels to contain difference in its allocated, safe space ''between'' the sexes.

Gallop's article moves out of this safe space and text into another, more troubling text illustrated by a perhaps even more troubling painting: Annie Leclerc's ''La Lettre d'amour,'' an extended love letter to another woman, and the painting to which the text consistently refers—Vermeer's "Lady Writing a Letter and her Maidservant." In the painting, a woman is handing a (love?) letter to her maid.

The last five pages of Gallop's article perform an elaborate reading of the painting through Leclerc's text. Gallop's analysis focuses both implicitly and explicitly on the question of the otherness of the maidservant, on the otherness produced by class difference and reproduced as sexual desire in Leclerc's piece. Otherness also permeates the structure of Gallop's essay, which moves metonymically from *Writing and Sexual Difference* and the paintings that frame it to "La Lettre d'amour," to the painting of the other woman within its frame.

Gallop preserves throughout the sexual dimension of otherness its challenge to heterosexual love and to what heterosexuality construes as "sexual difference." She reads Leclerc's desire for the other woman as it is problematized by class difference:

> (Leclerc) contemplates the difference between these women (in the painting) and rather than feeling guilt at this difference, rather than feeling pity, she feels desire. She writes, "I love the woman servant . . . oh no, not out of pity, not because I would take up the noble mantle of redressers of wrongs . . . but because I want to touch her, to take her hands, to bury my head in her chest, to smother her cheeks and neck with kisses." (Annie, p. 9)

Difference, recast, produces desire; class becomes an erotic, a "sexual" difference. The maidservant in the painting, seen through a series of mediating concentric circles, frames, texts, comes to embody desire and the absences and lacks that constitute it.

The concentric nature of this article's textuality repeats itself in the topography of its sexuality. After discussing the possible "problems" with Leclerc's desire for the servant ("there is a long phallic tradition of desire for those with less power and privilege"), Gallop inserts herself and her own desires into the text—parenthetically:

> Despite these problems I have with Leclerc's desire for the maid (an erotic attraction to women of another class which I share, I should add), I think it is valuable as a powerful account of this sort of desire. (Annie, p. 9)

Gallop places herself last in a chain of desirers that through a series of differences announce their attractions to the maid. Like the woman colleague in Stimpson's essay, Gallop appears only briefly, parenthetically, near the end of the essay. Gallop's entrance into the text as a narrative "I" simultaneously confirms the maidservant's otherness, her position as object to a telescopic series of readers and desirers, and announces Gallop's own otherness to her text. Gallop becomes her own sexually disruptive, parenthetically contained other. Her intrusion into this multiple scene of desire marks her, sets her off in the very act of identifying with Leclerc, with Vermeer, and with the maid. The "should" of the doubly parenthetical "I should add" foregrounds the problematics of textual self-insertion as effectively as Stimpson's announcement that the closing anecdote of her text will be "difficult." There is coercion in Gallop's "should" that is itself difficult, hard to locate. Who is telling Gallop to confess? Perhaps the prescriptive teleology of feminist discourse demands that a place be made for the "I" and for its (her) desires. Like Stimpson, Gallop promises an "I" only to give us a "she"; like Stimpson the "she" is subsumed under the signature of the "I" as the other woman becomes other than other.

Gallop ends this essay that explores sexual difference as a space between women with a fragment of the quotation from Spivak with which she ended "Monster" and which she has already placed so securely in the body of this essay. She ends with the "necessarily double and no less urgent questions of feminism: "not merely who am I? But who is the other woman?" By repeating Spivak's questions at the end of the essay, Gallop obviously underscores their centrality. By making them central, by placing them in, as it were, her mosaic, she is denying that they are other. By ending two essays with the words of the same other woman, she is rendering Spivak's words familiar and welcoming her into the family. The mirror that so frighteningly replicates women in "Monster" is held up to Spivak's face. In looking over Spivak's shoulder, Gallop sees Jane Gallop. The question "Who is the other woman?" transforms itself on the surface of the mirror into the questionable statement, "The other woman is myself."

If Gallop closes her essay with the integration of the other woman into the self, Julia Kristeva's *Des Chinoises,* translated as *About Chinese Women,* opens with a series of rhetorical and structural gestures that recast the self as other.[6] *Des Chinoises* is a collection of impressions recorded by Kristeva during a visit to China; part travel book, part anthropological treatise, part cultural criticism, it is carefully divided into two parts: "From This Side" (De Ce Côté Ci"), and "Chinese Women" ("Femmes De Chine"). "From This Side" situates the authorial voice in the West, admits that she is speaking from the West, that she is, as it were, from or perhaps even on a different side than the Chinese women who are nominally at least the subject of the book. More important, however, "From This Side," which begins with a short subsection entitled "Who is Speaking?" ("Qui Parle?"), directs toward the West the scrutinizing gaze usually reserved for foreign cultures by presenting a short history of and meditation on what for Kristeva is the West's constitutive ideology: capitalist monotheism. By placing the West under scrutiny, Kristeva refuses to take it for granted and, by her silence, to posit it as a norm. This destabilizing through scrutiny of the Western point of view, which we might call disorientation, recasts the familiar as foreign and transforms her discussion of capitalist monotheism into a journey through a strange country.

The issue of point of view, the idiom of looking, gazing, and being gazed at structures what might be called the text's primal scene, the scene that haunts Kristeva as, back in France, she tries to capture her Chinese experiences on paper:

> Sitting here in front of the typewriter, trying to write about my experience in China, I am haunted by one scene in particular. It makes me hesitate at each touch of the keyboard; but it excites me as well. Not to lose sight of it; to make it transparent on every page: such are the stakes in the course that follows. (Kristeva, p. 11)

This scene, which she must not "lose sight of" ("ne pas perdre la vue"), is a scene itself of looking, a scene where she and her fellow Westerners become the object of a disorienting gaze. Kristeva, who is part of a group of tourists from the West, travels to the Chinese capital of Huxian to look at an exhibition of peasant art in the city's main square. The scene describes the process by which the Westerners themselves become exhibits as they are stared at by the Huxian natives:

> An enormous crowd is sitting in the sun: they wait for us wordlessly, perfectly still. Calm eyes, not even curious, but slightly amused or anxious: in any case, piercing, and certain of belonging in a community with which we will never have anything to do. They don't distinguish among us man or woman, blonde or brunette, this or that feature of face or body. As though they were discovering some weird and peculiar animals, harmless but insane. . . . "A species—what they see in us is a different species," says one of the group . . . I don't feel like a foreigner, the way I do in Baghdad or New York. I feel like an ape, a martian, an *other*. (Kristeva, pp. 11–12, italics Kristeva's)

From the first page of this text, Kristeva is herself the other, constituted as more-than/less-than foreigner by the gaze of a group of Chinese peasants. The politics of the gaze that turns self into other are the politics of dehumanization; to be other is to be non-human, an "ape," an "animal," or a "martian." The radical otherness at work in this scene transcends the lexicon of the human.

To invoke otherness, however, is for Kristeva, for feminism, for French feminism in particular, at least in some sense to invoke the fundamental human category of gender and the opposition between the normative masculine and the feminine other. If Simone de Beauvoir identified women as "other" to masculine culture, Kristeva has named otherness itself "woman."

One would expect in a book whose gender-marked title *Des Chinoises* is, in the original French edition, underscored on the title page by the syntactically parallel name of the publishers, "des femmes," that the text's primal scene, like the primal scene in psychoanalysis, might be a locus for the exploration of sexual difference as it is usually understood. So tempting is it to see the haunting encounter in the Huxian square as a meeting between a patriarchal West and an exoticized, feminized East that Gayatri Spivak, in her critique of *Des Chinoises,* turns the staring peasants into staring *women.*[7] The scene as it is written, however, is explicitly gender-neutral; neither the tourists nor the peasants are identified by sex. The gaze of the collective peasants refuses, in fact, to recognize gender as a category: "they don't distinguish among us man or woman, blonde or brunette."

If we misread with Spivak and call the gazing peasants "women," we fail to grasp the radical otherness of this encounter. The Chinese peasants cannot/will not recognize Western men as men or women as women; they do not look or speak as women or as men in a sense recognizable in the West. To recognize any distinctions at all in a group already marked as "other" is to assume that one's categories—in this case gender, variations in coloring or feature—operate across cultures; to introduce distinctions is, in other words, to introduce the possibility of sameness. The refusal of white Americans to distinguish among blacks is only one example of the way in which resistance to differences among entire populations of others preserves the radical disjunction between self and other. In refusing to distinguish women either among the tourists as they are gazed at by peasants or among the peasants as she tries to recreate them for the text of *Des Chinoises,* Kristeva carefully marks out the difference between "sides" and between the two parts of her book. Despite the text's refusal to designate male and female, women do, in fact, have a place in the scene in the Huxian square; perhaps it would be more accurate to say they *define* a place or a position within it. Women enter the scene retrospectively, not as peasants or tourists, but as a name for the otherness already in place between East and West:

> Women. We have the luck to be able to take advantage of a biological peculiarity to give a name to that which, in monotheistic capitalism, remains on this side of the threshold of repression, voice stilled, body mute, always foreign to the social order. A well deserved luck, for, in fact, in the entire history of patrilineal or class-stratified societies, it is the lot of the feminine to assume the role of *waste,* or of the hidden work-force in the relationships of production and the language which defines them. But a *limited luck,* because, others, men, since at least the end of the nineteenth century . . . realize that they have been the "women" of the community. (Kristeva, p. 14, italics Kristeva's)

Women appear on and in the scene, not as what Kristeva will later call "the female sex," or as biological entities, but as a position that can be filled by anyone—man, woman, martian, or ape—who is defined by capitalism as "waste." This is the familiar move of poststructuralism, the move away from what is perceived as a dangerous biological essentialism that reduces women to the fact of their "biological peculiarity."

"Women," whoever they might be, also have a place in the visual economy of the scene. Recent accounts of the semiotics of the gaze have shown it to be marked by, indeed constitutive of, gender-positioning. To gaze, to take upon oneself the directive power of the eye, is to place oneself in a cultural position designated as male; to be looked at is to become, in the Kristevan sense, "woman." In making herself, in making the West, the object of a disorienting gaze, Kristeva positions the West as woman. In making the West the other, the exotic, the foreign, she feminizes it, opens it up to scrutiny. In this text, women become the name for those being looked at: the name "woman" will pass from the West in the first half of the book to China in the second half.

But with a difference. In the first few pages of *Des Chinoises,* where Kristeva justifies her choice of subject and her means of entry into Chinese culture, she offers two reasons why she has chosen to write specifically about Chinese *women*. Predictably, given the careful choreography of otherness that characterizes her structuring arguments, one reason has to do with the Chinese "themselves," with Chinese culture, the second with the culture of the West. She begins with China:

> . . . the studies of specialists, my own impressions, and the most recent developments in the cultural revolution prove that . . . the role of women, and consequently, that of the family, have a particular quality in China which is unknown in the monotheistic West. To observe that particular aspect of China is, therefore, to try to understand what makes China unique: a focus which seeks to measure the distance which separates me from Huxian. No way at all to understand China if one is not sensitive to the women, to their condition, to their difference. (Kristeva, p. 13)

In this passage Chinese women become both metaphors and metonymies for the difference between East and West: they simultaneously embody difference and act as points of entry to "larger" cultural differences. Simultaneously difference and ways into or ways of understanding difference, Chinese women mediate between East and West, providing access to the mysteries of Chinese culture. This role of sign and mediator, vessel and metonymy, is eerily reminiscent of the role of the Virgin Mary whom Kristeva discusses in "From This Side" and elsewhere as a figure for abjection.[8]

When Kristeva turns toward the West for another reason to write about women, she also implicates them in issues of difference:

> Second, and perhaps especially, I make this choice because the *otherness* of China is invisible if the man or the woman who speaks here, in the West, doesn't

position him/herself some place where our capitalist monotheistic fabric is shredding, crumbling, decaying. But where? . . . Women. We have the luck to be able to take advantage of a biological peculiarity. (Kristeva, pp. 13–14)

If women in the East are the measure of the distance between places, of difference from the West, "women" in Western culture stand for difference *within* the West. Chinese women, who appear in this passage at least to be biologically female, represent, indeed measure, otherness to the West; Western "women, who do not have to be female, embody otherness to the dominant culture. Both are explicitly defined as other to the dominant culture of capitalism."

Throughout the text of *Des Chinoises,* Kristeva privileges the recognition of otherness and difference. This is true, as we have seen, in the very structure of the book, where she acknowledges by the separation of her discussions of East and West the unbridgeable gap between them. On the level of content Kristeva constructs for both the East and West a politics of difference, which becomes, through the use of the same synecdoche that allows Chinese women to stand for Chinese culture, explicitly sexual difference. The problem with Western culture, we find in "From This Side," is that by and large it represses sexual difference, that it has "forgotten the war of the sexes." Those who do remember and work with sexual difference, notably analysts "faithful to Freudian pessimism," err in the opposite direction, "preach(ing) the impossibility of communication between the two (sexes)." (Kristeva, p. 23) According to Kristeva, we can neither gloss over difference nor allow it to silence communication between the sexes; her metaphor for the always problematic, always hostile, but always vital effort to communicate is war:

> The solution? To go on waging the war of the sexes without respite, without a perverse denial of the abyss that marks the sexual difference or a disillusioned mortification at its depth, while some other economy of the sexes works itself out; but not before it has revolutionized our entire logic of production (class) and reproduction (family). (Kristeva, p. 23)

For Kristeva, the difference between West and East lies precisely in their strategies for the management of (sexual) difference. The Chinese yin and yang, which in the West have, significantly enough, become catch phrases for an effortless and benign androgyny, stand in the Kristevan model of Chinese culture for the always present, always charged opposition between male and female principles. The Chinese sexual economy, in stark contrast to the sexual economy of the West, forbids the incorporation of one into the other:

> Such an economy, based on the *jouissance* of the woman without sacrificing that of the man, proceeds from the idea that the sexual relationship is not a relationship of identification, absorption of one by the other, negation of differences. In other

words, nothing of the sexual-psychological relationship here corresponds to the
Western medieval concept of love. (Kristeva, p. 63)

Again we can identify the outlines of a familiar sexual topography where the
difference between the sexes is represented by one of the sexes, by woman. In
this case woman's *jouissance* simultaneously "belongs" to woman and is a
sign of her difference, a difference that is carefully inscribed within the Chinese
sexual economy.

We have come, in the privilege of the acknowledgment of difference, to the
center of Kristeva's political and psychodynamic agenda: to repress difference,
or to silence exchanges between the sexes by positing an absolute difference, is
to set up a perverse sexual economy that depends on fetishism and female
masochism. To acknowledge and participate in the war between the sexes is to
become part of a dynamic economy that allows for women's pleasure.

One cannot escape the fact that the Kristevan economy of sexual difference is
an economy of heterosexual difference, an economy based on women's
differences from men, on "women's" differences from male culture. It is an
economy that betrays an unease with homosexuality, consistently figured as a
sort of sexual homogeny, an unease that betrays itself whenever the word
"homosexuality" enters her text:

> And we know the role that the pervert—invincibly believing in the maternal
> phallus, obstinately refusing the existence of the other sex—has been able to play
> in anti-semitism and the totalitarian movements that embrace it. Let us remember
> the fascist or socialist homosexual community (and all homosexual communities
> for whom there is no "other race"), inevitably flanked by a community of
> Amazons who have forgotten the war of the sexes and identify with the paternal
> word and its serpent. The feminist movements are equally capable of such
> perverse denials of Biblical teaching. We must recognize this and be on our
> guard. (Kristeva, p. 23)

This passage, rich with a privatized series of connections, is hard to untangle
without a recognition of the politics of difference at work within it. Although
she seems to make a distinction between homosexual communities "for whom
there is no 'other race'" and others that presumably make a place for sexual
difference, homosexuality and lesbianism, whenever they appear in *Des
Chinoises* are guilty—in Kristeva's own biblical idiom—of the sin of sameness.

Kristeva's construction of homosexuality here is not itself immune from
dangerous homology. The move in this passage from what is presumably a
historical reference to all-male Nazi communities to groups of "Amazons" that
"flank" them is revealing, both for its flight from historical specificity and for
the ease with which Kristeva's argument moves between the sexes. In a text so

preoccupied with retaining the energy of sexual difference it is an odd slip indeed. The chain of association that links Nazis to Amazons to contemporary feminists is especially suspect since Kristeva, like Luce Irigaray, is usually eager to distinguish between male homosexuality and lesbianism; if she does not, like Irigaray, consistently pun on the maleness of "hommosexuality" by introducing a second "m" into the word, she does, even in *Des Chinoises,* distance herself from the homology between male homosexuality and lesbianism with deliberately awkward phrases like "that which we commonly call female homosexuality." (Kristeva, p. 29)

It is in her later discussion of the psychodynamics of lesbianism that Kristeva's argument, dependent, as we might expect, on the vexed relation between sameness and difference, self and other, becomes most troubling. It is also here that she takes on the most troubling issue in the book: relations among women. Kristeva's account of lesbianism, closely tied to her discussion of masochism, frames it as a denial of sexual difference, of the "otherness" of female sexuality. Women's "otherness" here, as elsewhere, is defined in relation to male sexuality. What Kristeva describes as the multiple "twists" of "female homosexuality" are worth quoting at length:

> In her fantasy, the girl obtains a real or imaginary penis for herself; and the fantasy penis seems here to be less important than the access she gains to the symbolic dominance which is necessary to . . . wipe out the last traces of the dependence on the body of the mother. Obliteration of the pre-Oedipal phase, identification with the father, and then: "I am looking, as a man would, for a woman," or else, "I submit myself, as if I were a man who thought he was a woman who thinks she is a man." Such are the double or triple twists of what we commonly call female homosexuality. The oral-sadistic dependence on the mother has been so strong that it now represents not simply a veil over the vagina, but a veritable blockage. Thus the lesbian never discovers the vagina. . . . Artist or intellectual, she wages a vigilant war against her pre-Oedipal dependence on her mother, which keeps her from discovering her own body as other, different, possessing a vagina. (Kristeva, p. 29)

The lesbian, then, is imperfectly woman, imperfectly other. By repressing sexual difference she slips painfully and unconvincingly into the position of a man.

While it would be easy and perhaps fruitful to compare Kristeva's account of the male-identified lesbian with popular misogynist and gynophobic stereotypes, what interests me here is the heterosexism of Kristeva's notions of difference and otherness. There is no room in this discussion of lesbianism, or indeed in the book as a whole, for otherness between women, for differences among them. Chinese women become defined as other to Chinese men, as other to male culture; lesbians become themselves men, take up male positions.

"Woman," seemingly a fluid and fertile term that carries with it the promise, the energy, and the anger of otherness, becomes petrified in a single binary relation of same and other. No difference, no joy, no sex, is possible between women. The lesbian, other to non-lesbians, becomes strangely cast as the same; she is other in her sameness, in her non (hetero)sexual difference. The Kristevan textual economy opens itself up to difference, to disorientation, without moving from the painful recapitulation of the other as the same. *Des Chinoises* becomes not so much a book by a woman about other women, but a book about other women's relation to men by a woman defined in terms of male economy. The other woman is only other to men; differences in culture, class, and sexual preference between women telescope into a heterosexually defined otherness.

I want to end my examination of otherness in feminist theory with, although of necessity not in, the voice of she who is figured and has figured herself as other in two of the essays discussed above: Gayatri Chakravorty Spivak. Moreover, I want to look specifically at the essay that has contained and announced that otherness, her "French Feminism in an International Frame" which appears so uncomfortably as a vehicle for the other woman at the end of both Gallop essays and takes on, in the name *of* the other woman, Kristeva's *Des Chinoises*. Despite the positioning of Spivak within, or more properly outside and inside, Gallop's work, hers is by no means the last word on female otherness; my replication of the Gallopian gesture, at least as far as the placement of Spivak last in my series of feminist theorists is concerned, is not intended to suggest that Spivak, in her presence or in her argument, is, finally, the other woman whose voice, once properly accommodated or included, resolves the problem of the other within feminism. Indeed, the reason I chose this essay of Spivak's instead of one on the surface more "other" to Western feminism, less concerned with the West, is because it so carefully problematizes the author as other: to the West, to India, to writing itself.

Spivak's essay, like Stimpson's, begins with the introduction of an other woman in the form of a colleague, in this case a young Sudanese woman who has just "written a structural functionalist dissertation on female circumcision in the Sudan." (Spivak, p. 154) Unlike the colleague in Stimpson's essay, this woman is explicitly the object of a series of distancing mechanisms at whose emotional and political center is the question of otherness, of collegiality. Spivak invokes distance almost immediately with a complicated and painful triple irony: "I was ready to forgive the sexist term 'female circumcision.' We have learned to say 'clitoridectomy' because others more acute than we have pointed out our mistake." (Spivak, p. 154) The irony is triple because it points simultaneously to the colleague, the author, and to those acute and unnamed "others." Spivak, in placing herself in the position of one who can—and does—forgive, already problematizes her status as "Third-World" other, the status that gives sanction to her appearance at the end of Gallop's essays. How did Spivak get into a position where her forgiveness of another "Third-World woman"—Spivak herself engages cynically with the term—is an issue? Is she forgiving on behalf of the Western academy or on behalf of the victims of the practice (and perhaps the language) of "female circumcision?" Who are these others and where do they position themselves? The word "acute," functioning both in reference to the pain of clitoridectomy which Spivak will describe in the next paragraph, and to an intelligence that sees this pain as it really is, is itself double, itself troubling, itself destabilizing of the opposition between self and other that is not allowed to operate in the opening of this essay.

Choosing to "forgive" her colleague for her sexist language, Spivak does, nevertheless, take a critical stand on the methodology of her project: "Structural functionalism takes a 'disinterested' stance on society as functioning structure. Its implicit interest is to applaud a system—in this case sexual—because it functions." (Spivak, p. 154) Spivak goes on to quote a description of a Sudanese clitoridectomy from Nawal El Saadawi's *The Hidden Face of Eve* to show how it is "difficult" for Spivak "to credit that this young woman had taken such an approach to clitoridectomy." (Spivak, p. 154) By using the authority of Saadawi's text, Spivak uses the work of a third (world) woman to distance herself from her colleague; by quoting a fairly lengthy and extremely painful description of clitoridectomy, Spivak mobilizes a series of mechanisms for distancing and denial: horror, shock, indignation are let loose on the practice of clitoridectomy and of writing about it from a structural functionalist point of view. The female colleague comes to share the force and the direction of the reader's, "our," outrage at the process she so brutally misnames.

As soon as our horror and our anger are in place, as soon as the colleague is in place as other, Spivak returns with an "I" that disrupts the symmetry of our anger: "In my Sudanese colleague's research," she says, "I found an allegory of my own ideological victimage." (Spivak, p. 155) The unfamiliar form "victimage" underscores the disorientation that takes place here: if Spivak is victim, then so is the Sudanese colleague. They are victims like—although perhaps not in the same way as—the victims of clitoridectomy in the Sudan. The term "allegory," like metaphor, with its textured play of sameness and difference, should alert us here. What does it mean for one woman's experience to be an "allegory" of another's? An act of appropriation and identification, this allegory sets off a chain of others, a chain of other women who, like Spivak in some ways, but radically different in others, haunt the text of this essay with the impossibility of complete identification.

The allegorization of her colleague's experience allows Spivak to tell us the history of her own victimage, her own intellectual and political "choices" (for Spivak the term is always contained between quotation marks):

> The "choice" of English Honors by an upper-class young woman in the Calcutta of the fifties was itself highly overdetermined. Becoming a professor of English in the U.S. fitted in with the "brain drain." In due course, a commitment to feminism was the best of a collection of accessible scenarios. The morphology of a feminist theoretical practice came clear through Jacques Derrida's critique of phallocentrism and Luce Irigaray's reading of Freud. (Spivak, p. 155)

Like her colleague's, intellectual choices are, for Spivak, bound up in Western systems of thought and complicitous in a Western-based economics. The "young woman in the Calcutta of the fifties" who is—or will become—Gayatri Spivak, reminds us of "the young woman" the essay opens with; her story, structurally speaking, is analogous to her colleague's; they are both, in fact, a celebration of structure and function, a testimony to the descriptive if not the moral powers of structural functionalism. Western culture *works* and works so well that both Spivak and her colleague can articulate no convincing relation to Third-World women, but are "caught and held . . . in a web of information retrieval inspired at best by: 'what can I do *for* them?' " (Spivak, p. 155, italics Spivak's)

It is this question that radically separates Spivak (and her colleague) from the women of the Third World—whoever they may be. Spivak's essay seeks to "re-articulate" the question and, perhaps, to locate these women, who are always other to the process of knowing and writing as it takes place in the West. Spivak's "something like a solution" to the dilemma of writing as a "westernized Easterner" is contained within parentheses at the heart of a sentence that is in the process of breaking down under the weight of its own syntactic and orthographic hesitations:

> The complicity of a few French texts in that attempt could be part both of the problem—the "West" out to "know" the "East" determining a "westernized Easterner's" symptomatic attempt to "know her own world"; or of something like a solution—reversing and displacing (if only by juxtaposing "some French texts" and "a certain Calcutta") the ironclad opposition of East and West. As soon as I write this, it seems a hopelessly idealist restatement of the problem. But I am not in a position of choice in this dilemma. (Spivak, p. 155)

Spivak's announced, if muffled, project of juxtaposition, the bringing together of "some French texts" with and against "a certain Calcutta" is easy neither to understand nor to carry out. Western readers might know or suspect what those French texts might be; one can, at any rate, look to the footnotes of this article. The phrase "a certain Calcutta" gives us little but a play on the two most opposite meanings of "certain."

The structure of Stimpson's essay should prepare us here for a certifying gesture grounded on the anecdote; in fact, Spivak proceeds almost immediately from an admission that the following pages will be "fragmentary and anecdotal" to the recital of "an obstinate childhood memory." The "obstinate childhood memory," like Stimpson's "difficult anecdote," is about an other woman, in this case two other women: a pair of "ancient washerwomen" beating clothes dry on the stones of a river on Spivak's grandfather's estate on the Bihar-Bengal border.

> One (washerwoman) accuses the other of poaching on her part of the river. I can still hear the cracked derisive voice of the one accused: "You fool! Is this your river? The river belongs to the Company!"—the East India Company. (Spivak, p. 156)

Spivak notes that these women were technically incorrect, and that India had become a republic in 1950. She acknowledges, however, that "their facts were wrong but the fact was right. The Company does still own the land." (Spivak, p. 156) The rightness, the wisdom of these women serves to ground the problem of this essay, the problem of how feminism can speak to "the millions of illiterate rural and urban Indian women," without denying their existence or romanticizing them:

> The academic feminist must learn to learn from them, to speak to them, to suspect that their access to the political is not merely to be *corrected* by our superior theory and enlightened compassion. (Spivak, p. 156)

The trope of the "obstinate childhood memory" fixes the washerwomen at the moral and emotional center of the article; like the Chinese peasants in Kristeva's account of her journey to China, the washerwomen would seem to articulate the article's primal scene. These peasant women, unlike the crowd in the Huxian square, are indeed women; the anecdote leads metonymically into a discussion of the place of Indian women—we do not need Kristeva's woman as metaphor to understand their appearance at the center of Spivak's text.

We must not, however, place them at the center too quickly, too solidly. The washerwomen appear, in fact, everywhere but at the article's physical center. Once mentioned, they give way to three discussions of Western texts—"some French texts": Kristeva's *About Chinese Women;* Elaine Marks' and Isabelle de Courtivron's *New French Feminism;* a series of interpenetrating texts by Derrida, Lyotard, Blanchot, Cixous, Kofman, and Irigary. The (un?)"certain Calcutta," then, is replaced by familiar faces and voices from the West, a line-up of the usual suspects. Indeed the Third World itself disappears immediately after Spivak's sustained and convincing critique of Kristeva's ethnocentrism in *Des Chinoises.*

Throughout Spivak's intelligent and uncompromising exploration of the differences between Kristeva and Cixous, Derrida and Lyotard, and other pairs of French thinkers, the question of the differences between them and the washerwomen is never addressed. Like Gallop who marks off the (re)appearance of Spivak as other woman at the end of her text with blank space, Spivak reintroduces women from the Third World at the end of her article in a section orthographically separate from her examination of French feminism. She opens her final section with a warning:

> As soon as one steps out of the classroom, if indeed a "teacher" ever fully can, the dangers rather than the benefits of academic feminism, French or otherwise, become more insistent. Institutional charges against sexism here or in France may mean nothing, or, indirectly, further harm for women in the Third World . . . let me insist here that here, the difference between "French" and "Anglo-American" feminism is superficial. (Spivak, p. 179)

The last sentence tells us that "difference" has a different valence in this section of the article than it does in its center, where differences between Western thinkers are so carefully explored. We are now in a territory where differences are greater, more dangerous, and may work in unexpected ways. Spivak describes some of these ways in a footnote to her enigmatic assertion that "charges against sexism here or in France may mean . . . further harm for women in the Third World." She explains in a place even further separated from the physical center of the piece:

> To take the simplest possible American examples, even such innocent triumphs as the hiring of more tenured women or adding feminist sessions at a Convention might lead, since most U.S. universities have dubious investments, and most Convention hotels use Third World female labor in a most oppressive way, to the increasing proletarianization of the women of the less developed countries (Spivak, p. 179)

The women upon whose labor academic feminists depend reassert themselves at the end, at the foot, of Spivak's article; their second apprearance closes the frame of Spivak's text, enclosing, insulating, isolating, and perhaps even surrounding Western voices, producing an "International Frame" for French feminism. We cannot read the French theorists and the differences between them except through a frame of greater, more painful and "acute" difference. It is here that Spivak speaks the familiar words that will close Gallop's essays: "I see no way to avoid insisting that there has to be a simultaneous other focus: not merely who am I? But who is the other woman?" (Spivak, p. 179)

But Spivak, unlike Gallop, does not close here. Indeed, both passage and essay continue, the passage for several sentences, the essay for several pages. The line that follows immediately upon what I now think of as "Gallop's" words is particularly interesting, since, unlike Gallop's texts and like parts of *Des Chinoises,* it sets up a reciprocal dynamic of gazing and naming. The passage continues: "How am I naming her? How does she name me?" The other woman, like the Medusa, looks back and transforms the gazer and the gaze. She disorients, constructs, and reflects; the other woman is not a projection of the woman within the family; she is a woman who thrusts familial discourse back upon itself.

Once again, Spivak's essay refuses to end, to close on the issue with which it opened—clitoridectomy and the deployment, the "functioning" of female sexuality. Spivak ends with a discussion of clitoral versus uterine economies; her discussion, like female sexuality itself, breaks through gestures of closure and teleology: it is, in Spivak's words, a "reclaim(ation)" of the "excess" associated with female nonreproductive pleasure.

It is in the discourse of that pleasure, in the idiom of excess, that Spivak draws her essay to a provisional close that takes the form, ironically enough, of a Stimpsonian list-with-a-difference. A heterogenous "sex-analysis" that allows for pleasure will be problematic:

> will not necessarily escape the colonialism of a First World feminism toward the Third. It might, one hopes, promote a sense of our common yet history-specific lot. It ties together the terrified child held down by her grandmother as the blood runs down her groin and the "liberated" heterosexual woman who, in spite of . . . the famous page 53 of *Our Bodies, Ourselves,* in bed with a casual lover . . . confronts, at worst, the "shame" of admitting to the "abnormality" of her orgasm: at best, the acceptance of such a "special" need; and the radical feminist who, setting herself apart from the circle of reproduction, systematically discloses the beauty of the lesbian body; the dowried bride—a body for burning—and the female wage-slave—a body for exploitation. There can be other lists . . . (Spivak, p. 184)

This list, which hints at other lists to come, is not, like Stimpson's, an essay in seamless integration. The syntax itself tells us how difficult, how painful, this list is to hold together in the most utopian feminist imagination, how difficult it is to forget the dependent clauses, the syntactic hesitations, the precarious references, in the production of a united if multiple feminism. Nonetheless, it is the female body and the deployment of female pleasure that allow for and produce lists like the one Spivak offers above. It is the issue of female sexuality that, finally, allows Spivak to close her essay one sentence later with another, seemingly less vexed list of two: "For me it is the best gift of French feminism, that it cannot itself fully acknowledge, and that we must work at; here is a theme that can liberate my colleague from Sudan, and a theme the old washerwomen by the river would understand." (Spivak, p. 184) The never quite identified "it" of this passage, which points back to but fails to summarize the first, problematic list, is the first sign of hope for the promised juxtaposition of France and Calcutta. The reentry of the washerwomen, like the disappearance of the semicolons and dashes that mark the previous list, signals closure, compromise, and, to borrow a Spivakian hesitation, a *certain* utopia. The Sudanese colleague, brought into an erotic dialogue with the washerwomen, learns from them, from the juxtaposition of French feminism and information from the Third World. French feminism and lived experience of the Third World themselves form a list of two that are other to each other.

If Spivak's article ends hopefully, it does not end easily. If she, like Gallop, turns to other women, to women of the Third World to end with, it is not because the position of the "other woman," the "Third-World woman," has remained unexamined. The chain of women, other to each other, who take us into the Third World and out again in this essay, is infinitely iterable; otherness is infinite regress, cannot occupy one place, one body, one woman. Otherness is, at best, a dangerous gift that women pass on—sometimes blindly—to each other.

Inter-Chapter 5

Elizabeth and Helena

I, like Catharine Stimpson, begin with the rape of another woman: not a colleague, but a prostitute, a heroin addict, a carrier of the HIV virus, a woman whose scarred body was literally marked with the signs of otherness in the form of bruises, gashes, injection sites. I call up the names "prostitute," "heroin addict," and "carrier" because these were the terms I heard before I heard her name: it was—perhaps still is, for she might still be alive—Elizabeth.

I was counselor for a Rape Crisis Center on my first "companion call"—a visit to a hospital or court as an advocate for a rape survivor. I had worked for seven years at a battered women's shelter and for a year at the Rape Crisis Center, mostly dealing with survivors over the phone. This was my first face-to-face contact with a rape survivor in my capacity as advocate.

Anxious, disoriented, fairly new to the city, I arrived at the hospital in a part of town I had never seen before. Part of my companion training had involved practice runs by car and by bus to the city hospital where the police take most rape survivors. She had not called the police, so she had gone to the hospital closest to her. When I finally identified and passed through the right set of swinging doors to the emergency room—marked "hospital staff only"—the nurse on duty gave me a pair of gloves and told me on no consideration to touch Elizabeth because the sores on her legs were oozing. The gloves were too big; they made my hands look enormous, white, unfamiliar, a parody of doctors' hands.

I passed through the length of the emergency room, curtained booths on either side of a narrow white hallway. Most of the curtains were open, revealing men and women, mostly black, attached to IVs. No one was screaming or groaning; there was a lot of blood, but no one actually seemed to be bleeding. The blood stood still in scabs on faces, arms, bare torsos. It was surprisingly quiet and still.

199

Elizabeth was in a room at the end of the hall—the only room with a door. I knocked, heard something that might have been "come in" and entered. Elizabeth was lying across the width of a cot, her legs pulled close to her chin. I hadn't known where to expect the "oozing sores"; they were all over her arms and legs. Suddenly I realized they were not wounds from her attack but infected needle marks, signs not of what I was there for, but of a life before the rape.

It is one of the moral and political absolutes of feminist crisis counseling that the counselor not judge the survivor. This means believing she was raped, accepting her choices about her body, her life, what she wants to do. One is usually tempted into judgment about little things; for many people it starts with cigarettes. All advocates from this particular center, no matter what our position on smoking, travelled everywhere with packs of cigarettes in our pockets in case a survivor might want to smoke. I recall clutching at the pack of Kents I carried when I saw the scars, remembering that I had chosen Kents because my mother smoked them and I have, since I was six, tortured and belittled her for smoking.

I do not remember much of what we said at first; the first few words are always the hardest but they are quickly over. Most women seem to want to talk about the rape, but others want to ignore the topic or to be completely silent. I was there to do what she wanted to do. She did tell the story of the rape; a john had raped and robbed her. She knew the man; he was an addict, he had robbed her to get money for drugs. Her stories were full of people: women she lived with, johns, her husband who lived with her sometimes, friends and enemies. The one word she never used was "addict"; she did not have to use it to distinguish one person in her story from another. Everyone she mentioned was an addict. This was at the height of Nancy Reagan's campaign against drugs; the Police Athletic League had just tried to sell me a "Just Say No" bumper sticker along with six different kinds of homemade jelly.

I asked her what she wanted me to do. She was quick with the answer: "Get me into a program." It was then I realized that, despite the cigarettes in my pocket, I had come unprepared. I had no money—none: not even a quarter to make phone calls. We were supposed to keep them with our cigarettes. I spent about fifteen minutes getting permission to use the doctor's and nurse's phones, and two hours trying to locate a drug program. Most of them were closed for the weekend. The few that were open asked if Elizabeth had insurance. I had to ask her, knowing it was a ridiculous question but fighting against assuming anything about her. Finally, I found a place that would take her on Monday. I told her this; she said only "two days is a long time."

I could not get her into a program. I could not get the doctors to respond to her requests for painkillers. "She's an addict," they said. She seemed to like talking, but mostly she asked questions about me. "Was I married?" "Yes," I said. "Did I have children?" "No." "Did I think my husband cared for me?" "Yes, I think so." "Had I ever been to Assateaugue Island to see the ponies?" "No, but I've always planned to go." The conversation was slow and gentle; after telling me once about the rape, she seemed to have no desire to elaborate. She asked me if I could stay until evening. After I agreed to stay, she asked me how I was planning to get home without any money. I told her I thought my husband or a friend could pick me up. "You could go to dinner," she said. I thought about the linguine with clam sauce at my favorite restaurant and then about things I had eaten for dessert over the course of my life: chocolate melted on the radiator with coconut or raisins when I was little, pink birthday cakes shaped like hearts as a teenager, apple pies in graduate school where I would make the filling (lemon, brown sugar, and raisins) and my friend would make the crust (the way her grandmother taught her with as little water as possible), the beautiful and elaborate chocolate cakes my husband would start making at midnight, the crème brûlée with pears featured in yuppie restaurants that year.

At five o'clock she got very hungry. I asked a nurse about getting her dinner, and she told me that Elizabeth hadn't been in the hospital long enough to qualify for a meal. "She'll be leaving soon," the nurse told me, and then, in a slightly different tone, "She can't stay." I had failed to get her in a drug program, I had failed to find her friend at home. Getting her a meal became my mission; I saw this in myself and was ashamed that I was responding not only to her desire for food but to my desire to be successful in providing it. Nonetheless, the food would be food. I argued for an hour with three nurses and a doctor; I paged a social worker who was away for the weekend. I paged a social worker who came and signed the appropriate form with a wide lipsticked smile. The food came quickly and smelled—unexpectedly—delicious. The linguine with clam sauce faded from my mind as Elizabeth peeled back the tinfoil cover and lovingly lifted soft spoonsful of macaroni and cheese out of a square container. Next to the macaroni were glazed carrots and a small airline salad with a shockingly luscious looking tomato slice. "I hate carrots," she said. Taking for granted that I would eat them, she slid them over to me.

Elizabeth seemed especially to enjoy dessert; a small square of coffee cake, and a cup of coffee, which she drank slowly with sugar and cream. "I feel bad," she said, in a gentle, far-off voice. "About what?" I asked, wondering if she were going to mention the rape. "About that coffee. It's the first cup I've had in two months. I'm trying to stay off the caffeine."

After dinner, I argued with the same people to get a taxi voucher to take Elizabeth back home. The arguments were shorter and less energetic; in the end I wondered whether I had forced the argument to make me feel as though I were accomplishing something. I waited for her taxi and waved goodbye before using the nurse's phone to call my husband for a ride. We walked around for a while but did not end up at my favorite restaurant; my power to fantasize and to direct my experiences toward a fantasy were strangely tired. The restaurant we finally walked into looked cleaner than any place I had ever been: not hospital-clean, with its sense of something to be cleaned up lurking underneath the surface, but food-clean—hygienic but nurturing. I don't remember what I had for dessert, but I do know that I drank coffee: for a change, caffeinated coffee. I could not sleep that night for the caffeine singing through my veins.

NOTES

Introduction

1. Roland Barthes, *Mythologies,* trans. Annette Lavers (New York: Hill and Wang, 1972), p. 151.

2. I use "we" with hesitation because it is under interrogation here. I want, however, to align myself with feminists and with feminism from the beginning so that I might combat from inside the notion that this might be an anti-feminist project.

3. Gayatri Chakravorty Spivak, "Three Women's Texts and a Critique of Imperialism," *Critical Inquiry* Vol. 12, No. 1 (Autumn 1985), p. 253.

4. Bonnie Thornton Dill, "Race, Class, and Gender: Prospects for an All-Inclusive Sisterhood," *Feminist Studies* 9, No. 1 (Spring 1983), pp. 131–150.

5. Elizabeth Spelman, *The Inessential Woman* (Boston: Beacon Press, 1988), p. ix.

6. Mary Daly, *Gyn/Ecology: The Meta-ethics of Radical Feminism* (Boston: Beacon Press, 1978), p. 1.

7. Joyce P. Lindenbaum, "The Shattering of an Illusion: The Problem of Competition in Lesbian Relations," in *Competition: A Feminist Taboo?,* ed. Valerie Miner and Helen Longino (New York: The Feminist Press, 1987), pp. 195–208, and, in the same collection, Daphne Muse, "High Stakes, Meager Yields: Competition Among Black Girls," pp. 132–60.

8. Luise Eichenbaum and Susie Orbach, *Between Women* (New York: Viking, 1988).

9. Janice Raymond, *A Passion for Friends: Toward a Philosophy of Female Affection* (Boston: Beacon Press, 1986), p. 13.

10. Christine Downing, *Psyche's Sisters: Re-Imagining the Meaning of Sisterhood* (San Francisco: Harper and Row, 1988).

11. Iris Marion Young, "The Ideal of Community and the Politics of Difference," in *Feminism/Postmodernism,* ed. Linda J. Nicholson (New York: Routeledge, 1990), pp. 300–23.

Chapter 1

1. James Willing and Leonard Rae, *Jane Eyre, or Poor Relations,* unpublished manuscript, The Lord Chamberlain's Collection, The British Library (1879), p. 52.

2. Martin Meisel, *Shaw and the Nineteenth-Century Theatre* (New York: Limelight Editions, 1984), pp. 22–26.

3. Toni A. H. McNaron ed., *The Sister Bond: A Feminist View of a Timeless Connection* (New York: Pergamon Press, 1985), p. 4.

4. Stephen P. Bank and Michael D. Kahn, *The Sibling Bond* (New York: Basic Books, 1982), p. 10.

5. Christine Downing, *Psyche's Sisters: Re-Imagining the Meaning of Sisterhood* (New York: Harper and Row, 1988), p. 4.

6. Carroll Smith-Rosenberg, "The Female World of Love and Ritual: Relations Between Women in Nineteenth-Century America," in *Disorderly Conduct: Visions of Gender in Victorian America* (New York: Alfred A. Knopf, 1985), p. 64.

7. Margaret Morganroth Gullette, "The Puzzling Case of the Deceased Wife's Sister: Nineteenth-Century England Deals with a Second-Chance Plot," *Representations* 31 (Summer 1990), pp. 142–66.

8. Allen Horstman, *Victorian Divorce* (New York: St. Martin's Press, Inc.), pp. 21–23.

9. Mrs. (Sarah Strickney) Ellis, *The Prose Works Vol. I* (New York: Henry G. Langley, 1844) (reprint of London edition by Fisher, Son & Co.), p. 69.

10. Charlotte Yonge, *Womankind* (London: R. Clay & Sons, 1876), p. 27.

11. Nina Auerbach, *Ellen Terry: Player in Her Time* (New York: W. W. Norton & Company, 1987), p. 54.

12. Wilkie Collins, *No Name* (New York: Dover, 1982), p. 127.

13. Christina Rossetti, "Goblin Market," *The Complete Poems of Christina Rossetti Vol. I*, ed. R. W. Crump (Baton Rouge: Louisiana State University Press, 1979), p. 26, lines 462–65.

14. Thomas Hardy, *Tess of the D'Urbervilles*, ed. Juliet Grindel and Simon Gatrell (Oxford: Clarendon Press, 1983), p. 536.

15. George Eliot, *Middlemarch*, ed. David Carroll (Oxford: Clarendon Press, 1986), p. 7.

Inter-Chapter 1

1. Winifred Gerin, *Emily Brontë* (Oxford: Clarendon Press, 1971), p. 35.

2. Elizabeth Gaskell, *The Life of Charlotte Brontë* (Harmondsworth: Penguin Books, 1975), p. 87.

3. Charlotte Brontë, "Editor's Preface to the New Edition of *Wuthering Heights*," reprinted in Emily Brontë, *Wuthering Heights* (New York: W. W. Norton & Company, 1972), p. 12.

4. Charlotte Brontë, "Biographical Notice of Ellis and Acton Bell," reprinted in *Wuthering Heights*, p. 6.

5. Margot Peters, *Unquiet Soul: A Biography of Charlotte Brontë* (New York: Atheneum, 1986), p. 308.

Chapter 2

1. William Wilkie Collins, *The Woman in White* (Oxford: Clarendon Press, 1975), pp. 180–81.

2. Luce Irigaray, "The Sex Which Is Not One," *The Sex Which Is Not One* (Ithaca: Cornell University Press, 1985), p. 26.

3. For a discussion of class in sensation fiction, see Jonathan Loesberg, "The Ideology of Narrative Form in Sensation Fiction," *Representations* 13 (Winter 1986), pp. 115–38.

4. Mrs. Henry Wood, *East Lynne* (New Brunswick: Rutgers University Press, 1988), p. 114.

5. Mary Elizabeth Braddon, *Lady Audley's Secret* (New York: Dover, 1974), p. 57.

6. For an account of the relation between Catholicism and sexuality in *Lady Audley's Secret*, see Susan David Bernstein, *The Untold Story: Constructing Confessions of Women in Victorian Literature* (Unpublished manuscript), Chapter 4.

7. For comments on Braddon's obsession with her heroines' hair see "Sensation Novels: Miss Braddon," in *North British Review* XLIII (September 1865), pp. 94, 97, 99, 100.

8. For my discussion of the power of maternal inheritance, I am indebted to Beth Kowaleski-Wallace. See *Their Fathers' Daughters: Hannah More, Maria Edgeworth and Patriarchal Complicity* forthcoming from Oxford Univesity Press, Chapter 6.

9. I am indebted to Jonathan Loesberg for the suggestion that "M. V." could stand for "Mme. Vine."

10. For a discussion of the Victorian governess' painfully double position, see Mary Poovey, *Uneven Developments* (Chicago, University of Chicago Press, 1988), pp. 130–136, and my own *The Flesh Made Word* (New York: Oxford University Press, 1987), pp. 46–52.

11. For a useful definition of sensation novels as novels with a secret, see Kathleen Tillotson's introduction to *The Woman in White* (Boston: Houghton Mifflin, 1969).

12. Thomas Hardy, *Tess of the D'Urbervilles* (Oxford: Clarendon Press, 1983), p. 21.

Chapter 3

1. The term "lesbian novel" is, of course, a problematic one and the subject of much debate. While I want to resist a totalizing definition of the term, I want to proclaim the status of "lesbian novel" for *Rubyfruit Jungle*. Proclamation is, in fact, the key term: the publication and dissemination of *Rubyfruit Jungle* was a community-forming event; not only was it a novel by a self-proclaimed and highly visible lesbian about a character who became comfortable with the label, but it was, as far as I can tell, absolutely central in the construction of lesbian identity for many American women. A study of the effect of *Rubyfruit Jungle* on the identity formation of individuals and communities would, I think, be very useful to ethnographers and historians of lesbianism in the United States.

2. Rita Mae Brown, *Rubyfruit Jungle* (New York: Bantam Books, 1977), p. 7.

3. John Boswell, *Christianity, Social Tolerance, and Homosexuality* (Chicago: University of Chicago Press, 1980), p. 73.

4. See Louis Crompton, *Byron and Greek Love: Homophobia in 19th Century England* (Berkeley and Los Angeles: University of California Press, 1985).

5. Adrienne Rich, "Compulsory Heterosexuality and Lesbian Existence, " *Powers of Desire: The Politics of Sexuality,* ed. Ann Snitow, Christine Stansell, and Sharon Thompson (New York: Monthly Review Press, 1983), p. 192.

6. Other attempts to see gayness as a series of possibilities ranged along a political and sexual spectrum include Eve Kosovsky Sedgwick's notion of the homosocial. See her *Between Men: English Literature and Male Homosocial Desire* (New York: Columbia University Press, 1985).

7. I have chosen to use the spelling "fem" instead of "femme" because of this chapter's debt to Joan Nestle who spells it this way. (See Note 10.)

8. Esther Newton and Shirley Walton, "The Misunderstanding: Toward a More Precise Sexual Vocabulary," *Pleasure and Danger: Exploring Female Sexuality,* ed. Carole S. Vance (Boston: Routledge and Kegan Paul, 1984), p. 247.

9. Amber Hollibaugh and Cherrie Moraga, "What We're Rollin Around in Bed With: Sexual Silences in Feminism," *Powers of Desire,* p. 396.

10. Joan Nestle, "The Fem Question," *Pleasure and Danger,* p. 236.

11. Members of SAMOIS, ed. *Coming to Power,* 3rd ed. (Boston: Alyson Publications, Inc., 1987), p. 281.

12. Audre Lorde and Susan Leigh Star, "Interview With Audre Lorde," *Against Sadomasochism: A Radical Feminist Analysis,* ed. Robin Ruth Linden et al. (San Francisco: Frog in the Well Press, 1982), p. 68.

13. Karen Sims and Rose Mason with Darlene Pagano, "Racism and Sadomasochism," *Against Sadomasochism,* p. 101.

14. Elly Bulkin and Joan Larkin, eds. *Lesbian Poetry: An Anthology* (Watertown, MA: Persephone Press, 1981), pp. xxi–xxxiv.

15. Adrienne Rich, *Of Woman Born: Motherhood as Experience and Institution* (New York: Bantam, 1976), p. 234.

16. Adrienne Rich, "A Woman Dead in Her Forties," *The Dream of a Common Language* (New York: W. W. Norton & Co., 1978), p. 53.

Chapter 4

1. Again, I find Bonnie Thornton Dill's political ironizing of the term "sister" useful here.

2. For a discussion of various black women writers' reluctance to talk about sexism within the black community, see Claudia Tate, *Black Women Writers at Work* (New York: Continuum, 1983), in which Tate interviews fourteen black women writers and asks many of them what they think of feminism, of sexism in a black culture, and of the advantages of talking about these issues to an audience that includes white readers.

3. Anne Hostetler, "The Aesthetics of Race and Gender in Nella Larsen's *Quicksand*" *PMLA* 105, no. 1 (January 1990) pp. 35–46.

4. Nella Larsen, *Quicksand* (New Brunswick: Rutgers University Press, 1986), p. 27.

5. For a discussion of black women's bodies and their shifting relations to notions of background and foreground, see Sander L. Gilman, "Black Bodies, White Bodies: Toward an Iconography of Female Sexuality in Late Nineteenth-Century Art, Medicine, and Literature," *Critical Inquiry* Vol. 12, No. 1 (Autumn 1985), pp. 204–42. For the constructedness of "race" as a category, see Henry Louis Gates' Introduction to the issue, "Writing 'Race' and the Difference It Makes."

6. Deborah McDowell offers a compelling discussion of sexuality in *Quicksand and Passing* in her introduction to the Rutgers University Press edition of the novel. According to McDowell, the neatness and symmetry of both novels are undercut by a powerful subtext about the taboo subject of female sexual awakening. While the novels try to deflect the question from sex to race, sexuality continues to haunt them, surfacing in certain scenes like the Harlem party in *Quicksand* which I discuss below.

7. Nella Larsen, *Passing* (New Brunswick: Rutgers University Press, 1986), p. 148.

8. Toni Morrison, *Sula* (New York: Bantam Books, 1973), p. 13.

9. Joseph H. Wessling, "Narcissism in Toni Morrison's *Sula*," *College Language Association Journal* Vol. 31, No. 3 (March 1988), pp. 281–98. Barbara Smith, "Toward a Black Feminist Criticism," *The New Feminist Criticism: Essays on Women, Literature, Theory*, ed. Elaine Showalter (New York: Pantheon Books), pp. 175–83.

10. Deborah McDowell, " 'The Self and the Other': Reading Toni Morrison's *Sula* and the Black Female Text," in *Critical Essays on Toni Morrison*, ed. Nellie Y. McKay (Boston: G. K. Hall, 1988), pp. 77–89.

Inter-Chapter 4

1. *Sports Illustrated*, 3/7/88, p. 40.

2. *The Washington Post*, 2/28/88 p. D-5.

Chapter 5

1. Laurel Richardson, *The New Other Woman* (New York: Macmillan, 1985), p. ix.

2. Luce Irigaray, *Speculum of the Other Woman*, trans. Gillian C. Gill (Ithaca: Cornell University Press), pp. 101, 103.

3. Catharine R. Stimpson, "Feminism and Feminist Criticism," *The Massachusetts Review*, Vol. 24, No. 2, p. 275.

4. Jane Gallop, "The Monster in the Mirror: The Feminist Critic's Psychoanalysis," originally delivered at the English Institute, September, 1983.

5. Jane Gallop, "Annie Leclerc Writing a Letter, with Vermeer," *October* (Summer, 1985), pp. 104–05.

208 *Notes*

Julia Kristeva, *Des Chinoises* (Paris: des femmes, 1974). Translations are from *About Chinese Women,* trans. Anita Barrows (New York: Urizen Books, 1977).

7. Gayatri Spivak, "French Feminism in an International Frame," *Yale French Studies,* No. 62 (Fall, 1981), p. 158.

8. Julia Kristeva, "Stabat Mater," trans. Leon S. Roudiez in *The Kristeva Reader,* ed. Toril Moi (New York: Columbia University Press, 1986), pp. 160–87.

CREDITS

Artwork

Cover: Roger Fenton, *The Princesses Helena and Louise* c. 1857. Courtesy of the Royal Photographic Society

Fig. 1. Branwell Brontë, "The Pillar Portrait," c. 1835. Courtesy of the National Portrait Gallery, London

Fig. 2. Branwell Brontë, "The Gun Group." Courtesy of the Brontë Parsonage Museum

Fig. 3. Front cover, The Judds, *Why Not Me*. Courtesy of BMC Music

Fig. 4. Back cover, The Judds, *Heartland*. Courtesy of BMC Music

Fig. 5. Front cover, *The Judds' Greatest Hits*. Courtesy of BMC Music

Fig. 6. Front cover, The Judds, *River of Time*. Courtesy of BMC Music

Lyrics

GRANDPA (TELL ME 'BOUT THE GOOD OLD DAYS)
By: Jamie O'Hara
Copyright © 1985 Cross Keys Publishing Co., Inc.
All rights administered by Sony Music Publishing
Reprinted by permission

ONE MAN WOMAN
Words and Music by Paul Kennerly
Copyright © 1989 Rondor Music (London) Ltd.
All rights administered in the U.S. and Canada by Irving Music, Inc. (BMI)
All Rights Reserved. International Copyright Secured.

HAVE MERCY
Words and Music by Paul Kennerly
Copyright © administered in the U.S. and Canada by Irving Music, Inc. (BMI)

INDEX